THE FIRST 200 YEARS OF MONTY PYTHON

The First 20~~0~~ Years

of MONTY PYTHON

KIM
"HOWARD"
JOHNSON

Plexus, London

All rights reserved including the right
of reproduction in whole or in part in any form
Copyright © 1989 by Kim ''Howard'' Johnson
Published by Plexus Publishing Limited
26 Dafforne Road
London SW17 8TZ
First printing 1990

Johnson, Kim
    The first 200 years of Monty Python.
    1. Television programmes. Comedies
    I. Title
    791.455

    ISBN 0-85965-107-X

Published by arrangement with St Martin's Press, New York.
A Thomas Dunne book

Design by Jaye Zimet
Printed in Great Britain by the Bath Press

CONTENTS

FOREWORD

The First 20X Years of Monty Python by Kim "Howard" Johnson has got to be the greatest book ever written. I particularly like the writing in it—it has lots of writing in it, and another thing I like is the color of the outside jacket. It's "really" great. The typeface is particularly good—very good, and I like this book much more than Salman Rushdie's book which had larger type and was not about Monty Python (well not much of it was about Monty Python). A great work by a truly great writer, and "Howie" Johnson will be remembered long after other great writers have been forgotten for his contribution to the fast food industry.

—George Harrison

PREFACE

Kim "Howard" Johnson has been pestering us for years, coming round "interviewing" us, asking "questions" and generally writing damn-fool "things" about "Python." Now he is "publishing" it all for "money." Well what else can you expect from a man who sticks quotation marks in the middle of his name? Still, good luck to him, though I don't think Boswell will be turning in his grave. . . . At least now you have a chance to see what we've had to put up with all these years. The patience of saints I'd call it. Beats me why anybody'd write a book about Python, let alone read it. Have they nothing better to do? Are they all mad? Is this enough words for a Foreword? Is the cheque in the Post?

John Cleese once told me he'd do anything for money: so I offered him a pound to shut up. And he took it. 'Nuff said.

—Eric Idle
London

AUTHOR'S NOTE

*I*n keeping with the finest American tradition, when I was a kid, I ran away from home to join the circus. This, however, was a flying circus, and it was run by Monty Python. So much for tradition.

Actually, I started watching *Monty Python's Flying Circus* almost from its first American broadcast. I was flipping through the dial when I accidentally came upon a still picture of the larch tree. This segued into a town full of Supermen where the local hero was a bicycle repairman, a children's show host reading the youngsters rather twisted tales, and a very bizarre restaurant. I was hooked. It wasn't *The Ed Sullivan Show*.

Word of mouth was spreading, and the show soon became PBS's top-rated entertainment program. By the time *Monty Python and the Holy Grail* opened in 1975, the group had developed a sizable core of fans, and the team flew into New York to promote the film. During the publicity tour, I met Terry Jones and Graham Chapman very briefly at a Chicago theater appearance, and wrote to the pair of them afterward. Terry invited me to New York early the next year, when the group would be performing at the City Center. He took me backstage before the show, and I had the opportunity to meet the entire group.

Slowly but surely, I began amassing information about the group with clippings, photos, letters, and whatever other materials I came across. In early 1978, I put out the first of a three-volume Python fanzine (highlighted by a phone interview I did with Michael Palin while he was working on *Saturday Night Live*), which was the forerunner of this book. Response from the Pythons themselves was most encouraging and flattering; at the end of his letter, Michael Palin foolishly stated "If you're ever in London, look me up." I left the next month. While in London, I visited nearly all of the group as they were preparing to leave for Tunisia to shoot *Life of Brian*. I eventually ended up going to Africa for the main portion of the filming, living and working with them on location—truly a once-in-a-lifetime experience.

During the subsequent years, I have done numerous interviews with the Pythons for magazines and radio, attended and participated in the Hollywood Bowl shows, and gotten to know the group members personally and professionally. Thanks to them all, the results are in these pages.

Since my original contacts with the Pythons, I have gone on to various writing and performing projects. Somehow, Monty Python has been responsible, either directly or indirectly, for most of my successes.

We all have gurus in our lives who help us along the way, providing advice, encouragement, or opportunities. Most of the time, however, we aren't able to pay them back for all their help. This book is one small attempt, a twentieth birthday present, to thank the Pythons for all of the guidance, inspiration, and above all, laughs.

Graham Chapman died of cancer on October 4, 1989, just one day before the twentieth anniversary of Monty Python. It was the only occasion his timing was less than perfect.

His fans, friends, and family all have their special memories of this kind, generous, wonderfully silly man whose work will be enjoyed for a long time to come.

Not long before he died, Graham read the manuscript of this book and was very happy with the result; I hope this book serves as a tribute to his life and his career.

And somehow, I think Heaven has become a slightly sillier place.

ACKNOWL-EDGMENTS

This exhaustive (and exhausting) look at the Python television shows would not have been possible without the assistance of many people. First and foremost are Graham Chapman, John Cleese, Terry Gilliam, Eric Idle, Terry Jones, and Michael Palin, for their support, encouragement, and time. Also essential for her assistance was Anne James and everyone else at Mayday Management, particularly Steve Abbott, Alison Davies, and Ralph Kamp. Thanks also to Charles Alverson, Connie Booth, Carol Cleveland, George Harrison, Neil Innes, Charles McKeown, Lorne Michaels, Hazel Pethig, David Sherlock, John Tomiczek, and Barry Took.

Special thanks also go to Dominick Abel, Mike Carlin, Del Close, Max Allan Collins, Roland Coover, Jr., Mark Evanier, Mike Gold, John Goldstone, Bob Greenberger, Harvey Kurtzman, Nancy Lewis, Barbara McCoury, Dave McDonnell, as well as everyone at *Starlog*, Valerie Miller, Dana Snow, Don and Maggie Thompson, and my parents, Ken and Marge Johnson, who never quite understood what it was about . . .

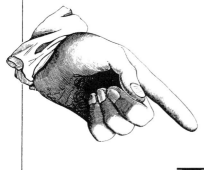

INTRO-DUCTION

*I*t has now been over twenty years since *Monty Python's Flying Circus* was first broadcast to a small portion of the world. In its original late-night time slot on the BBC, where it was often pre-empted (or not run at all in the provinces), it slowly but surely took hold of an influential segment of the British public, a following that gradually began to grow.

From such humble beginnings (Michael Palin claims their first viewers were insomniacs, intellectuals, and burglars), Python gradually became a phenomenon. Their TV shows were popular around the world, while their films became critical and box-office hits.

Even more important is the way Python shaped and changed comedy for a new generation of viewers. The original shows sideswiped traditional TV conventions—there were no guest stars, very little music, and the sketches did not always have a beginning, middle, or end—at least not in that order.

Even stranger was the form the shows developed—there was very much a stream-of-consciousness approach to each program; any given show was linked by means both obvious and subtle, including Terry Gilliam's animations. Characters from one sketch could turn up much later in a different sketch; performers could step out of character and talk to the camera. And, lest the shows be deemed a triumph of style over substance, it should be noted that the group broke new comedic ground in their use of such less-than-traditional themes as cannibalism, royalty, and dismemberment. They waged a battle with the BBC over their innovative use of sex, violence, and language.

As brilliant as the subsequent films, records, and stage shows are, it is the forty-five TV shows that established Monty Python as one of the most significant comedic forces in decades. Those shows are full and rich in their material, and represent a high-water mark in British comedy. *Monty Python's Flying Circus* was to British TV comedy in the '70s what *Beyond the Fringe* was to British stage comedy in the '60s, or *The Goon Show* to British radio comedy in the '50s. Although *All in the Family* and *Sanford and Son* were based on English TV shows, Python was the first British comedy successfully broadcast intact in America. It was seen and noticed by the creators of such shows as *Saturday Night Live* and *Cheers*, and has had its effect on countless writers and performers in the years since.

Monty Python's Flying Circus will doubtless continue to influence our comedy in years to come. This volume is an effort to salute those forty-five classic shows that are still seen daily across America, as well as the films, books, and records that followed. As much as is possible, the Pythons themselves discuss in their own words the concepts, writing, and performing that went into their series. Although in some cases one recollection may contradict another, each has been recorded as faithfully as possible, in hopes that the individual perceptions will prove enlightening. The interviews and research have continued for over a decade, and ultimately this book would not have been possible without the ongoing support of the group members themselves over the years.

THE FIRST 200 YEARS OF MONTY PYTHON

Part One

THE GATHERING STORM

BEFORE THE BEGINNING

*B*y 1969, the six men-who-would-be-Pythons had been writing and performing for the BBC in various capacities. John Cleese and Graham Chapman had just finished *At Last, the 1948 Show*, while Terry Jones, Michael Palin, Eric Idle, and Terry Gilliam had wrapped up *Do Not Adjust Your Set*, a BBC children's show that had also featured Neil Innes and the Bonzo Dog (Doo Dah) Band.

Accounts vary, but the BBC was reportedly interested in doing a series with John Cleese, while Cleese had wanted to work with Michael Palin. The two groups got together, and thanks to the efforts of producer Barry Took, they had the opportunity to do an as-yet-undefined comedy show.

"Mike was the connecting element that got our two different groups together," recalls Gilliam. "John had this standing invitation from the BBC to do a program—I don't think they knew who all of us were. They knew we'd all been writers, we'd worked on stuff for Marty Feldman and David Frost, but John was always the one they liked the most.

"Mike, Terry, and Eric were all intrigued by the animation, and the idea of having this element in the show. I don't know if John and Graham were interested at all." He laughs.

Michael Palin remembers getting a phone call one evening

that got it all rolling. "John Cleese asked what we were all doing. He was sort of kicking his heels, and said 'Why don't we try something all together?' We'd also done the animation with Terry Gilliam, and since John had also worked with Terry, we said 'Fine, let's talk about it.'

"At the time, Barry Took was sort of a father figure for us younger writers, and he was working for the BBC as a script editor. He provided our first entrée to the BBC. He got us in to talk with Michael Mills, who was head of comedy at the time, and we just had a meeting. The BBC suddenly said 'Well, you can have thirteen shows for the late night slot.' So saying, they left the room!" Palin laughs.

Took had known all of the group since their early days with the BBC. A number of writers and performers were emerging from the stage revues at Oxford, Cambridge, and elsewhere, and Took was aware of this surge of creativity. In addition to smoothing the way at the BBC, Took also helped throw together the most interesting creative groups he saw at the time.

"It struck me that of the twelve or fifteen very talented men around, I thought the people who had the most influence on each other would be John and Graham on one hand, and Michael and Terry on the other. Fundamentally, it would be the impact of those two different sorts of brainwaves coming together that would make the comedy. They added another couple of ingredients, to become Monty Python," says Took.

"I went to them all and said 'Would you like to do a program with these other people?' and they all said yes. They all had qualms about it, and didn't want to feel trapped by a group show that they could not then get out of, so I said 'If you don't like it, there's nothing to hold you, you can leave.' I wanted to have a very free feeling.

"If one has people with talent, I say 'Go with that,' don't ask what they're going to do—let them do what they feel is absolutely apt. I wanted to impose the antithesis of censorship or control. It sounds a contradiction, but I wanted to say to them 'Look, if you let people run free, they'll produce better work than if they're constrained in old-fashioned formulas.' They say 'You can't do that because it's never been done before,' but the other side of that is 'We must do that because it's never been done before.' I said [optimistically] that once we gave these young men their head . . . 'They're so bright, how could it not work?' . . . before it ever happened. And every piece of evidence suggests that the initial guess was the right one," Took points out.

The first meeting of the six was encouraging, recalls Graham Chapman, and although they had not all performed together, they tended to be familiar with the others' work. "When Barry Took hit on the idea of putting us all together, it was fine by us—although at that stage, I knew nothing about Terry Gilliam at all. I'd seen him a couple of times on *Do Not Adjust Your Set*, and that was about it—a shadowy figure!

"The first meeting was a convivial affair. We knew of each other and what kind of work the others had put out for such things as *The Frost Report*. There was already a working relationship, even though we'd never actually worked together.

One of the very first group photos taken of the team shows (left to right) a young John Cleese, Graham Chapman, Terry Jones, Eric Idle, and (seated in front) Michael Palin. Missing from the picture, Terry Gilliam's initial role in the group was unsure; in fact, the very first shows listed Gilliam's name only under the "animation" credit. **Photo copyright BBC and Python Productions**

So, after the very first meeting, which was really just saying 'Hello,' and 'Yes, it would be a good idea to work together,' we went away and had a sit-through, and looked at all of the old material we had left over from *The Frost Report*." Chapman laughs. "Just to see how much material we would have for our first few shows . . . Actually, there was quite a bit, which made us feel safer. We knew we had some bankers, as it were, in the way of sketches that we knew were good and hadn't been used to that point. So we began writing more, meeting together, and reading stuff to each other. That's how the whole process began."

Once the BBC approved the idea of such a show, it was up to the six Pythons to decide just what the show should be. As Michael Palin recalls, they already had a time slot, but they didn't know what shape their program would take. One of the most important influences was Spike Milligan's series *Q5*. Milligan had been an idol of the group ever since his *Goon Shows** aired on BBC radio in the '50s, and the stream-of-consciousness approach of *Q5* was closely noted. In fact, the Pythons asked for *Q5*'s Ian MacNaughton to direct their new show, and MacNaughton ended up handling all but the first four shows (which were directed by BBC staff producer John Howard Davies).

The unique structure was most intentional. After working under the constraints of TV comedy at the time, the group members were chomping at the bit to bite the hand that had been feeding them. And when they were unleashed, they did just that.

The show distinguished itself immediately with its use of animation, used to present short Gilliam

bits and to connect sketches that could not be linked in any normal manner. As Michael Palin notes, "For a couple of weeks, Terry Jones and Terry Gilliam were very keen on this stream-of-consciousness approach. Gilliam was very influential in those early days in setting the style of Python."

While Palin, Jones, Gilliam, and Idle—the *Do Not Adjust Your Set* group—emphasized stream of consciousness, Chapman and Cleese had their own thoughts on the shape of the show that complemented the others' ideas.

"Partly because of *At Last, the 1948 Show*, John and I already had in mind what it should *not* be, and that was conventional," Chapman says. "We'd gotten further away from most TV sketch shows by ignoring the conventions established over the years—that sketches must have a beginning, middle, and end, and a punch line, above all. They must also be interspersed with songs and dances—that was always the tradition, a holdover from stage variety or stage revue. We protested that—it was laziness on the part of the writers to say 'And now over to a song' when we could conceivably have half-an-hour's worth of television

*Other original *Goon Show* members included Michael Bentine, Harry Secombe, and Peter Sellers.

British comedy hero Spike Milligan joins the Pythons for a cameo in Life of Brian, *the comedic equivalent of Chuck Berry and Little Richard joining the Beatles onstage for a jam session. From the far left: Jones, Carol Cleveland, Gilliam, Palin, Milligan (in white beard), Cleese, and Idle (standing behind Cleese).* **Photo copyright Kim Howard Johnson**

show which was *all* funny. 'You *can* take it,' we thought. It's just that people weren't industrious enough to write it. So, we did want each part of the show to be worthy of its place on the basis of comedy.

"We had gone further and further with the *1948 Show*. We got quite a long way indeed from the conventional formats by sending them up, quite often, by having silly announcers—they were obvious ciphers. A running thread throughout one show was the 'Make the lovely Aimi MacDonald a Rich Lady Appeal.' We also added a sort of supernumerary pleasant-looking lady each week . . . and those girls would say even less, some being given [only] the word 'and'—which often proved difficult for them." Chapman laughs. "When you've only got the one word, you'd better get it right. Of course, that creates awful tension!"

"Anyway, we did slightly send up those old formats, to get away from them and mess around with the shapes. Also, no one up to that point, really, had decided to write something for television—forget all that film and stage nonsense—think about television, what one can do with it. And, that's the way we should be doing our comedy.

"Of course, we were influenced by the anarchic school of comedy as represented by *The Goon Show*, and particularly Spike Milligan's *Q5*. So, to an outside observer, some of the strange links and the weirdness, and the bits of obvious television that we left in, like shots of cameras that said quite obviously 'This is television and we don't mind' were quite reminiscent of Spike Milligan. It was nice to find that we were moving in the same direction."

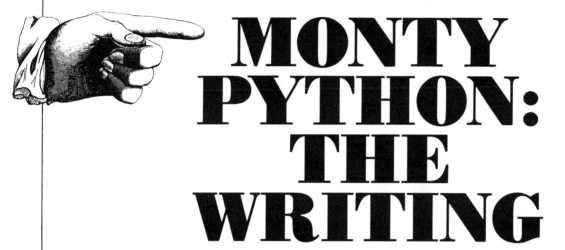

MONTY PYTHON: THE WRITING

*I*n a way, Monty Python was formed as a writers' collective. As Eric Idle has said, the individual members began performing somewhat out of self-defense to protect their material.

Graham Chapman and John Cleese had written together since their Cambridge days, and tended to do so throughout most of Python. Likewise, the Oxford pair of Michael Palin and Terry Jones wrote together for most of the Python shows. Eric Idle was left to write—and present—material largely on his own, while Terry Gilliam was so independent that the others seldom knew what he was working on until he walked into the studio on taping days with his completed reels.

Still, as the series continued, the writing partnerships would temporarily shift to keep everyone fresh and to stave off boredom. Yet they always managed to revert back to Chapman and Cleese, and Jones and Palin.

"Toward the end of the first series, I tried to break up the writing partnerships, because I thought we'd get more original material by going with the different pairings," explains John Cleese. "Michael and I wrote the 'Hilter' sketch, the 'North Minehead Bye-Election,' Eric and I wrote the 'Sir George Head' mountaineering sketch, and I think Mike and I wrote the sketch about the Army protection racket with Luigi Vercotti.

"Then, for some reason, we drifted back into the original pairings—which I regretted, because I thought it was much more fun to keep breaking them up."

During the Python days, Terry Jones admits it was his own lack of self-assurance that prevented him from writing with different members of the team. "I always felt very unconfident about material that I'd written," he confesses. "It was only when Mike had okayed it that he and I worked it out, and I felt more confident. Mike always used to read our stuff at meetings, and he was certainly much better than I was."

Still other changes would occur in writing partnerships for various reasons.

"It was just for the sake of change sometimes, or if someone was absent for some reason or another, or someone wanted someone else to help work on a particular idea—that would happen, too," Graham Chapman recalls. "I would do little bits with Michael or Eric from time to time, though I never really did anything with Terry Jones or Terry Gilliam."

The teams were useful for a more pragmatic reason, however. When the group met to decide on what material to use in each show, they would vote—which left Idle at a disadvantage.

"Eric's problem was that he always wrote on his own. He always felt that he only had one vote. On the whole, if we read out material that we had written as a pair, we would both vote for it. Eric was always a bit sore, he was a bit outnumbered," says Cleese.

Idle concurs, and figures it was fifty percent harder for him to get his material in the shows. "I didn't have somebody to laugh when I came to the joke bits." Idle smiles. "Michael would read out, and Terry would fall about laughing. But, since everything had to be really auditioned, I don't know how much difference it made.

"It probably didn't matter much on the TV shows, but it always made more difference on the films, because we'd constantly rewrite them. Therefore, I'd have to do it again each time, and

I'd have to sell it several times to finally get a piece into the film.

"So, I got whittled away more on films. There was so much more material on TV—where we'd be doing thirteen shows—that if it finally got some kind of laugh, it would be in one of the shows. But I guess I had a higher percentage wipe-out rate."

Idle says that since he was on his own, he couldn't really conspire with a partner to get votes, but the group setting was very useful for them to advise each other. "If it worked and we got laughs, there it was—it was obviously funny. And if it didn't get laughs, or if it only got a few laughs, then we had immediate advice: 'I can help this sketch go here,' or 'What it needs is this.' And we could do it in a rewrite, or someone else could take it on. That happened a few times."

John Cleese says there was a slight contrast in style between the Palin/Jones team and Idle, Chapman, and himself, and he may have picked up votes at times due to a slight Oxford/Cambridge bias. "We always valued the other peoples' styles—it was just that if there was a disagreement as to whether a sketch should go in or not, the voting was often along Oxford/Cambridge lines," Cleese notes.

"The split was *always* between Oxford and Cambridge," emphasizes Terry Jones. "It was always John and Graham and Eric who tended to like something when Mike, Terry Gilliam and I didn't. Terry was sort of 'honorary Oxford.' The split was *always* on those lines. It *never* happened that Graham joined us, for example. It was just a question of taste."

The one Python who usually escaped such politicking was Terry Gilliam. His involvement in planning the main body of the shows was usually peripheral, but he took advantage of his freedom within the group.

"When the others were working on ideas for a program, I always had things I wanted to do as well," Gilliam explains. "Sometimes when we were putting together a program, I'd say 'Well, I've got this idea of doing that,' which would get them to say 'Let's stick that in there, that sounds like it might work.' But, most of the time they would run out of steam, so I had to get them from that point to the next bit.

"I would go away and do what I was doing, and they would see it on the day of the show. I'd arrive with this can of film under my arm, and in it went! They would be confused. I think John was always vaguely intimidated by visual things, and he would never make obvious comments like 'It doesn't work,' or 'It's utterly awful,' because he didn't know whether it was or it wasn't! I escaped a lot of criticism because people just seemed to be too uncertain about these matters to pass judgment!" He laughs.

Gilliam was obviously the most independent member of a very independent group. His role was very different from that of the other five Pythons, and his method of production further encouraged that status. "It was always very difficult to comment about what I was doing until I'd done it, so in most cases it was a fait accompli—there it was.

"Whenever I actually talked to Mike or Terry, who were the most sympathetic to what I was doing, and tried to explain what I was working on that week—well, I would tell it very badly." Gilliam laughs. "I would explain it in the worst possible way, and they would immediately start panicking, thinking 'Oh, oh, he's really done it this time!' And after a while, they really just didn't want to know what I was doing."

Although several Pythons might work on various stages of a sketch, they never attempted to write an entire sketch all together. The only complete group efforts were usually short, linking material.

"When we were assembling sketches into shows, we inevitably needed to rewrite the top, tail, and maybe another part of a sketch, because we wanted an interruption from an earlier or later sketch to come into it," says Graham Chapman. "We didn't usually spend a great deal of time rewriting while we were all actually together. Usually, if a whole sketch needed rewriting, we knew the direction it needed, and those responsible would go off and do that. But we would do the two or three lines in between each sketch when we were there as a team. And at that stage, a lot of the structuring and original ideas for new short sections—or even longer pieces—came up. There was a lot of cross-pollination there."

The principal difference between the two contingents was that between visual (Oxford) and verbal (Cambridge) humor, at least during the early shows, although Jones and Palin (Oxford) were, along with Gilliam, also more concerned with the stream-of-consciousness structure of the series.

"Mike and I tended to write silent film things. My heart was in the visual stuff in those days, and we tended to write more inconsequential stuff," says Jones. "Also, we were interested in the whole shape of the show, whereas John and Graham were always much more interested in verbal humor. They wrote really tight idea sketches."

Working with each other as closely as they needed to often resulted in each influencing the others, a phenomenon that increased with each season. As a result, there is really not a typical Jones/Palin sketch, for both subtle and overt reasons, according to Terry Jones.

"What was a typical Jones/Palin sketch, when we started writing, is now no longer a typical Jones/Palin sketch," Jones says. "In the early days, it was a sketch without many words, and was mostly visual; it was 'Pan over countryside and play music' a lot. Gradually, John and Graham would send us up so much about this, that we tended to stop writing visual sketches, and got more into verbal sketches.

"And at the same time, they did the opposite. They started writing more visual sketches while we got more verbal. I think the real difference is that Mike and I will tend to write things that we can't justify, so far as writing from a gut feeling. There isn't a rationalization of the concept, whereas John is a very rational person.

"John introduces amazing sketches which are terrifically funny to me, but they'll have a very rational base . . . and [you can] say 'That's why it works.' I think John has a need to seem to be explaining a problem; the actual sketch is the result of a rational process that one [can] analyze," Jones says.

"When John relaxes, he writes some of the most wonderful, absurd things. He loves absurdity, but he likes it to have this rationality behind it. He doesn't like stuff that Mike and I write that can't be explained, like the 'Spam' sketch. I don't think John or Graham ever particularly liked that, because it doesn't have any rationale behind it."

The writing didn't always go easily but, without a doubt, the most worrisome problem that developed was Graham Chapman's dependency on alcohol. His battles with the bottle, and his subsequent recovery, have been well documented elsewhere, especially in his own *A Liar's Auto-*

biography. His drinking naturally affected his Python teammates.

"Graham has now gone on record as having gone through an alcoholic phase," says writing partner Cleese. "Obviously, that introduced certain difficulties, just because he tended to be a bit vague about what we were writing."

Michael Palin affirms that, of all of them, Chapman has changed the most since the television days, and much for the better. "Graham would be the first to admit that going off the booze has done wonders for him. He was always a very funny man, and a good writer of inspired silly material. But he's got his act together now.

"If anyone has changed, it's Graham, because his whole life did change when he went off the drinking. Basically, he's doing what he was doing before much more efficiently. He just doesn't crawl under tables and bite waiters."

The other major difficulty that evolved during Python writing sessions was a virtual polarization within the group, with John Cleese and Terry Jones at opposite extremes. The two had radically different temperaments, and used to lock horns over material, or even the form the shows should take.

"They were real extremes—extreme right-wing and extreme left-wing!" Eric Idle jokes. "They always argued as if the entire world depended on it, and they *are* both extreme characters.

Though their working relationship had suffered some strains during the TV shows, by Life of Brian, *Cleese and Jones were back on track.* **Photo copyright Kim Howard Johnson**

"But it was good, because John could actually stand up to Terry. Terry is very Welsh. When he's very emotional about what he thinks and feels, it's impossible to change his mind. If he says A, you say B; he says A, you say C; he says A, you say D. You're trying to give in, because he's still saying A!" He laughs. "John was good at standing up to that, 'cause he'd always see it as emotional pressure, and analyze it, and not give in to it.

"So work was actually more fun with the others. I think it was easier, but the work, in fact, was not so good after John left, because the balance wasn't there."

Looking back on it now, Cleese admits he and Jones were at the opposite ends of the spectrum. "This came out of the fact that we were *completely* different temperaments, and we didn't, perhaps, have that little greater understanding of ourselves that we have in middle age.

"Jonesey was really the romantic, and I was really the classicist; that's a reasonable way of describing it. We used to lock horns, which neutralized us, and then the others could jump on the scales and make the decision. I heard from one or two of the others that when I left the group Jonesey became a bit too dominant at one point, because he always believed in everything very strongly. I always used to say to him, 'Terry, have you ever believed in something *not* very strongly?' Because I often *didn't* believe in things very strongly, but I'd got fed up with being steamrolled.

"Terry always had such strong emotions backing up his argument. We gradually began to get over that around *Life of Brian*, when I realized that we often disagreed because we didn't quite understand what the other person was saying. It's a temperamental thing. Jung wrote a book about psychological types because he was fascinated with why he and Freud split; there was something in the way they approached the world that was so radically different. With Terry and me, we had differences of opinion that resulted from that. And it was often hard for us to understand exactly what it was the other person wanted. I discovered that I could listen more to Jonesey and then understand more of what he wanted, and then I began to realize that most of the time, we were *not* in disagreement."

Jones says he wasn't really aware of the strong differences with Cleese toward the beginning of the series. "I suppose I felt that John didn't really get on with me as well as he might have. Maybe we were on slightly different wavelengths.

We certainly used to have fights, but I only threw a chair at him once!" he says, laughing.

"At the beginning, I was very concerned about the shape of the show, getting this flow. That didn't mean anything at all to John; he used to get a bit irritated by that. But as things went on, he began to realize that it was important to the series. I always had such a respect for John's material—I always thought it was such good stuff!" says Jones.

The years have mellowed them all, though, and the two enjoyed their most recent collaboration immensely. Jones, while directing *The Meaning of Life*, was encased in a huge costume as Mr. Creosote, which he says was like trying to direct from inside a cage. "Every morning, I'd come in and set up the first few shots, then go and have three hours of makeup while they were setting up for lights, camera, and sound. Then I'd come out and get into my costume, which was about six feet around—the world's fattest man—and I couldn't really move. It was quite horrible." Jones

An early generic group shot, minus Terry Gilliam, and one of the very first publicity shots taken by the BBC to publicize their new comedy show, **Monty Python's Flying Circus** *(left to right: Cleese, Chapman, Jones, Idle, and Palin in the foreground).* **Photo copyright BBC and Python Productions**

laughs, but points out that the only other Python around consistently was Cleese, who helped him enormously.

"I really enjoyed the week working with John on Mr. Creosote," Jones says. "Quite often, John and I are poles apart, but working together was really pleasant. John was in top form, producing very funny stuff and coming up with ideas and suggestions. It was really good fun!"

Whatever creative differences existed between Jones and Cleese, it seems that in the long run they probably helped the show. "I think it was good to have that tension going on, though it had all eased up by *Meaning of Life*," says Jones. "At the time, I never saw it as being between me and John, but other people have told me that's what the situation was. As long as there was a fight going on, there was a dynamic happening within the group."

Writing with Cleese and Chapman

Graham Chapman describes a typical writing session with him and John Cleese:

"There was very little variation; it either took place at John's or my house. I would be half an hour late, even at my own house. John was usually fairly punctual, but forgetful about everything else.

"John would lose entire sketches with ease, even on his own desktop, and they would never be found again, even if we went through his entire house. It definitely had disappeared. It was probably a shredder or some kind of sketch-like Black Hole that existed somewhere around, but material that John thought needed rewriting somehow magically disappeared . . . We never found it again, so we did have to rewrite it, which often worked out to our benefit. Other than that, John was just forgetful and disordered in dealing with actual physical objects around him, though mentally he kept a fairly tidy mind!

"In the first half hour or so, we would both try to avoid work, really. It's an awkward moment when we actually had to commit ourselves to saying 'Well, what are we going to write today? What is the subject going to be?' And, we're committed to writing down something which is hopefully going to be funny. So, we'd talk about any subject that came into our heads while having loads of coffee. We could be chatting about newspapers, television news, or literally what had happened on the way to work while trying to decide whether what we were working on yesterday was any good or not. Frequently, if there was a glimmer in it, it was a good idea to start out working on that, because at least we'd have a foot in the door, and might actually get something finished before lunchtime.

"That was always the aim, to go off for a satisfied lunch. But quite frequently lunchtime got very close before anything had been achieved at all. In moments of real desperation, when *no* ideas seemed to come, then *Roget's Thesaurus* or the *Bible*, or any sort of reference book, would be taken out and thumbed through, in the hopes that something would spark off an idea—and often, they did!

"Between John and me, he would be the one to do the actual physical writing on paper 99.99999 percent of the time. I was rather inhibited about that, because I was afraid that no one else would be able to read what I had written, and also slightly inhibited because of my scientific, rather than artistic, schooling. I never really worried too much about spelling or grammar. I knew about it perfectly well, but couldn't really bother to think about it and write neatly. Getting the facts down in a rush was the important thing.

"I also found it a bit inhibiting. I'd rather be

able to let my mind wander, and not have to concentrate on the actual physical work at all. So, John would write them down and lose them, and we would read out the rewritten sketch at the next meeting. In the end, we probably wrote out three sketches a week, which is not an enormous amount."

Python Meetings

"The basics of a Python creative meeting was to read out what we had just written, separately, to each other," explains Graham Chapman. "Rather like still being at school, we would mark the sketches like essays.

"They would get three ticks if they were very good and made everyone laugh, two if they were very good but could be improved, one if it was good enough to be in a show somewhere but probably needed a bit of work, and then none if it was really a waste of time. I suppose that latter category is not a lot of stuff that we really all regret throwing out, although each of us has his own pet in that batch of material.

"But it was like the marking of essays at school. Whether it made me laugh and observing whether it also made the others laugh is how we arrived at what we regarded as quality material," Chapman explains.

"We would spread it around a little bit, so that we'd had a couple of good ones in each show if we possibly could. We didn't always have that luxury—sometimes they were a bit thin around show nine or ten, I suppose. Then, there was a little bit of a revival toward show thirteen at the end, as we kept a little of the good stuff back, or else just saw the light at the end of the tunnel, and we would start writing very silly stuff again."

No matter how the writing went, though, the group could also switch around sketches and shows—and often did. Individual scenes were changed around from show to show regularly, and shows were not always broadcast in the order they were recorded, for an assortment of reasons.

"Sometimes it would have to do with pure timing—we were over-length, or whatever. We had to be fairly exact about that at the BBC, though less exact than we would have had to be at a commercial network," Chapman says.

"The weight of individual shows was another reason. If we'd found we'd got a lot of really good stuff in one show, and another one was a bit thin . . . we'd sometimes mix them around . . . to try and get some good laughs in it.

"It happened for a variety of reasons. Sometimes there had been an objection in the form of 'No, you can't do that' because of something happening in the news, like an airplane crash when we'd just done a sketch about an airline. We'd say 'Well, we can't put that out for a week or two!' That sort of thing happened a little, and some sketches were also removed because of censorship, though I've found it very hard to be specific about that. . . ."

Speaking Up for Cartoons

The greatest contribution the other Pythons made to Gilliam's creations usually occurred after he had finished the animation. Acknowledging their verbal superiority, he would occasionally recruit his teammates to do voices for his footage.

"A lot of times I would have the stuff, and a vague script with actual lines of the characters. I'd grab John in the hallway or something, and say 'Can you say this?' And he would say that, plus other things. The stuff would grow, and they would invariably improve upon it verbally," says Gilliam.

"Terry had the animation so clearly worked out in accordance with his own ideas for the week, that we didn't even know what the pictures were," says Cleese. "We never saw the animation until we actually got to the studio on the day of recording, where they'd play it about three. We just trusted him. There was no point in making suggestions because we didn't know what the pictures were. Three or four of us would suddenly get called into some room, and he'd ask us to do screaming, or arguing, or running up stairs. . . ."

Strangely enough, another major source for Gilliam's voices, and virtually *all* of his sound effects, was Gilliam himself. "I did do a lot of voices on the animation myself, because I couldn't always get my hands on the others. I made all the sound effects myself.

"I'd sit in my flat with a microphone and a blanket over my head, making all these terrible noises—getting kitchen utensils and banging, and shrieking, and doing whatever was necessary," Gilliam says. "I also had the advantage of the BBC sound effects library if I wanted . . . It's very crude stuff to listen to. I got away with it on television, because it's coming out a little three-inch speaker, but if one really listens to it in the cinema, it's shit! But because it was crude, it was effective and made an impact—it wasn't subtle. I did everything. I'd edit the stuff, and it was great—I was doing everything myself!"

PERFORMING

*T*he Pythons always tried to get each series of thirteen shows written before going into production each season. The bulk of the shows *had* to be scripted beforehand, so that the group could shoot the film segments before going into the BBC studio for thirteen weekly turnarounds. About five to eight weeks before recording the shows in the studio, the Pythons would go off to film. The first season's film was shot in two weeks, nearly four week's shooting for the second series, and then five weeks of filming for the third series.

"We gradually used more and more film as the budget allowed, but we had to write everything well in advance, because we obviously couldn't film show thirteen if we hadn't written it," says Graham Chapman.

"By the time we actually went into the studio to shoot the first one each season, we would have about eight shows absolutely mapped out, four of them written, typed up, and in the office, then gradually attack the others. We would have enough material for almost all of the shows."

Monday would see the group going into the studio to start work on the week's show. "We rehearsed mornings only, then spent the afternoons doing bits of rewriting or, if we were lucky, doing nothing!" Chapman laughs.

"On Saturday, we would go into the studio for rehearsal with cameras. Sometimes we would get a full camera rehearsal, but often not. Then we would do the show in front of a studio audience that night. They allowed us an hour and a half of studio time. We could go up to two hours, but the next half hour would cost us time and a half or double time. They just wouldn't allow us to go over two hours, because by then we would be past the time when the electricians could actually just black out the whole studio—and if it looked like we were going on, they would! It was something of a limitation."

As Python developed a following, fans packed the studio to attend tapings. However, the audiences for the first few shows were not exactly Python followers.

"The BBC ticket unit was responsible for getting people into shows, and most of the BBC audiences were the type of ladies who went to holiday camps," explains Michael Palin. "The audience was not a Python audience in age, education, or whatever—not the audience that one would spring something new on at all! They liked the comfortable, familiar old comedians telling the old jokes, and they liked a bit of music.

"Those were the people we got for the first two or three shows, until they realized what Python was. So, we'd have some moments where there was practically no audience reaction at all—except for Connie Booth (John Cleese's first wife), who we could hear laughing a mile away. She really ought to get a credit! One sees those early shows, one can always hear Connie—great noise . . . In those early shows, we could hear our friends laughing politely. We could hear Terry Jones's brother laugh quite a lot!"

The studio tapings were always preceded by comics doing rather traditional audience warm-ups, which pleased the early audiences not as familiar or comfortable with the more unorthodox Python style.

"Python hadn't been assimilated, and hadn't permeated the great British public, and so audiences were quite happy to listen to someone tell a few jokes," says Palin. "Increasingly, we used to make appearances during the warmups, and eventually we ended up almost doing the warmups ourselves. By the second or third season, we realized the people wanted to see us, and we'd go out and do a little bit ourselves. But we had other people. We'd come back with a musician that we'd met on holiday—'Oh, I met this wonderful person in Mykonos and I said he could play the guitar before the show.' 'Oh, did you? All right.' That's what would happen toward the end."

The actual taping of the shows was similar to live theater, according to costumer Hazel Pethig. "The studio was great and exciting, like doing a stage show, with the music, and audiences, and quick changes. It was much more like theater than television, because we had a limited amount of time. There was a wonderful theatrical feeling. The dressers all enjoyed it in terms of the number of quick changes—except for the suit of armor, with the chicken. Getting them in and out of that quickly was always a trial."

Terry Jones confirms that they tried to present it all as a real show, while the limited time they had in the studio helped to move things along.

"It seemed very important to keep the audience boiling with us all the time," Jones explains. "The show was usually shot in order; we usually had just the length of the film clips to change into the next sketch, so it was important to get the audience looking at the film inserts. We did stop and start, though, we didn't shoot continuously.

"Mike, Eric, and I had just come out of *Do Not Adjust Your Set*, which was shot on a very low budget. [On that program] they didn't want to cut the tape, so we actually did these as live shows—everything was done to real time. Coming out of that background, we tried to do Python that way and keep it moving. Inevitably there would be moments when we'd have to stop at the end of the sketch. But it was very exciting."

As much as Jones enjoyed the writing process and taping the shows in the studio, he preferred shooting the film segments because of the control they could exercise. "We could have much more of a hand in the filming. Usually Mike or Terry Gilliam and I would go with Ian Mac-Naughton to scout locations, and we worked closely when we were actually filming it all. Ian and I could discuss it as we were doing it."

There was a great feeling of camaraderie filming on location, recalls costumer Hazel Pethig, and the cast and crew all worked and played together. "They were always very generous, taking us out to supper. They didn't pick and choose who they were going to be nice to—it didn't matter who you were. Whether it was the driver, the dresser, or whoever, there was no discretion at all."

Although the budgets were small in the TV days, they all managed to get along. "We were very much the poor relations at the BBC, so I had very few facilities," Pethig says. "I once had a lorry that had literally been used as a cattle truck, and I'd be changing people in that! One minute they'd be in a muddy field, and the next sequence would be in white shirts!

"Terry Jones and Mike used to be suckers, really. They used to do stunts like jumping off a bridge in the middle of winter while wearing a funny costume. They were always willing. All of them were important, but I felt that Terry and Mike, in a physical way, held Python together. All of them contributed something different, in terms of holding it together. Terry and Mike were like schoolboys full of energy, with their physical ability to keep it going, because it was really trying. And with costumes like the pantomime goose—Graham was often the pantomime goose—they were unspoiled; they coped with it better than they might do now. They were willing to throw themselves into any problem that I had. Even though they had done so much, I felt they shouldn't have to do everything themselves," says Pethig.

The filming was always enjoyable for the group, but the loss of control when they moved into the studio particularly concerned Terry Jones.

"Once we got into the studio, we were totally in Ian's hands as to how to shoot something. We had less input by then, we were really just performers, keeping an eye on the monitors and thinking 'God, that's not quite right,' and sneaking up to the control room and suggesting to Ian, 'Maybe we should do something over there,' " Jones says.

The shows were usually edited later in the week, immediately following the recording. From the beginning, Jones tended to take a strong interest in the process, recognizing the importance of the timing to the laughs. He accompanied director MacNaughton to the editing sessions to provide the input from the Pythons.

"In many ways, I think I enjoyed the editing most of all," Jones says. "It was difficult to begin with, because Ian used to have two hours booked, and wanted to get out of it quickly. He didn't like me going along and sitting there looking over his shoulder while he was editing.

"But the shows were really made in the editing. We could tighten up gaps and pauses, and we could segue into things. Ian began to realize that I wasn't undercutting him when I sat in on the editing—it was just part of the whole creative process. By the second series, and particularly the third series, Ian had really gotten into the editing, and knew to take a day. We'd spend a day in front of the video machines, cutting it down, trimming it, taking out pauses, and making everything work. . . . One can see that in the shows. The editing in the first series is rougher, whereas by the later shows, it really flows by," says Jones.

Undoubtedly, the same part of Jones that drove him to become a director made him look harder at the technical, behind-the-scenes aspect of the Python shows, unlike the rest of the group.

"I don't think the others realized how important it was, to begin with, or else they were more interested in the performing and writing. I'd always felt the editing was crucial. We could write and perform a funny script, but if it wasn't shot right, or if it was shot in the wrong location or something, then it wouldn't work if it wasn't edited properly," says Jones, who still likes to work with the editors on his own films today.

RECURRING FAVORITES

*A*s Python developed, certain characters and conventions came along and proved popular—or useful—enough for return appearances. The Pepperpots and the Gumbies, discussed elsewhere at length, certainly fall into this category, as do Graham Chapman's Colonel, Michael Palin's "It's" Man, Terry Gilliam's Knight with the rubber chicken, and Terry Jones's nude organist, along with such less obvious characters as Cleese and Idle's Mr. Praline and Mr. Badger. The more traditional show business convention, however, carried with it some dangers, according to Graham Chapman.

"We were quite conscious of the heritage of the worst aspects of the earlier shows we'd been associated with, particularly the radio show *I'm Sorry, I'll Read That Again*. It was obviously too easy to rely on the same character appearing, and thereby getting an easy laugh, whether a laugh of recognition or whatever. A person could say 'Well' and they could get a laugh. So we wanted to avoid that easy, catch-phrase reaction.

"We did try to keep it to a bare minimum, but there are characters that did crop up more than once. Obviously, the Colonel was a very useful linking figure in that he was able to stop something, and start something else off without there being a logical connection between the two—yet, it seemed reasonable that he should do so. . . . He could also forestall possible complaints by actually complaining about something, or stopping it himself, saying it's gotten too filthy or it's too silly, then stopping it and going on to something else, hopefully disarming a potential Mary Whitehouse,* or BBC censor!" Chapman laughs.

Despite their usefulness, running characters like the Gumbies were not enjoyed by everyone. "They were useful to come back and link, or comment on something we'd done, but they were never great favorites of mine," says Eric Idle. He says he has no favorite characters or sketches because he was too close to the proceedings.

"We weren't really fans—we just did it," Idle says. "I don't really have favorites because I don't sit there and watch my own work: 'Aren't we wonderful here?' . . . By and large, my memories are not of the shows, but of actually doing them—bits of filming where it was raining, and we were stuck in a pub for six hours dressed in strange costumes. It isn't like we sat around watching the show together, going 'Oh, I loved that.' So, favorite bits are not really relevant in this context."

It's

One character that started in the very first show, and appeared in nearly every program following, was the appropriately named "It's" Man, who would run up to the camera and gasp "It's" just before the opening titles rolled. "There was really no reason why we did it," says Michael Palin, who brought the character to life, "but of course, there was a reason why we did things for no reason at all. I'm sure the 'It's' Man must have been born of that," says Palin.

The "It's" Man wasn't a parody of any other program, however, but a new invention for Python. "We were always quite keen to split up the show in slightly nonsensical ways, like cutting to a Viking saying 'the' in the middle of a sentence. The 'It's' Man was rather like that. Instead of having a smooth presenter saying 'Now it's *Monty Python's Flying Circus*' or 'Welcome to the show,' we started with the antithesis of smoothness. This was a hunted, haunted, ragged, tattered creature, obviously in the terminal stages of fear and exhaustion, coming toward the camera—but we only let him say 'It's,' he never got to say the rest," Palin explains.

"It was rather like this character who, maybe one day many years ago, had been a presenter, and had been allowed to say whole sentences. But he'd fallen on hard times, and was now cut off immediately after he said just the first word. In fact, one of the titles of the show was 'It's,' so he must have been in there fairly early on. On a list of titles I've got scribbled in a notebook was 'It's' and just 'It,' so that's probably where he came from," Palin says.

The "It's" Man segments were shot along with the other filmed portions of Python, generally on locations, and later inserted into the studio part of the show. The "It's" Man was usually filmed wherever the group happened to be at the time.

"The first one I remember was at a place called Cool Harbor in Bournemouth, with very nice, sunny weather," recalls Michael Palin. "Unfortunately, the 'It's' Man had to emerge from the sea. I had to get dressed up in all these rags and tatters, walk into the sea, wait for a cue from the director, get down under the water, count ten, and then come staggering out.

"But we were at a place called Sandy Bay, or something—very aptly named, because it was all sand; there was hardly any sea there at all. I walked out to where I thought I'd be underwater. I'd gone out several hundred yards, and it was still just below my knees! By the time I found enough water to submerge in, I was out of earshot, and everything had to be done with waving hands, and screams, and shrieks. I just felt very silly. I was

*The Phyllis Schafly (or self-appointed monitor) of British TV.

dressed like this, and there were a few holiday-makers who looked extremely bewildered, as this terrible figure strode out, trying to get lower and lower, occasionally ducking down in the water to find that my back was still showing, so I had to go further . . . That was baptism of water!

"The nastiest 'It's' Man of all, though, was where I had to be hung up on meat hooks. In those days, we couldn't really afford harnesses or anything—I was just hanging. I can understand why they kill things first, because it's extremely painful to be hung up on these bloody hooks if you're still alive."

Women's Institute Applause

Another bit that frequently recurred through the entire series was a two- to three-second film sequence showing a group of older ladies applauding, stock footage of a Women's Institute meeting. The bizarre shot was intercut to reveal the ladies clapping at a Python sequence that the real women would probably never have anything to do with. But, the film was peculiar enough to occur in a great number of shows, often more than once per show.

"We had a researcher in the first series, Sarah Hart Dyke, who probably got these bits of film. There's an awful lot of that stuff in the BBC film library," says Palin. "It was rather good, I must say. It was rather like our own audiences [at the start]."

"The Python Theme Song"

BY JOHN PHILIP SOUSA

Yet another Python trademark around since the first show is the use of John Philip Sousa's *Liberty Bell March* as the Python theme song, a curious but somehow appropriate choice to accompany the show's titles and credits.

"We chose that off an album in an office at the BBC," says Palin. "We obviously had to get something that was out of copyright. I think Terry and I chose that because we wanted something that was rather like brass band music, something lively."

Terry Gilliam maintains there was no actual thinking behind the decision to use the Sousa march. "Like most of the stuff, it was all spur of the moment—if we liked it, we did it. We might have been talking about marches, or something martial, while trying to think of music for the opening. I just remember sitting there listening to a lot of music, when suddenly that thing came on, *The Liberty Bell*. I thought 'That's got to be it,' it was wonderful, just exactly right.

"So, we got it and I cut it down to thirty

seconds; we rearranged it and cut sections out. It was the bell at the beginning that did it for me. *Bong!* It was a great way to start something. We cheated the bell so it's actually much louder than it is on the original recording," Gilliam says, and smiles as he points out that it is in the public domain.

"It was free; a lot of people just don't know that the song is Sousa, but he deserves full credit—it's a wonderful tune! Before Python, I don't remember hearing that song, but now I hear it all the time. The International Horse Show in London, a big thing every year on TV, inevitably plays *The Liberty Bell*, and they play it at football games. It's always now associated with Python, not with Sousa. To me, that is now Our Song and nobody else's."

The march turns up in many unexpected places, to the delight of Python fans, but Michael Palin has one special memory. "A wonderfully Pythonesque moment happened on one of the endless programs during the wedding year of Charles and Diana, the wonderful royal couple we all know and love. There was an in-depth interview in a room overlooking the Horse Garden Parade in London, where they were talking about 'Where will you live?' and 'How will you educate your children?' Suddenly, from down below, one could hear this band practicing, and up came the music! It must have been the Guards practicing. It's just subliminally in there, but it was quite a wonderful moment to anyone who knew Python! They were going on answering these questions, while we heard the music drifting up. It was a real absolute delight!"

Helping out with the Montgolfier Brothers, Carol Cleveland found herself hanging from an airbag by the fourth season of Python. **Photo copyright BBC and Python Productions**

Carol Cleveland

The Pythons weren't able to play all of their parts themselves, and were lucky enough to have a very talented stable of supporting players to back them up. But, whether they appeared in one show or dozens, none is as dear to the hearts of Python fans as their Number One Ingenue, Carol Cleveland.

"Carol, of course, was excellent. She was the unsung heroine because she was so spot on," says Michael Palin. "We never had to tell her how to play a scene, she just had a Python way of thinking about it. She instinctively knew how to get all those laughs out, which is not necessarily by going over the top or mugging. It's all teamwork, sharing the laughs with the others. She was so very good when she was in love with the pantomime horse! 'Oh, pantomime horse, I do love you so!' Things like that, she did very well indeed—she was never, ever, upstaged."

Although she was born in England, Carol was raised in America. Half American, she had show business in her blood, and her parents met on a film set. "My mother wasn't a pushy, theatrical mom, but I think she was delighted that I went in that direction," Carol says.

She began taking ballet lessons at about five, but in her early teens decided she would rather be an actress. "I was the leading dancer in an amateur production, and played Cinderella at the last minute when the girl that was supposed to do the part broke her leg. That was a great turning point for me, and I decided acting was a lot of fun. From that moment on, I've never really wanted to do anything else."

Carol had been doing a fair amount of comedy, playing the "glamour stooge" in various television comedy shows, working with people like Spike Milligan, Peter Sellers, and The Two Ronnies. Although she had done drama as well, she claims to have fallen into comedy early on, and her name came up when the Pythons were first putting their show together.

"I'm not quite sure who introduced me to the whole setup. Someone suggested my name when they were looking for a female. They had only written five episodes so there wasn't a lot to do, but they wanted someone. I didn't know any of the lads, I'd never met or worked with any of them, but someone put my name forth as a possible choice. I was interviewed by the producer, John Howard Davies, who was

Carol Cleveland had a chance to work on her tap dancing at the Hollywood Bowl, while Neil Innes plays "I'm the Urban Spaceman." **Photo copyright Kim Howard Johnson**

Complete with showgirl costume, Carol Cleveland introduces Cleese at the Hollywood Bowl. Photo copyright Kim Howard Johnson

going to direct the first four episodes at the time, and he cast me," Carol says.

"I was only supposed to do five shows according to my contract, but by that time the fellows decided they liked me, and I seemed to fit in with what they were doing. I must admit that, the first couple of episodes, I didn't understand what the hell was going on, I didn't understand what it was all about! But they liked me and I fit in, so they kept me on as their regular female. It was the fellows who decided they wanted me around, which was really very nice.

"I loved working with them, once I got used to it. I was baffled to begin with, but I think everyone was rather baffled to begin with. But, I just loosened up and decided that, whatever it was all about, I'd just enjoy it, and I got into the zaniness of it all. I thought it was splendid and I loved doing it."

Despite their unorthodox use of women, costumer Hazel Pethig confirms that Carol was gradually accepted and embraced by the group. "I remember always having to strap women's boobs up to make them look big. It wasn't a very emancipated show." She laughs. "But Carol was gradually given character roles. In the beginning, she wasn't very comfortable, but she got used to it. It was great being able to dress her up as a character, and forget the fact that she was young and glamorous. She fitted in very well."

Although most of her time today is taken up performing in theater and occasional British TV, Carol says she is obviously best known in America for her Python work. "I come across Python fans in America who keep talking about sketches which I have long since forgotten. I think 'Oh my goodness, yes, that was a funny one, I'd nearly forgotten about that one.' For me, the favorite one that I did was the very funny send-up of 'Scott of the Antarctic.' That was one of the few long sketches that worked, because on the whole, the long sketches in Python have been the least funny. But this was very funny, and we all played these very definite, extremely funny characters. I played a film starlet à la Marilyn Monroe, all blonde and kooky. I had to stand in a trench when the film director comes up to me and says, 'We think we'd like for you to play this scene out of the trench today,'" Carol says, and goes into her character voice.

"'You want me to play the scene out of the trench? But I've never acted out of a trench before! It's dangerous, I might fall over!' Lovely things like 'I'm terribly sorry, I just can't remember my lines, my doggie's not well.' For me personally, that was the one that I enjoyed doing most of all.

"Monty Python was one of the happiest experiences I've ever had. Little did anyone know at the time what a great fantastic success it was going to be. I just thought 'Well, this is fun.' But, I've never loved anything quite so much."

Neil Innes

Neil Innes was involved with the members of Python before Monty Python actually existed, and then became reinvolved when the series was underway. He eventually did music for the records, all of the stage shows, and the films as well. Innes, however, was rather well known before his Python career began.

While at Goldsmiths College in London around 1965, Innes became involved with a group of other art students that formed the now-legendary Bonzo Dog (Doo Dah) Band. They began playing in pubs around London, doing '20s dance tunes and rock and roll, with instruments that included banjos, saxophones, tubas, and spoons, in addition to guitar, piano, and drums. Their high-energy, fast-paced playing was accented by their costumes, stunts, gags, and explosions by the time of *Gorilla*, their first album in 1967. They played concerts with Cream and the Bee Gees, and appeared with the Beatles in *Magical Mystery Tour*.

The Bonzos also began performing on *Do Not Adjust Your Set*, the children's series that also featured Terry Jones, Michael Palin, Eric Idle, and

Neil Innes runs through some of his numbers at the Holly-wood Bowl dress rehearsal. **Photo copyright KHJ**

Terry Gilliam, shortly before Python came into being. They all became friends, but wound up being pulled in other directions.

Innes and the Bonzos had become quite popular in England, but seemed to lack the business acumen to become financially successful. In 1969, they did two tours of the United States, and played the Fillmore West with the Byrds and Joe Cocker. Although they always went over well in the States, nobody on the industry side seemed to appreciate them, with management apparently deciding there was no market for them. During this final period (their last performance was in January 1970), they had become more committed to rock. Innes began to come into his own as a musician and songwriter, talents he would carry over into his post-Bonzo work. He joined the short-lived group The World in 1970, followed that by working with Grimms in 1971, and the Bonzos reunited in 1972 for one last album.

Increasingly on his own, Innes became more drawn to his Python friends. "When they all formed Python, the Bonzos sort of packed up,"

**Neil Innes relaxes in a casual moment offstage.
Photo copyright KHJ**

Innes explains. "I met up with them later, when Eric rang me up and asked if I'd like to come along and do a warmup at the BBC. I said 'I don't do warmups,' and he said 'It's twenty-five quid,' and I said 'Done!' Their regular man was ill. I've never done a warmup since," he says, laughing.

Innes worked with the group during their stage shows, and during the fourth series he wrote some musical material and cowrote two sketches for the shows. He then did the music for *Monty Python and the Holy Grail*, where he also performed onscreen, chiefly as the minstrel who sings "The Ballad of Sir Robin"; he acted in *Life of Brian* as well, most memorably as the scrawny Samaritan who battles the gladiator.

Innes actually became a Python regular earlier with his appearances in all of the stage shows. He performed songs like "How Sweet to be an Idiot," "The Old Gay Whistle Test,"* and the old Bonzo favorite "I'm the Urban Spaceman" in costumes which suggested the Bonzo days. Although the Bonzo albums are hard to find, Innes can be heard performing solo on the *Drury Lane* import and the *City Center* live albums, as well as *Monty Python Live at the Hollywood Bowl*.

After the breakup of the Bonzos, Innes says it was fortunate to have another funny, talented group to collaborate with. "I much prefer working with a group of people," he explains. "It was very good for me after the band ended, to meet up with another group of people who were just as silly and clever in their own way, a very good thing to move on to from the Bonzos. There was the same sort of anarchy. Whereas the Bonzos were completely anarchic, though, the Pythons knew how to get things done in front of the camera."

Innes and Idle continued collaborating, particularly on Idle's *Rutland Weekend Television* series in 1974 and the soundtrack album released at the same time.

The greatest Idle-Innes collaboration, however, is undoubtedly "The Rutles," their Beatles parody that developed out of a film done for *RWT*. Idle conceived the group, and Innes wrote and helped record all of the Rutles music for the Warner Brothers soundtrack album *The Rutles*. Idle had turned the concept into a full-length "docudrama," *All You Need Is Cash,* which aired on NBC March 22, 1978, and also featured Dan Ackroyd, John Belushi, George Harrison, Mick Jagger, Bill Murray, Michael Palin, Gilda Radner, and Paul Simon, with Idle, Innes, Rikki Fataar, and John Halsey as the Pre-Fab Four. The album was nominated for a Grammy for Best Comedy Recording of 1978.

Innes also starred in his own comedy/music series in 1979, *The Innes Book of Record*, which included an appearance by Michael Palin. A soundtrack album of the series was released in Britain on Polydor Records.

*"The Old Gay Whistle Test" was a late '60s-early '70s TV rock show.

And a Cast of Many

The Pythons generally drew their supporting cast from a pool of friends and colleagues, and even wives—Connie Booth made several appearances in sketches, along with Mrs. Idle. Booth and Cleese were married just before Python began, and she began appearing early in the first series.

"I don't remember my first sketch, but I think it was a Canadian scene, with the Mounties, and me singing. I had to learn an English accent for one thing, but I mostly did little tiny bits," says Booth, who is a native of Indianapolis. She says her appearances were rather sporadic, due to the nature of the show.

"I didn't think I was that suited for much of the stuff, but if something came up that they thought I was right for, I did it. Carol Cleveland was hired to be their steady lady, while I was only in for little bits. Carol was also very good at different voices, and I usually only did American parts.

"I never really felt that Python wrote for women. They wrote for men to do women, and they played women much better than women did," she explains.

"I was very flattered to be amongst Python, because I admired what they were doing, but I always felt I was never particularly funny. They

***Connie Booth** with former husband Cleese in Tunisia, writing the second series of* **Fawlty Towers**. **Photo copyright KHJ**

were the funny ones, and I was always the fall guy, the dumb blonde, and they were the ones being eccentric or interesting."

Of the supporting men, probably no one made more appearances on the TV show than Ian Davidson.

"Ian was a friend of Terry and myself from the same Oxford University Revue. Now he writes for the BBC, and in fact does a lot of work with Barry Humphries," Michael Palin says.

"It was generally friends that we used back then. There was a guy named David Ballantyne who appeared in a number of sketches. He was a very nice, presentable-looking lad, more presentable than any of us, with a nice haircut. He was a very good, straightish guy found by Ian Mac-Naughton.

"There was a chap named John Hughman who was immensely tall, and used to appear in things like 'Spot the Looney.' Terry and I had used him in *The Complete and Utter History of Britain* for his enormous size. Generally, people we liked were invited back a second time. They had to be people who were just prepared to go along with it and not complain—they had to like it or lump it!"

HELP!

*I*n early 1965, Terry Gilliam was working as associate editor for Harvey Kurtzman's *Help!* magazine in New York City. John Cleese was in the same city, where he appeared on Broadway for several weeks in *Cambridge Circus*.

The magazine regularly ran a fumetti feature—essentially a comic book using photos, rather than illustrations. For an upcoming feature, Cleese was tapped to portray Christopher Barrel, a young executive who falls in love with his daughter's doll. One of Gilliam's duties was to supervise the shooting of the feature, and for the first time Cleese and Gilliam worked together on a comedy project.

The meeting proved to be significant for the both of them, and for comedy lovers everywhere. It was that meeting which led to Gilliam's eventual collaboration with the five Englishmen. Without Gilliam's animation and contributions to the structure of the show, *Monty Python's Flying Circus* would have looked quite different—if it had even come about at all.

Gilliam kept in touch with Cleese, and when he journeyed to England, after a series of jobs, he looked up Cleese in hopes of working in television. Cleese referred him to a BBC producer, and Gilliam's persistance resulted in TV work. This eventually led to work on *Do Not Adjust Your Set*, and meetings with Eric Idle, Terry Jones, and Michael Palin—and the rest is history.

But that history began in the May 1965 issue of *Help!* magazine, and "Christopher's Punctured Romance." Although brief portions of it have been presented in the past, this significant piece of Python history has never been reprinted in its entirety, until now. It holds up very well indeed, and Cleese's expressions are a wonder to behold. One can almost hear that familiar voice mouthing the lines.

But now one can judge for oneself. For the first time since 1965, "Christopher's Punctured Romance."

Behold Christopher Barrel, returning dutifully home to his wife, Wilma Barrel — with a case of ennui. Look at him. This sort of thing happens to a man. Too much sameness, too much tedium, too much everything everyday, and then the ennui sets in. Some survive, some never get out of it and some never notice; but to some there is An Occurrence . . .

CHRISTOPHER'S PUNCTURED ROMANCE

BY DAVE CROSSLEY
JOHN CLEESE AS CHRISTOPHER BARREL
CINDY YOUNG AS WILMA BARREL
MARTIN   IGER, PHOTOGRAPHER

"Christopher's Punctured Romance." **Photo copyright Harvey Kurtzman**

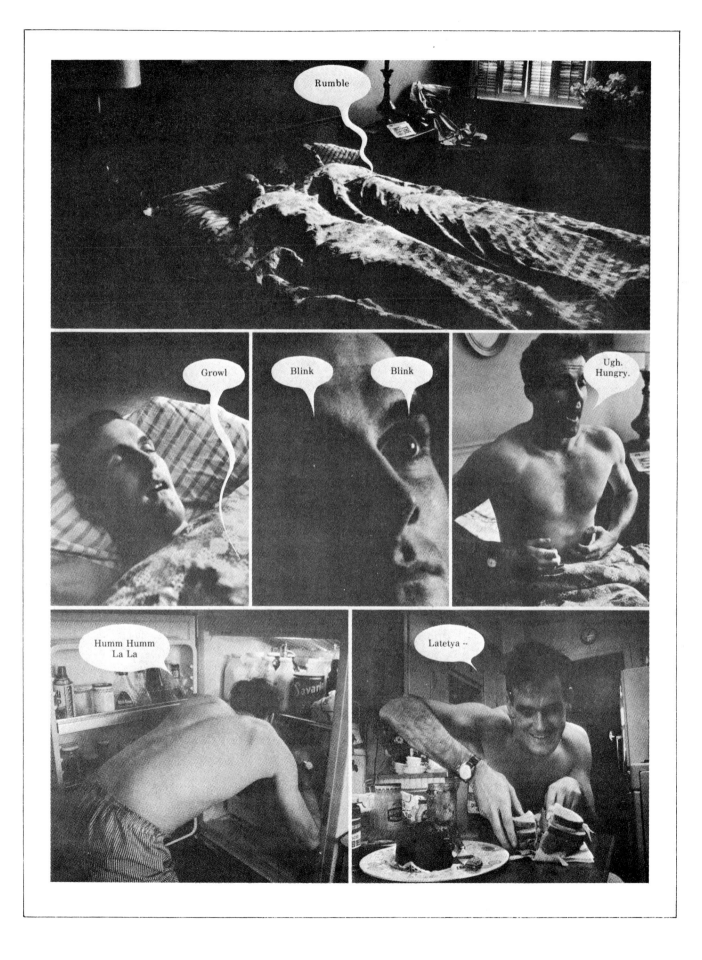

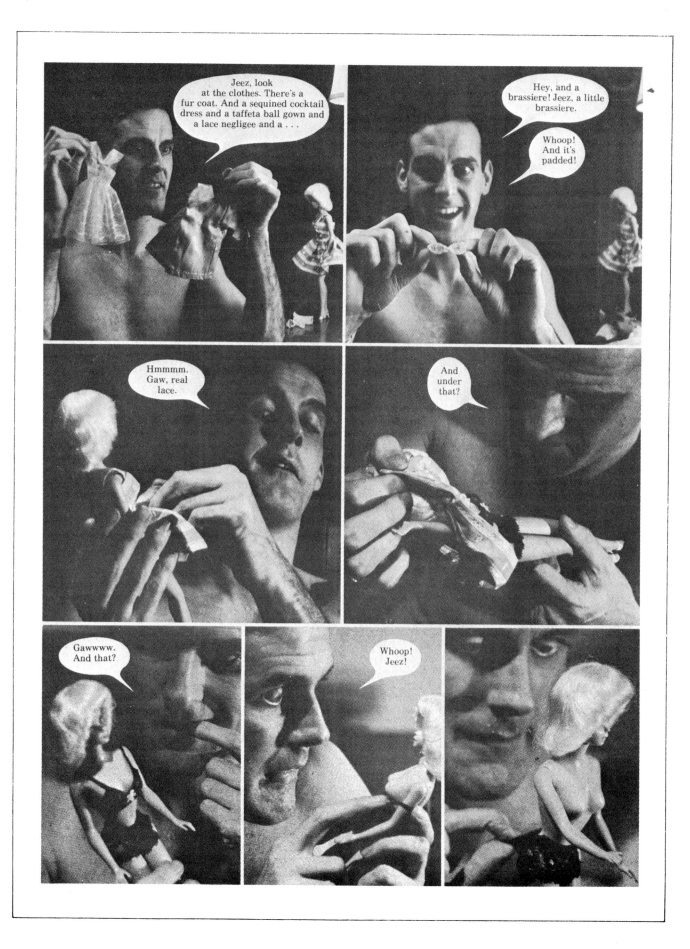

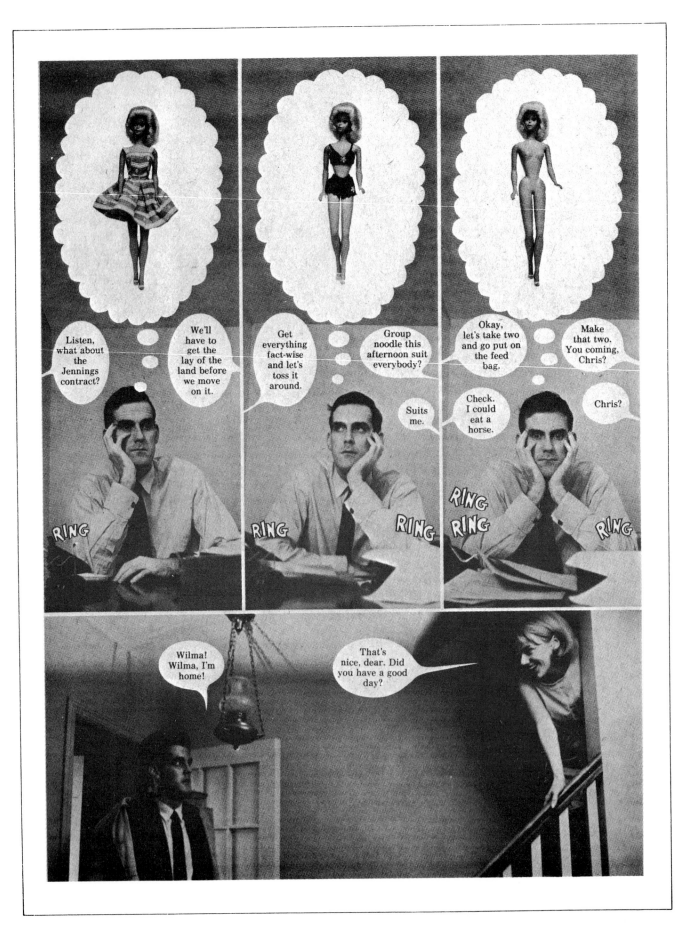

39

41

42

Part Two

THE CLASSIC FORTY-FIVE SHOWS AND MORE

THE FIRST SERIES

*AIRED OCT. 5–OCT. 26, 1969,
AND NOV. 23, 1969–JAN. 11, 1970*

When all of the groundwork had been laid, and all of the advance filming completed, it was time to go into the BBC studios and record the first show. Although Michael Palin had remembered it as being less than successful, when he checked his 1969 journal, he discovered that everyone was actually quite optimistic about it all. Palin writes:

Barry Took won the audience over with his warmup . . . At 8:10, Monty Python's Flying Circus *was first launched on a small slice of the public in Studio 6, Television Centre. The reception from the start was very good indeed, and everybody rose to it, the performance being the best ever. The stream-of-consciousness links worked well, and when, at the end, John and I had to redo a small section of two Frenchmen talking rubbish, it went even better—the audience really seemed to enjoy it!*
It went better than we'd ever hoped, but have yet to see a playback. Afterwards, there was the usual stifling crush in the

bar, with genuine congratulations, polite congratulations, and significant silences. Our agent, Kenneth Ewing, did not appear to like it, and he's probably waiting to hear what other people think. About sixteen of us finished the evening in a festive mood, a pool of relief. This evening I felt very, very happy.

Palin writes that on September 1, 1969, he went to the BBC in the afternoon to watch a playback of the show:

It looked very good. Sagging in a few places, but these can be edited out because we over-ran by about four or five minutes. It looked very relaxed, it was well directed by John Howard Davies, whose reputation now seems totally restored.

NOTE: The following show synopses are based on the rehearsal scripts, as well as repeated viewings of each of the programs; any dubious-looking spellings can be attributed to those scripts.

Wherever possible, the initials of the actors will appear next to their characters, though in some cases they could not be determined. This is particularly true in the case of various extras, mostly without speaking parts, whose names are buried in the bowels of the BBC. Even most of the roles played by the Pythons themselves in the two German shows could not be determined, as most of the information on the two programs was gleaned from the scripts in the Python office.

Keen-eyed viewers may notice apparent discrepancies throughout various shows (i.e., Supt. Harry "Snapper" Organs of "Q" Division changes his rank and his division during his several appearances). Consistency was not highly valued by the Pythons, and will be viewed with similar disdain within these pages.

And now, the classic forty-five shows. Pay attention—there may be a quiz!

Show 1—Sex and Violence

RECORDED AS SERIES 1, SHOW 2—PROD. #53440

The "It's" Man (MP) dashes through a field laden with trap doors, running up to the camera and announcing "It's"
  Titles
  Part Two   Sheep
  A city Gentleman (TJ) talks with a Farmer (GC) about his sheep, which are up in the trees under the misapprehension that they're birds. This leads into a pair of Frenchmen (MP and JC) who lecture in pseudo-French on the commercial possibilities of aviation by sheep, and several Pepperpots (Python old ladies) on film discuss the French and their philosophers.
  An animation sequence follows involving "The Thinker," and "I think, therefore I am."
  Eric introduces the next sketch with "And now for something completely different." It is an interview with Arthur Frampton (TJ), a man with

three buttocks. The Questioner (JC) attempts to get him to drop his pants ("Our viewers need proof!"), with no success, even after switching back to him several times. Eric introduces several other people, including a man with three noses (GC), who blows his stomach, and there is the familiar stock film of the Women's Institute group applauding.
  An unctuous MC (MP) introduces Arthur Ewing and his musical mice, consisting of twenty-three highly trained white mice that each squeak out a different tone when Ewing strikes them with a large mallet. He attempts a song, but is dragged offstage before the indignant crowd.
  The Marriage Guidance Counselor (EI) is visited by Arthur and Deidre Putey (MP and CC). The Counselor and Deidre hit it off, and they send the mild-mannered Arthur out of the room as they

step behind a screen, removing their clothing. Outside, Arthur is met by a man in black cowboy garb (JC), who tells him to be a man and go back in for his wife. Determined, Arthur goes back inside, but when ordered away, he meekly complies. The caption reads "So much for pathos!"

In the north country, Ken (EI) goes home to visit his parents (GC and TJ). Ken ran off to work in the coal mines, instead of laboring in the theater like his parents, who "fill their heads with novels and prose" and are worn out with "meeting film stars, attending premieres, and giving gala luncheons." His father is afflicted with writer's cramp, and finally throws his son out.

The downstairs Neighbor (MP) pounds on the ceiling with a broom handle, and introduces a Scotsman on a horse (JC), who is applauded by the stock Women's Institute film. The man with three noses (GC) blows his elbow, and an animated sequence features Harold, the flying sheep.

"The Epilogue" (introduced by JC) features Monsignor Edward Gay and Dr. Tom Jack, Humanist (author of *Hello, Sailor!*), wrestling to determine the existence of God. Arthur Waring (EI) is master of ceremonies for the bout, and while it continues, the Host (JC) begins a gun battle with an animated cowboy.

The animation continues with a political speech being closed down, a baby coach that devours old ladies, and "The Lovers" statue that becomes musical.

"The World Around Us" (hosted by MP) focuses on the "Mouse Problem"—men who dress as mice, eat cheese, and squeak. Harold Voice (TJ) interviews Arthur Jackson (JC), who describes how he came to terms with his own mousehood, while clips are shown of historical figures who were also mice. There are hostile opinions by the man in the street, and secret film

of a mouse party, climaxed by a farmer's wife cutting off their tails. The Host (MP) shoots Harold the sheep, who lands on his desk.

The "It's" Man (MP) runs away as the credits roll, and a voice-over announces the existence of God by two falls.

ALSO APPEARING: Carol Cleveland

Two Frenchmen (Cleese and Palin) explain the intricacies of flying sheep, while trying to maintain their composure. **Photo copyright BBC and Python Productions**

☞ The BBC script is actually titled "Owl Stretching Time," but the title is crossed out on the inside page, where "Bunn, Wackett, Buzzard, Stubble, and Boot" is handwritten in its place.

☞ Further Pepperpot dialogue on the French philosophers (vs. German philosophers— "Would you swap Descartes for, say, Hegel and Heidegger?") is cut from this show.

☞ The "Musical Mice" sketch was not in the original script, but inserted by hand; Arthur Putey is variously referred to in the script as Arthur Posture and Arthur Pewtie; and a panel of nuns was cut from the final version of "The Epilogue."

☞ A Linkman (MP) interviews "The Amazing Kargol and Janet" (TJ and CC), a psychiatrist/ conjurer act, in a scene that followed the Jackson "Mouse Problem" interview; it was also cut from the final show.

☞ A filmed sketch called "The Wacky Queen" was intended for this show, just before "Working Class Playwright." Silent with voice-over by Alfred Lord Tennyson, it featured Queen Victoria (TJ) and Gladstone (GC) walking along the lawn at Osborne. The slapstick bit begins with the Queen pushing the gardener into a manure-filled wheelbarrow, and squirting Gladstone with a hose, whereupon Gladstone dumps whitewash on the Queen. The cake-throwing climax ends in a freeze-frame that turns into the photo on the mantle in the "Working Class Playwright."

☞ THE MOUSE PROBLEM AND PETER SELLERS'S MILKMAN

The "Mouse Problem" sketch had been written earlier by Graham Chapman and John Cleese; they had held onto it, knowing it could be used at some point in the future.

"We'd always been rather fond of it," Chapman explains, "and it cropped up in Python. I was always quite fond of mice, or little rodents of any kind.

"In actual fact, we had written the sketch for the Peter Sellers movie *The Magic Christian*. He had liked the item very much indeed, but he went off it the very next day, when his milkman didn't like it."

Show 2 — Whither Canada

RECORDED AS SERIES 1, SHOW 1—PROD. #53346

The "It's" Man (MP) runs out of the sea, and says "It's"

Titles

An announcer (GC) walks onto a set and sits on a pig; a picture of a pig is crossed off a blackboard.

"It's Wolfgang Amadeus Mozart" features Mozart (JC) presenting the deaths of historical characters, complete with judges and a sidekick, Eddie (EI), to recap the scores. Deaths include Genghis Khan (MP) and Mr. Bruce Foster (GC), by request, and the finale is the demise of Admiral Nelson, who is hurled off a building. A pig is heard squealing as he hits the pavement, and a teacher (TJ) in an Italian language class crosses another pig off the blackboard.

The teacher attempts to instruct his students, but all of them are Italian and speak it fluently, except for a German student (GC) wearing lederhosen, who is in the wrong class. The teacher then sits on a pig. A pig on the blackboard becomes animated, and runs away before it can be crossed off, leading into a commercial where Pepperpots claim they cannot tell the difference between Whizzo Butter and a dead crab.

"It's the Arts," hosted by a Linkman (MP), begins with an interviewer, Tim (JC), conducting an interview with celebrated film director Sir Edward Ross (GC). After calling him Eddie Baby,

Sweetie, and other too-familiar terms, he walks off the set. The Linkman promises an upcoming film of Picasso painting live on a bicycle, and then shoots a pig.

Another Interviewer, Michael (EI), talks with composer Arthur "Two Sheds" Jackson (TJ) about his nickname, ignoring his music. The first Interviewer then joins Michael after Two Sheds protests, and they throw him out. The Linkman introduces an Eddie Baxter type (MP), who stands in front of a map of Picasso's route describing his plans. On the Guilford Bypass, Reg Moss (EI) talks with British cycling champion Ron Geppo (GC) on Picasso's strategy, as there is no sign of the painter yet. Sam Trench reports live from another location, where several cycling painters go by, but Picasso has apparently fallen off his bicycle and failed in his first bid for international cycling fame, ending "It's the Arts" as the closing credits roll.

The closing credits are interrupted by Victorian animation ("Sit up!"), with heads flying off bodies, dancing soldiers, and a pig falling on a man.

Earnest Scribbler (MP) writes the funniest joke in the world and dies laughing. His mother (EI) discovers it and also falls over dead. A man from Scotland Yard (GC) tells an Interviewer (TJ) that he will enter the house, aided by somber music and laments by men of Q Division, in case he accidentally looks at the joke. The army becomes interested during World War II, and the joke is tested and carefully translated into German. On July 8, 1944, the joke is first used in combat with fantastic success, while a German joke is unsuccessful against the Allies. A Gestapo Officer (JC) and his assistant Otto (GC) interrogate a Prisoner (MP) to discover the joke, Otto providing the sound effects of slapping. His captors fall victim to the joke, as does a German Guard (TG), who bursts into the room to stop him. The Germans were found to be working on their own joke as the war ended, when joke warfare was outlawed and a monument was erected to the Unknown Joke.

At "The End" the "It's" Man is poked with a stick and rises from the beach into the water, as the credits roll.

ALSO APPEARING: Carol Cleveland
Terry Gilliam

Pigs 9   British Bipeds 4

☞ Some sequences here were trimmed, and several other bits were scheduled to be in this show. Taken out and used in other shows were the "Lingerie Shop Robbery," the "Holiday Camp MC," "Donkey Rides," and the "Restaurant" sketch, set to follow "It's the Arts," as well as Johann Gambolputty de von Ausfernschpledenschlittcrasscrenbonfriediggerdingledangledonglebursteinvonknackerthrasherapplebangerhorowitzticolensicgranderknottyspelltinklegrandlichgrumbelmeyerspellerwasserkurstlichhimbleeisenbahnwagengutenabendbitteeinnurnburgerbratwurstlegerspurtenmitzweimacheluberhundsfutgumberaberschonendankerkalbsfleischmittleraucher Von Hauptkopf of Ulm.

☞ The "Italian Lesson" featured a longer sequence in which a fight breaks out in the class over which city is better, Milano or Napoli; the "Killer Joke" originally had a Churchill speech, as well as a modern-day BBC interview on German jokes coming through Britain.

☞ The Scribblers' house is located on Dibley Road, Dibley coming from Gwen Dibley; Michael Palin originally wanted to name Python *Gwen Dibley's Flying Circus* (see Dibley Notes).

☞ HISTORY COMES ALIVE

"I always liked the famous deaths, which I introduced as Wolfgang Amadeus Mozart. I was particularly fond of the death of Nelson at the Battle of Trafalgar. We'd gotten this enormous model of Nelson and threw him out of the top window of this modern bloc, and as he sails through the air, he shouts "Kiss me, Haaardyyyy . . . '" says Cleese, and slaps his hands to indicate a splat.

☞ THE DEADLIEST JOKE IN THE WORLD—REVEALED!

"It was actually German gibberish," Eric Idle explains. "It's written-down gibberish, because we all had to learn the same thing, yeah, but it's gibberish! It doesn't mean a thing at all. At least, I don't *think* it does . . ."

But, for the souls brave enough to withstand it, here is the Deadliest Joke in the World, revealed for the first time in print: Venn ist das nurnstuck git und Slotermeyer? Ya! Beigerhund das oder die Flipperwaldt gersput!

Show 3—How to Recognize Different Types of Trees From Quite a Long Way Away

RECORDED AS SERIES 1, SHOW 3—PROD. #53376

The "It's" Man (MP) runs through a forest, says "It's"

Titles

Episode 12B—How to Recognize Different Types of Trees from Quite a Long Way Away

Number One: the Larch.

Harold Larch (EI) is in court, giving a long, impassioned speech about freedom, but the Judge (TJ) points out that it's only a bloody parking offense. Mr. Bartlett (JC), a barrister arriving late, tries to question Mrs. Fiona Lewis, who delivers rambling, gossipy testimony before being led out of the courtroom. A coffin containing the late Arthur Aldridge is brought in and questioned, but the Judge accuses the barrister of dumping bodies in his courtroom. Bartlett calls in Cardinal Richelieu (MP) as a character witness, but Inspector Dim of the Yard (GC) gets the Cardinal to confess that he is actually Ron Higgins, a professional Cardinal Richelieu impersonator. Dim sings "If I were not in the CID,* something else I'd like to be . . . ," but when Bartlett starts to sing, he is hit with a rubber chicken by a Knight in armor (TG).

Number One: the Larch.

Mr. F.G. Superman (MP) lives in a town inhabited entirely by Supermen. But when the need arises, he becomes their greatest hero, Bicycle Repairman.

The Commentator (JC), wearing a jacket and tie, and sitting at a table in a garden, goes into a tirade against Communists, and eventually flails about, as the Knight (TG) follows him offscreen.

*Criminal Investigation Division.

In "Storytime," the Host (MP) begins reading several stories for children, but stops as they all contain sexual assault, transvestism, contraceptives, discipline, and nudity. The childish animation at the end turns violent, and an animated priest hammers a parishioner into the ground with his forehead.

"Donkey Rides" at the beach is featured briefly, while the unctuous Host (MP) introduces the "Restaurant" sketch.

A couple of (GC and CC) dining at a three-star restaurant point out a dirty fork at their table. Gaston the waiter (TJ), Gilberto the headwaiter (MP), and the Manager (EI), all apologize and beg forgiveness (Gilberto orders the entire washing-up staff fired). Mungo the cook (JC) storms out of the kitchen and tries to attack the customers, when the punch line "Lucky we didn't say anything about the dirty knife," is delivered.

Back at the beach, the unctuous Host (MP) is hit with a chicken by the restaurant Customer (GC), who returns the chicken to the Knight.

An animated commercial is shown for "Purchase a Past"—for fifteen shillings one can purchase bits of other peoples' more interesting lives (including photos) and pretend they're your own. The plan falls apart when numerous animated relatives arrive and start filling up the house, and the animation is crumpled up.

A happy, whistling Milkman (MP) is led into the house of an attractive customer in a negligee (CC). She leads him upstairs, into a locked room where there are numerous other milkmen, some with long beards, others dead.

Newsreader Michael Queen (JC) is reading the evening news, when a shootout erupts around him. He continues reading, oblivious, as he, his desk, and his chair are wheeled out of the BBC Television Centre by the gunmen. He is loaded onto a truck, driven through town, and finally pushed from a dock, all while he keeps reading.

And now—Number One: the Larch. Number Three: the Larch. And now—the Horse Chestnut.

A man (JC) interviews three children (EI, MP, and TJ) in a "Vox Pops" film segment about trees, but they request Eric's "Nudge, Nudge" sketch.

Norm (EI) sits in a pub, making insinuations about another man (TJ) and his wife, asking about their personal lives, nudge, nudge, grin, grin, wink, wink.

The "It's" Man (MP) runs away from the camera as the credits roll.

ALSO APPEARING: Ian Davidson

☞ This show was originally called "Bunn, Wackett, Buzzard, Stubble, and Boot" in the BBC rehearsal script.

☞ In the original BBC rehearsal script, the "Larch" was not included, and the Harold Larch character was originally named Harold Millet; "Storytime" was to lead into the "Vocational Guidance Counsellor," rather than the "Restaurant" sketch; "Irving C. Saltzberg" originally followed the "Milkmen," with Saltzberg calling for the newsreader for the hijacking sketch.

☞ Graham was originally supposed to be one of four children in the "Vox Pops" scene just before "Nudge, Nudge."

The cast of "The Dirty Fork Sketch," another early generic group shot, though not as early as the previous generic group shot. (Left to right: Idle, Chapman, Palin, Cleese, Jones, and Gilliam, who wasn't involved in the sketch, and very rarely appeared on camera toward the beginning of the series.) Photo copyright BBC and Python Productions

FASTER THAN A SPEEDING LAWYER

"Bicycle Repairman" came about from the Jones/Palin tendency to think visually. "That sketch came from Mike and me thinking about rehearsals," Terry Jones recalls, "though it also came from thinking about what would look funny. And it *did* look funny seeing a lot of Supermen all walking around."

Although the "F.G. Superman/Bicycle Repairman" sketch involved groups of people in (what else?) Superman costumes, the group apparently met with no legal repercussions from DC Comics for the use of their character. Michael Palin explains that they had very little trouble from legal sources, especially in their first season. "When we used Spam, I don't think we ever got permission from them—we just used it. In the end they were very keen, and promised they would send us several tins of free Spam. We said 'No, that's all right, thanks anyway . . .' And, we had no repercussions that I can remember from the comics.

"We were not well known at all then, and there was no export potential to other countries. We were just a silly little late-night Saturday show, not even aired in all of Britain. The first series wasn't even seen in the Midlands—they got farming programs. Eventually, people in Birmingham got angry and felt they were missing something. But by the second series, the comedy lovers got the upper hand over the farmers."

Performing "Nudge, Nudge" live onstage had its problems—in this case, Jones and (standing) Idle are halted by the Colonel (Chapman). **Photo copyright KHJ**

Show 4— Owl-stretching Time

RECORDED AS SERIES 1, SHOW 4—PROD. #53485

The "It's" Man (MP) is hurled off a cliff. He crawls along the ground toward the camera and gasps "It's"

Titles

Episode Arthur   Part 7   Teeth

A Guitarist (EI) strums and sings "Jerusalem" live from the Cardiff Rooms, Libya, while he introduces the next sketch.

In "Art Gallery," Marge and her friend Janet (GC and JC) are trying to keep track of their children, who are running around the museum vandalizing great works of art. They discipline the kids just off-camera, and finally start to eat some of the masterpieces themselves. An Art Critic (MP) in the next scene starts nibbling at pictures himself, along with a girl assisting him in the discussion.

The Guitarist is seduced by a girl while trying to sing, and the slogan "It's a Man's Life in the Cardiff Rooms, Libya" is criticized by the Colonel (GC). He says it's too similar to the "It's a Man's Life in the Modern Army" slogan, and warns them against using it again. On his orders, the cameras cut away.

In "Changing on the Beach," a man (TJ) tries to change his clothes at the beach, in the under-cranked style of an old-time silent comedy. He tries to change behind trucks, stacks of chairs, etc., until he accidentally ends up onstage, where he takes the opportunity to do a striptease. The Colonel objects to the caption "It's a Man's Life Taking Your Clothes Off in Public," and orders the next sketch to begin.

In a gymnasium, a Sergeant-Major (JC) teaches a group of recruits (TJ, MP, GC, EI) self-defense against an assailant armed with various kinds of fresh fruit, and asks them to help demonstrate. He shoots Harrison (GC), who was armed with a banana, and Thompson (TJ), armed with raspberries, is struck with a sixteen-ton weight.

An animated operation sees spare body parts become two flunkys, who carry a sedan chair to the beach. The eighteenth-century Gentleman (EI) inside the chair exits, undresses, gets back inside, and is carried into the sea.

The post-coital Guitarist sings, introducing a man (JC) walking through the hills with "It's a Man's Life in England's Mountains Green," but the Colonel stops him before he can deliver his rustic monologue. The Colonel wants to see something about teeth.

A Tobacconist (EI) enters a bookstore, but the Bookseller (JC) says they are all out of books and tries to get rid of him, until the Tobacconist explains he was told to come there. The Bookseller gives the sign and countersign to no avail, and the Tobacconist says he was told to come there by a little old lady in a sweet shop. The Tobacconist starts to become suspicious, and asks for "An Illustrated History of False Teeth." He is accused of being a dentist, and Stapleton, the bookseller, pulls a gun on him. Another secret agent, LaFarge (MP), bursts into the shop, immediately followed by another couple dressed as a dentist and his nurse, all looking for the secret fillings. They all assure the Tobacconist that nothing is going on. Brian (TJ) then bursts in with a bazooka, getting the drop on them all, until the Big Cheese (GC) rolls his wheelchair in, shooting his pet bunny Flopsy. He threatens them all with death, but they break for lunch.

The Tobacconist reveals himself as Arthur Lemming of the British Dental Association. When a chorus sings a refrain about him, with the caption "It's a Man's Life in the British Dental Association," the Colonel stops the show. The "It's" Man is nudged with a stick and runs away as the credits roll, and is thrown off the cliff again.

ALSO APPEARING: Dick Vosburgh
Carol Cleveland
Katya Wyeth

☞ The original order and contents of the show were quite different in the BBC rehearsal script. It was to have led off with the "Bookseller/Dentist/Spy" sketch, followed by "Changing at the Beach," the "Art Gallery" and "Art Critic and Wife" link. The show then went to "Buying a Bed," used in Show 9, then the "Sedan Chair," into the "Hermits," also used in Show 9, to "Soft-Fruit Defense."

☞ ## HAUTE CUISINE

"Those picture frarnes that we ate were apparently some kind of pastry, made with flour and water paste," Graham Chapman recalls. "They weren't sweet, and they were rather dry . . ."

☞ ## TO LAUGH OR NOT TO LAUGH

Since the makeup of the early studio audiences was somewhat less than that of the typical Python fan, the sketches didn't always elicit the desired reactions. In fact, some of them played to a bewildered silence.

The group didn't let the reaction (or lack of such) distract them unduly, as a number of technical considerations were involved as well, and the Pythons simply had to rely on their gut instincts to judge their timing.

"We just had to watch it and say 'Is it funny or not?'" says John Cleese. "There is some stuff that doesn't work with a studio audience, yet I still feel is intrinsically funny. They're not the only criteria, not least because there's a certain way of presenting a sketch to a studio audience that they will laugh at, but there are other ways of doing it.

"For example, when they have to look up

to monitors when we've cut from studio to film—those pieces always play to dead silence. The audience is always looking at the wrong place at the wrong time. But those sketches can still be very funny at home."

 ### CHANGING ON THE BEACH

The Jones/Palin team had, by the time of Python, developed a visual style that was most apparent in their short silent film done for this show. Although it was funny and mostly successful, it was a far cry from the type of material usually included in Python, and Jones says it didn't really work.

" 'Changing on the Beach' doesn't seem like Python, really," he says. "There were certain bits that were never done quite right. I was wary of the part where they take the deck chairs away—it's just too slow, and we didn't undercrank it enough. I always liked silent film stuff, though. That was the kind of thing we'd been doing for *The Frost Report*—it was 'our' style of filming. But it didn't go down well with the others."

Jones (who is a big fan of Buster Keaton) also performs the first of the two stripteases that he does during the series. Both are hilariously convincing, despite his claims of inexperience. "One of the first days of filming was the striptease in this large theater . . . It was quite nerve-wracking, and I was frightened," says Jones. "I hadn't worked out at all what I was going to do. I don't think I'd even *seen* a striptease back then!"

Show 5—Man's Crisis of Identity in the Latter Half of the Twentieth Century

RECORDED AS SERIES 1, SHOW 5—PROD. #53947

The "It's" Man (MP) rows a boat toward the camera and says "It's"

Titles

A Suburban Lounge Near Esher

A middle-aged Couple (MP and TJ) call the vet for their cat, who is suffering from boredom—it just sits out there on the lawn. The vet tells them that their cat is in a rut, and badly needs to be confused.

They send for Confuse-a-Cat Ltd. The Sergeant (MP) drills the group, and the General (JC) orders the "funny things" out of their van. They build a stage in front of the cat, and put on an amazing show, one using locked cameras, undercranking, jerky motion, jump cuts, etc.; it includes Long John Silver, prizefighters that keep changing their identities, Napoleon, a traffic cop, and a penguin on a pogo stick. At the end of the show, the cat gets up and walks away. Credits are shown over a picture of the General, whose animated moustache grows, turning into yarn for knitting needles.

A Customs Official (JC) stops a suspicious-looking man (MP) who appears to be smuggling watches. The Official won't believe him, however, even when he confesses and shows him the watches. He makes the man go on through, but the next person, a Vicar (EI), is ordered to undergo a strip search in the next room.

"Vox Pops" one-liners follow on customs procedures, and the Chairman (TJ) of a TV discussion group on customs enforcement measures interviews a duck, a cat, and a lizard. Man-in-the-street interviews follow, including one by Mr. Gumby (JC) on law enforcement measures. Gumby is then hit with a chicken by a Knight (TG).

Police Constable Henry Thatcher (GC), with police dog Josephine waiting outside, raids the apartment of actor Sandy Camp (EI), looking for illicit substances. He drops a paper bag on the floor, but it is found to contain sandwiches, causing him to wonder what he gave his wife. Two more letters are read, and man-in-the-street interviews continue.

A BBC Newsreader (EI) reads an item about a man wanted for robbery, and the picture of the suspect shown on the Eidaphor screen behind him reveals it to be the Newsreader.

"Edited Highlights of Tonight's Romantic Movie" are seen by Bevis (TJ) and his girlfriend Donna (CC) while in bed; the film includes tall, soaring trees, waves crashing, a fountain, fireworks, a volcano, and other such symbolism. Finally, a caber is tossed, a plane falls, a tree crashes to the ground, and the tower at the beginning of the film collapses.

An animated commercial is shown for "Charles Fatless."

David Thomas (GC) applies at a Management Training Course where the Interviewer (JC) terrorizes him. He makes noises and faces, has him stand up and sit down several times, making him generally nervous and upset, and a team of judges score him. The Head of the Careers Advisory Board (MP) then begins talking about how he originally wanted to be a doctor or lawyer, etc.

A Burglar (EI) knocks on a door, but the Housewife (JC) doesn't want to let him in because she's afraid he's an encyclopedia salesman. Film of an unsuccessful encyclopedia salesman is shown, and he is thrown off a tall building.

The "It's" Man rows away, as the credits roll.

ALSO APPEARING: Carol Cleveland

☞ The cover of the script reads "Beware, Poison, Not to be Taken Internally."
☞ The BBC rehearsal script has the "It's" Man hurled off a cliff at the beginning of the show;

David Thomas's original name was Stig; and the "Ron Obvious" scene was to appear at the end of this show (it is now in Show 10), with the film of the "It's" Man shown at the beginning run backwards, while Vercotti sits on the beach.

☞ ## THE WAR AGAINST ANIMAL COMPLACENCY

Their working environment often had a major influence on Python writing, explains Graham Chapman. When John Cleese came over to his penthouse apartment to write one day, an idea was sparked off that became a classic sketch.

"I had noticed a neighbor's lawn for the last two weeks. It was very carefully tended—she even brushed it—but there was a cat on it, which was *always* in the exact same position. No matter what happened, it didn't move. It didn't even move in moderate rainstorms. It would just sit.

"So, I discussed this with John, and wondered what the problem was with the cat. We decided that it was complacent, and had seen it all, and therefore needed shaking out of its complacency. So Confuse-a-Cat, Ltd., were the guys for the job! That sketch came about purely from what was around."

Chapman says that when desperate, they often relied on reference books to spark ideas. "Whether from the news, from a book like *Roget's Thesaurus*, or from what was happening around us, all ideas have to come about through some sort of observation. It sparks an attitude, and some object or emotion causes a reaction in the other person. They think 'That's an interesting way of looking at it,' and then build a sketch out of it."

Show 6—The Ant—An Introduction

RECORDED AS SERIES 1, SHOW 7—PROD. #55307

The "It's" Man (MP) runs through the woods followed by explosions, as he announces "It's"

Titles

Part 2   The Llama   Live From Golders Green

A pair of South Americans (EI and TJ) sing a song in Spanish about the llama, while another man (JC) describes colorful facts about the animal. English subtitles are shown, and a Señorita (GC) wheels in a motorbike to end the scene.

A man (JC) in a dinner jacket sits at a desk behind Ada's Snack Bar, and announces "And now for something completely different." A man with a tape recorder up his nose (MP) plays *La Marseillaise.*

Arthur Wilson (EI) applies for a job on a mountain-climbing expedition with Sir George Head (JC), who unfortunately sees double of everything and assumes Arthur is twins. The expedition plans to search for traces of the previous year's expedition (led by Head's brother), which had hoped to build a bridge between the two peaks of Mount Kilimanjaro. The leader of the current expedition, Jimmy Blankenshoff (GC), tries to reassure the young mountaineer, but he climbs over the furniture in the room, knocking everything down and inspiring little confidence.

Led by Cleese, the Spanish quartet sings the praises of the llama. **Photo copyright KHJ**

Twins at two desks (JC) introduce a man with a tape recorder up his brother's nose (MP and GC), which is played normally and again in stereo.

An animated Clergyman sells encyclopedias, and is then awarded a kewpie doll.

A Businessman (TJ) visits a shop where the Barber, Bevis (MP), is afraid to cut hair for fear of slaughtering his customers. He tries several subterfuges, including playing a tape of haircutting sounds. The Barber explains that he hates cutting hair, and actually always wanted to be a lumberjack. He then sings a song about lumberjacks, backed up by an increasingly disgusted chorus of Mounties (six Fred Tomlinson Singers, along with GC and JC) as the song takes a transvestigial turn. This is followed by letters of complaint.

Prof. R. J. Gumby (GC) sings while hitting himself on the head with a pair of bricks.

Compère Henry Lust (EI) gives an elaborate, sniveling introduction for "someone whose boots I would gladly lick until holes wore through my tongue," Harry Fink—who isn't there. Instead he introduces Ken Buddha and his Inflatable Knees (TJ), followed quickly by the animated Brian Islam and Lucy, a pair of eccentric dancers.

Meanwhile, the Barber tells his customer

met in a pub about three years ago. He changes their music, insults Iris, and tells an off-color joke. He has also invited the next visitors, Brian and Audrey Equatol (JC and TJ), who sit on the cat. More unwelcome visitors include a poof* (TG), a disgusting Old Man (MP) and his sick goat, and a group of miners who gather around the piano and start singing "Ding Dong." When Victor orders them all to leave, Brian shoots him.

The "It's" Man runs back into the woods and is blown up, as the credits roll.

ALSO APPEARING: Carol Cleveland
Connie Booth
The Fred Tomlinson Singers

☞ In the original BBC rehearsal script, the show leads off with the "Barber," a version in which the entire cassette is allowed to play out through the end of the haircut without the customer wising up. This is followed by letters and Ken Buddha, and an earlier, rather different version of the "Visitors" sketch, in which a couple arrives seven hours late for dinner, and the pajama-clad, sleepy host tries to act as though nothing is wrong, remaining polite as long as possible.

Meanwhile, backstage a lovely senorita (Chapman) prepares to ride a motorcycle into the midst of the Spaniards. **Photo copyright KHJ**

about outdoor life, which leads into a hunting expedition where the hunters shoot at everything in sight. In driving game from the brush, they also flush out lovers, and fight a duel, and find a parachutist and an Indian.

The Knight (TJ) with the rubber chicken is told that he isn't needed this week, and walks away disappointed, passing the man at the desk (JC) in a chicken coop, who announces "And now for something completely different."

Victor and Iris (GC and CC) are timid lovers suddenly interrupted by the arrival of Arthur Name (EI), a strange man Victor

*Slang for gay.

Sir George Head (Cleese) interviews a prospective member (Idle) of his mountaineering expedition. Afflicted with double vision, he hopes to find traces of last year's expedition, which tried to build a bridge between the twin peaks of Mt. Kilimanjaro. **Photo copyright BBC and Python Productions**

👉 THE LUMBERJACK COMETH

Without a doubt, the "Lumberjack Song" is the most popular Python song and, along with the "Dead Parrot," is probably the most famous Python sketch. It has been included in all of the stage shows, with either Eric Idle or Michael Palin singing the lead role, and the rest of the group as the Mountie Chorus. The group has been joined in past shows by such celebrity Mounties as George Harrison and Harry Nilsson. It was even performed in German as the "Holzfeller Song," with a chorus of Austrian border police. When Harrison toured America in late '74, the "Lumberjack Song" was the last music played over the PA system before Harrison and his group began performing.

Michael Palin says he doesn't remember much about writing many of his sketches, but he does recall the day when he and Terry Jones wrote the "Lumberjack Song."

"We'd just had this very long work day trying to finish off the 'Barber' sketch. We were quite pleased with it—it had a nice manic feel, but we were stuck for an ending, or a link, or anything to take us out of it. It was such a looney sketch in itself, so surreal and strange, and it's always more difficult to link something that elusive in itself, rather than something more straight.

"It was about a quarter to seven in the evening, and we'd worked on a lot longer than we normally would. We were just about to give up, and someone shouted 'Supper in half an hour!' We were just ad-libbing, and had the barber say 'Oh, to hell with it! I don't want to be a barber anyway, I wanted to be a lumberjack!' And this huge spiel just came! Terry said 'Quick, we'll write

The hunting party, which claims heavy casualties among its members (Left to right: Chapman, Idle, Cleese, Jones, and Palin). **Photo copyright BBC and Python Productions**

it down!' And not only did the spiel come, it just seemed natural to go into a silly song, because, lumberjacks sing songs.

"I think the whole 'Lumberjack Song' was written by a quarter past seven . . . and we even had the tune for it, which we thought we'd written. It's just an amalgam of various of those sort of jolly musicals-cum-stirring march-type songs. And that's really how it happened. It was just one of those nice little flashes of inspiration. We just roared with laughter when we wrote it, so we knew we had something good there. How wrong we were . . . "

The original Mountie Chorus was made up of the Fred Tomlinson Singers, along with John Cleese and Graham Chapman.

"I wonder how we did get stuck there," Chapman muses. "I had no particular *wish* to be there, but I suppose it was quite jolly. And it was the end of the show, so I didn't really mind. I suppose John and I were tall-ish, and so the Mountie costumes fit."

Show 7 — Oh, You're No Fun Anymore

RECORDED AS SERIES 1, SHOW 6—PROD. #54006

The "It's" Man (MP) runs down a mountain and through brush, and he is prompted off-camera to say "It's . . . It's . . . It's . . . "

Titles

An interviewer, Peter (JC), quizzes Mr. Subways (EI), an unsuccessful camel spotter who used to be a yeti spotter. In seven years, he's spotted nearly one camel. He is actually discovered to be a train spotter, so Peter tells him "You're no fun anymore." Animation follows which includes an old band and more.

"You're no fun anymore" blackouts follow, including ones with Dracula (GC) whose fangs fall out, a man being lashed to the yardarm (EI), and Mr. Subways.

In "The Audit," Wilkins (MP), a very new chartered accountant, gives a financial report to the Board of Directors of the Multi-Million Pound Corporation and its chairman (GC). A sign on the wall reads "There is No Place for Sentiment in Big Business." The company has grossed a shilling, but Wilkins has embezzled a penny. When one of the board members (TJ) says "You're no fun anymore," Mr. Subways ties him to the railroad tracks for using his phrase.

Viewers are invited to complain to Mr. Albert Spim at a given address (the voice-over and caption don't match), and one-liners follow.

The "Science Fiction" sketch is introduced by an unctuous, red-jacketed Host (MP) in a near-empty theater, and begins with shots of galaxies and a voice-over. Mr. and Mrs. Samuel Brainsample (GC and EI) of New Pudsey are overlooked because they are so boring, and instead Harold Potter (MP), a gardener and tax official, becomes the first Earthling to be turned into a Scotsman by a flying saucer. Other victims include a Detective Inspector (TJ), a man at a bus queue, a policeman, mother and baby, a black jazz saxophonist, and a company of Welsh Guards; all are transformed into plaid clothes with kilts.

A scientist named Charles (GC) searches for a cure when his girlfriend (DR)'s father, Mr. Llewellyn, becomes a Scotsman. England is deserted, while an animated map of Scotland shows the crowding, with three men to a caber.

A tailor, Angus Podgorny (MP), and his wife, Mary (TJ), receive an order for forty-eight million kilts from the planet Skyron in the Andromeda Galaxy. Mary is eaten by what is found to be a

Blancmange* impersonator and cannibal named Jack Riley.

Charles discovers that since the worst tennis players in the world are Scotsmen, and several tennis players are eaten, the Blancmange means to win at Wimbledon. And Podgorny is the last human being left to challenge the Blancmange.

Angus is losing to the Blancmange at Wimbledon when Mr. and Mrs. Brainsample run onto the court and eat the Blancmange. Angus practices, and fifteen years later becomes the first Scotsman to win at Wimbledon, playing himself, as the credits roll.

ALSO APPEARING: Donna Reading

 WHAT'S MY MOTIVATION?

Critics have often cited Terry Gilliam's Python acting debut for its subtle nuances and understatement, and for good reason. During his first appearances, Gilliam was forced to emote through a medieval knight's helmet, with no more than a rubber chicken to react with. Still, with a successful career in animation assured, why did Gilliam decide on the additional career?

In his own words: "I wouldn't even rate the knight with the chicken as performing." Gilliam chuckles. "I was just filling up holes that nobody else wanted to step into. I had done all of my work, and was sitting around all day when everyone else was up there doing things. It was very tedious, and so it was better to keep busy doing something. I would just wear costumes and do the things nobody else would touch. It was really more out of boredom."

 LOTS OF SCOTS

If not for the foresight of costumer Hazel Pethig, the Blancmange's prey would have been very few indeed. Getting enough costumes was a common problem for the Pythons, and they often had to improvise. "I used to throw spare things onto this big van, and try to imagine what they might ask for, or what range of costume types I might need. I might need to outfit five Scotsmen in kilts, but if I found more, I'd throw on as many spares as I could, and anything that might relate to that kind of sketch.

"I can remember the whole crew dressing up as Scotsmen, and running onto the hillside. It was totally unethical and against union rules, but the crew was so happy on the show that they were quite happy to do it."

Show 8—The BBC Entry for the Zinc Stoat of Budapest

RECORDED AS SERIES 1, SHOW 8—PROD. #54772

A phone rings on a tree stump in the forest, and is answered by the "It's" Man (MP).
  Titles
  Next Week—How to Fling an Otter

*A kind of custardy pudding.

This Week—The BBC Entry for the Zinc Stoat of Budapest (Current Affairs)

The price of the preceding captions is shown and added up, as several more costly captions are displayed.

Arthur Figgis (GC) (first shown riding a bicycle with Arthur "Three Buttocks" Frampton in an earlier show) signs an autograph for a fan (MP), and the ink lines become animated as the scribble wriggles away, to eventually be shot from an animated cannon, whereupon it becomes Michelangelo's *David*, and the introduction to "It's the Arts."

Arthur Figgis introduces the program, which discusses the German baroque composer Johann Gambolputty de von Ausfernschpledenschlittcrasscrenbonfriediggerdingledangledonglebursteinvonknackerthrasherapplebangerhorowitzticolensicgranderknottyspelltinklegrandlichgrumbelmeyerspellerwasserkurstlichhimbleeisenbahnwagengutenabendbitteeinnurnburgerbratwurstlegerspurtenmitzweimacheluberhundsfutgumberaberschonendankerkalbsfleischmittleraucher Von Hauptkopf of Ulm.

An Interviewer (JC) questions his oldest living relative, Karl (TJ), who dies while attempting to say his name; the Interviewer, disgusted, throws away his microphone and begins digging. There are "Vox Pops" of different characters saying Johann's name, and the close of "It's the Arts" sees an animated hand reaching for the leaf covering *David*; a blue-nosed censor is underneath.

A gang of desperate-looking robbers (JC, GC, TJ,

A gang of vicious thugs hatch a brilliant, elaborate plot to buy a watch. Photo copyright BBC and Python Productions

EI) listen to their boss (MP) devise an elaborate plot to buy a watch. One of them, Larry (TJ), complains that they aren't doing anything illegal. Several short "Vox Pops" follow, with bank robbers, judges, and a police inspector (JC), who announces that he'll be appearing in the next sketch.

Sure enough, Inspector Praline and Supt. Parrot (JC and GC) visit the office of Arthur Hilton (TJ), the head of the Whizzo Chocolate Company, to question him about the Whizzo Quality Assortment, which contains such items as Crunchy Frog, Anthrax Ripple, and Cockroach Cluster. He is taken into the station, while Parrot becomes ill trying to warn the public.

The "Dull Life of a City Stockbroker" (MP) is next. As the Stockbroker leaves his house in the morning, his wife has an affair with two men, a Zulu tribesman throws his spear at his next-door neighbor (narrowly missing him), he buys a newspaper from a nude woman, is nearly killed by Frankenstein's monster while waiting for a bus, and is caught in the middle of an army battle before arriving at his office, where a number of violent deaths have taken place. He remains oblivious to it all, and begins reading a comic book, which becomes animated as a super-hero tries to break out of a panel. The curtain closes on the panel to begin the "Thea-

One of Cicely Courtneidge's fans (Idle), complete with bow and arrows, waits impatiently for her appearance, to the uncertainty of other theatergoers. Photo copyright BBC and Python Productions

ter'' sketch.

An American Indian (EI) in full warrior dress takes a seat (next to GC) in the theater. The Indian says he is a big fan of Cicely Courtneidge, explaining that the Redfoot tribe are mighty hunters and actors. When a theater spokesman (MP) announces that Cicely Courtneidge won't be appearing that evening, he is pierced with arrows.

The next morning, Mrs. Emma Hamilton (TJ) and Edgar (ID) read about the Indian massacre at the theater the previous evening. A Policeman (JC) enters, and does an advertisement for people seeking policemen as friends, and has Emma draw the next sketch from his hat. She chooses a Scotsman on a Horse.

Young Lochinvar (JC) rides through the countryside to a small church, where a wedding is going on. He arrives just in time, and carries away the groom (MP); there is stock film of Women's Institute applause.

Another animated sequence follows, with a vicious baby carriage that chases people, leading up to ''20th Century Vole Presents.''

Producer Irving C. Saltzberg (GC) talks to six writers (JC, EI, TG, MP, TJ, ID) about his next movie. The terrified writers quickly praise his every suggestion, but he begins throwing them out for the slightest hint of disloyalty, until the room is empty. He picks up the phone, and the phone on the tree stump rings.

The phone is answered by the ''It's'' Man, who runs away as the credits—all involving Irving C. Saltzberg—roll.

ALSO APPEARING: Ian Davidson

☞ The first sketch was originally three men in a pub (MP, JC, EI) trying to recognize a fourth (TJ), who looks very ordinary, with plastered-down hair and pinched spectacles. They ask him to repeat phrases to jog their memories, but he turns out to be Arthur Figgis, an accountant, rather than Jimmy Stewart, Eddie Waring, Anthony Newley, David Frost or their other guesses, and leads into Johann Gambolputty . . .

☞ The ''Dull Life of a City Stockbroker'' is not in

During a live performance of the Whizzo Chocolate Sketch, Gilliam (right) stands quietly, his mouth full of cold beef stew. **Photo copyright KHJ**

the BBC rehearsal script, while "Young Lochinvar" and "Irving C. Saltzberg" were written for earlier shows.

 ## BON APPETIT!

When the "Whizzo Chocolate" sketch was performed in the stage shows, Terry Gilliam usually took the Superintendent's role, but had no lines. The reason for this was evident at the conclusion of the scene, where TG vomited into his police helmet, to the delight or disgust of the audience. He then placed the helmet back on his head.

Backstage at the Hollywood Bowl, he was asked how he could stand to have the fake vomit in his mouth throughout the scene. "I don't know why everybody gets so grossed out by it," he said straight-faced. "It's only cold beef stew."

 ## HI-YO, SILVER!

The shots of Young Lochinvar on horseback were not actually done by Cleese; he didn't learn to ride a horse until fifteen years later, while making *Silverado* in New Mexico, for which he took several weeks worth of riding lessons.

"I actually did have some rather good riding shots in *Silverado*—I looked remarkably good on a horse—but they didn't fit in the film. They've actually got a shot of me leading a posse that I'm really proud of. My daughter Cynthia was obsessed by horses at the time, and I thought I could finally win a little respect from her! In fact, all of the wider shots in the film are stuntmen with crepe beards," Cleese says.

"In 'Lochinvar' there were closeups of me riding, but I wasn't on a horse; the long shots were done by a stuntman. I'm actually on a horse for all the closeups in *Silverado*, at least. In 'Lochinvar,' I think I was sitting on a bicycle."

 ## A DAY IN THE LIFE OF AN ORDINARY BBC COMEDY WRITER

"The whole 'Dull Life of a City Stockbroker' sequence was an interesting piece of writing," says Graham Chapman. "It obviously wasn't an ordinary day in the life, except—well, such extraordinary things happened around him, but he clearly never noticed, which is why he had such an extraordinary life. Quite a nice point to make, but a fairly straightforward one.

"That was actually written by Eric Idle and myself as a sendup of a Terry Jones/Michael Palin script. They wrote a lot of sketches for Marty Feldman with a Day in the Life of a Golfer theme—it was almost a genre with them. So we thought, 'Well, that's pretty easy, let's write one of those and see if they notice," Chapman laughs. "But they didn't say anything about it at the time, and when we finished up filming it, Eric and I just kept quiet about it."

I REMEMBER THE FACE, BUT THE NAME . . .

When they presented the rest of the group with the "Johann Gambolputty . . . " sketch, Michael Palin says there was surprisingly little grumbling over the frighteningly long name they would have to remember. "It was our University Revue background that made us take great pride in being able to cope with difficult things like that, difficult names and long speeches without cue cards.

"That was the stuff of University Revue. It was verbal dexterity, memorizing long speeches, talking without a break. So there it was, and we just had to learn it. There was never a question of anyone saying 'Well, it's got to be easier.' It was just 'That's it, that's what it is, and we'll learn it.' "

Only one of the troupe got lucky.

"I never had to do all of it," Eric Idle says, smiling. "I played an old man who died halfway through it, so I only had to memorize the first bit."

AN IRVING C. SALTZBERG PRODUCTION

"That was an early sketch, a holdover from old material that hadn't been used before. John Cleese and I had written it for *At Last, the 1948 Show*. People generally liked it, though we'd just read it through and hadn't actually cast it," says Graham Chapman.

"Suddenly, Marty Feldman wanted to play Irving C. Saltzberg, which was okay. I suppose I'd seen either John or I playing him, but we would, of course—we wrote it. Anyway, that was fair enough. But when we came to rehearse it, suddenly Marty wanted to pull out—he got nervous for some reason. I don't know quite why, but there it was. So, we used it later.

"I did enjoy it. The Colonel was fairly dominating, but Saltzberg was *overdominating*. We did feel a slight resentment toward the Hollywood moguls, who clearly couldn't tell Whizzo margarine from a dead crab, no way. That was largely due to our experience with *The Magic Christian*, although in the years after the . . . *1948 Show*, John and I spent a couple of years writing for movies. We wrote for *The Magic Christian*, and quite a chunk of *The Rise and Rise of Michael Rimmer* in that period, as well, and filmed it just pre-Python."

Show 9—Full Frontal Nudity

RECORDED AS SERIES ONE, SHOW 9—PROD. #54698

The "It's" Man (MP) sits in a lawn chair and is served a drink by a blonde in a bikini, who then hands him a bomb as he says "It's"

Titles
Episode
12B
Full Frontal
Nudity
Several "Vox Pops" on nudity and the permissive society introduce World War II footage from 1943, which leads into "Unoccupied Britain, 1970."

Private Watkins (EI) tells his Colonel (GC) that he wants to leave the Army because it's too dangerous. He was shocked to find out that they use real guns and bullets, and is afraid someone will be

Palin and Cleese, in drag, are two members of Hell's Grannies, geriatric delinquents terrorizing the younger generation. Such film segments were actually shot in the streets of London, to the astonishment, curiosity, or disinterest of the British public who happened by. **Photo copyright BBC and Python Productions**

hurt. He says he only joined for the water skiing and travel. A Sergeant (JC) introduces Dino and Luigi Vercotti (TJ and MP), who try to sell him protection for his Army and intimidate him. They say it would be a shame if someone set fire to his paratroops, and make other insinuations. The Colonel finally stops them, saying the whole premise is silly and badly written, and orders the director to cut to the next scene.

An animated Dirty Old Man goes to the theater to see full frontal nudity, but at the crucial moments, people stand up in front of him, and cars and trains pass by in front of the wom-

The Hells Grannies in action, terrorizing the townspeople. **Photo copyright BBC and Python Productions**

en. More "Vox Pops" follow on full frontal nudity.

An Art Critic (MP) discusses the place of the nude, and film is shown of the Art Critic strangling his wife (KW) in a field.

Running through the same field are a bride and groom (TJ and CC), who run into a department store to buy a bed, and are waited on by Mr. Lambert (GC) and Mr. Verity (EI). Lambert divides every measurement by three, and Verity multiplies them all by ten. They are then warned not to say "mattress" to Mr. Lambert, and instead say "dog kennel." When they say "mattress," he puts a paper bag over his head, and they all have to sing "Jerusalem" to get him to remove it. When they say "mattress" a second time, they have to get a large crowd to stand on a tea chest and sing, and there is stock film of a huge group singing. The bride says "mattress" a third time, but she begins crying and says it's her only line. The Colonel interrupts the show again, saying the show is getting too silly, and calls for a good, clean, healthy outdoor sketch.

Frank, a hermit (EI), talks with another hermit (MP) who lives in the cave just up the goat track. They discuss caves and moss, and the second hermit recommends birds' nests, moss, and oak leaves for insulation. The mountain where they are living is populated with several other hermits. Frank says he enjoys his lifestyle, and would never go back to public relations. The Colonel walks on and stops the sketch for being too silly, and chases the actors and camera crew off the mountain.

An animated broom sweeps the cast and crew figures into a meat grinder, where they emerge as the hair of *Venus Rising from the Sea*, who does a dance and falls into a fish tank at a pet shop.

In the pet shop, Mr. Praline (JC) tries to return a parrot which he claims is dead; the Shopkeeper (MP) disagrees. Say no more.

The Shopkeeper sends the man to his brother's pet shop in Bolton, which he thinks is Ipswich, but actually turns out to be Bolton. He complains to a Railway Clerk (TJ), but the Colonel stops the sketch.

A Newsreader (EI) introduces frontal nudity in a film featuring a Flasher (TJ), and then introduces a report on Hell's Grannies, a gang of old ladies who trip young girls, terrorize young people, and ride motorcycles through shops; their favorite targets are telephone kiosks. This is followed by vicious gangs of baby-snatchers and Keep Left signs, until the Colonel stops the show.

The "It's" Man's bomb explodes as the credits roll.

ALSO APPEARING:
Katya Wyeth
Rita Davies
Carol Cleveland

☞ "Buying a Bed," originally intended for an earlier show, was much longer in its previous version, and involved substitutions of several other words, such as "pesos" for "lettuce."

☞ In the original rehearsal script, following "Hell's Grannies," the Colonel presents a sketch he's written called "Interesting People," which is used in Show 11.

Cleese, with his pacamac fully buttoned, studies the ex-parrot. **Photo copyright BBC and Python Productions**

 **DEATH OF A PARROT**

With the possible exception of the "Lumberjack Song," the "Dead Parrot" sketch is probably the single best-known Python bit. It has been performed in all of the stage shows, and included on numerous Python albums. Although it was chiefly written by Graham Chapman and John Cleese,

Michael Palin says the origins of the expired Norwegian Blue actually go back further than that.

"I did a show with John Cleese, purely as an actor, called *How to Irritate People*," Palin explains. "It was written by John and Graham in 1968. There were some very funny sketches in there.

"I had told John about my experiences with the local garage guy who had sold me my car. He was one of those people who could never accept that anything had gone wrong. I was telling John that the brakes seemed to be gone, but when I told the mechanic this, he said 'Oh, well, it's a new car, bound to happen.' He had an answer for everything. He would never, ever accept any blame for anything at all. I'd say 'Well, the door came off while I was doing 50 mph,' and he'd say 'Well, they do, don't they?'

"John liked this character very much, and worked him into *How to Irritate People*. I played a guy selling a car, almost literally line-for-line verbatim what the garage man said.

"So when John and Graham were looking around for stuff to write for the first season of Python, they plundered that show. They felt they couldn't do a garage man again, though. I think Graham had the idea for the parrot, which was marvelous. Bringing back a parrot which is dead, to complain about it, is just a marvelous idea," Palin says.

The costume worn by Cleese was the finishing touch, recalls Hazel Pethig. "I thought John could wear a pacamac, a folded plastic raincoat, and it worked very well. It was a really odd cos-

tume. He buttoned it right up to the neck, and that made him look really odd—a creepy English character."

"Very good with animals, they were, John and Graham, good animal writers," says Palin. "They had a feel for animals—fish, parrots, strange animals like that. They did *awful* things to them!"

In a slightly different costume for the Hollywood Bowl performance of "Dead Parrot" (actually, Palin and Cleese are hurrying through a dress rehearsal). **Photo copyright KHJ**

Show 10—Untitled

RECORDED AS SERIES 1, SHOW 10—PROD. #55176

The "It's" Man (MP) is hanging among pig carcasses, and gasps "It's"

Titles

A Bandit (JC) and a Clerk (EI) wait impatiently on a store set, looking at their watches.

Frank, a Plumber (MP), sits in his kitchen reading a letter from the BBC, asking him to appear in a sketch. His wife (TJ) encourages him, and as he leaves to do the walk-on, she tunes in the sketch on her TV. Frank arrives at the BBC, and walks off the store set just before the Bandit walks in, and the sketch begins.

The Bandit is confused because he thought he was in a bank. When it turns out to be a lingerie shop, he leaves with just a pair of knickers.

David Unction (GC) laughs and welcomes everyone to the show, and introduces the glittering world of show business with Arthur Tree. "It's a Tree" is a talk show hosted by Arthur Tree, a talking tree, with several tree guests, including Scott Pine and the Conifers; the audience is a forest. Tree (who speaks like David Frost) welcomes his first guest, a block of wood. He also

features an animated Chippendale writing desk which does impressions, including Long John Silver, Edwood Heath, and a play by Harold Splinter.

Several animated curtains open to reveal the "Vocational Guidance Counselor" sketch, with the title sung in harmony. The Vocational Guidance Counselor himself (JC) joins in, as the scene begins in his office. He is visited by Mr. Anchovy (MP), a chartered accountant who says his job is too dull, tedious, stuffy, and boring. He wants to be a lion tamer, but when the Counselor shows him a picture of a lion, he screams and faints. The Counselor calls for a piece of wood and the larch tree is shown briefly. Anchovy continues to snivel. The Counselor asks people to send money to the League for Fighting Chartered Accountancy, 55 Lincoln House, Basil Street, London SW3.

David Unction is caught reading *Physique*, a body-building magazine, which he tries to hide; he argues with a Viking (TJ) over how butch they were.

The sea begins the story of Neaps End, who hopes to be the first man to jump the English

Channel. He is interviewed (by JC) and explains that he plans to jump into the center of Calais, even though his furthest previous jump is only eleven feet six inches. He is being sponsored by a British firm, and so is carrying fifty pounds of their bricks.

After failing that jump, his manager, Luigi Vercotti (MP), has him attempt other stunts, such as eating Chichester Cathedral, tunneling to Java, splitting a railway carriage with his nose, and running to Mercury. After he is killed, Vercotti says he is having Ron Obvious attempt to break the world's record for remaining underground.

A Customer (JC) wants to buy a cat at a pet shop somewhere near Melton Mowray. The Shopkeeper (MP) wants to make a terrier into a cat, but the man refuses. He then offers to do a parrot or fish job on the terrier.

A Vicar (TJ), another Man (GC) and a Lady conduct interviews in the town hall for a librarian. They question a gorilla for the job, but it turns out to be Mr. Phipps (EI), a man in a gorilla suit. The next applicant is a dog.

Several letters lead into "Strangers in the Night." Vera Jackson (TJ) and her Husband (MP) are in bed when a Frenchman, Maurice Zatapatique (EI), enters through the bedroom window looking for her. Roger Thompson (JC) then enters and confronts the two of them, while her husband sleeps on. Biggles (GC) and Algy enter also, to see Vera, as does a Mexican Rhythm Combo, which asks her husband for directions. He goes for a tinkle, and turns out to have a blonde stashed in the bathroom. Since he is gone, the rest of the characters in the bedroom see no point in continuing the sketch, and decide to end it.

Several animated animals devour each other, and the "It's" Man is carried away to the slaughter, as the credits roll.

ALSO APPEARING: Barry Cryer
Carolae Donoghue
Ian Davidson

☞ The "Vocational Guidance Counselor" sketch had originally been planned for Show 3, the "Lingerie Shop" was intended for Show 2, and "Ron Obvious" was set for Show 5.

☞ The "Accidents/Self-Destructing Room" sketch, in Series 2, Show 5, was originally intended for this program, between "Ron Obvious" and the "Librarian" sketch.

☞ **ANIMALS, ANIMALS, ANIMALS**

"Mutant animals are very much the Cleese and Chapman area," says Michael Palin. "They like stretching animals out, fitting things to cats and converting them to fish. The animal humor section of Python is quite strong and extensive— converting parrots to emus, and all that."

John Cleese and Graham Chapman both admit to a strange fascination with animals. "I've always thought that animals were funny, and I can't quite put a finger on why," says Cleese. "But *all* comics think animals are funny. One can never believe that God bothered to make them all. The very fact that they sometimes seem to behave with emotions that are connected with human emotions make them doubly funny.

"There are dogs that can't make up their minds whether to fight or not, and scratch themselves with a puzzled look on their faces before either running away or attacking the other dog. One sees that kind of behavior in people, in ways like tie-straightening. It's very funny to watch."

Strange animals pervade Python humor, some of them taken from real life. "A couple of items involving cats came in as a direct result of my trying to get a message over to John Cleese without saying so directly—that maybe the cats in his apartment were having parts taken away from them on rather too regular a basis," says Graham Chapman.

"They were almost becoming mechanical cats. Claws were going, and wombs. All right, we expect wombs, and perhaps [loss of] claws in a flat one can understand, but then the voice box? Taken one step further, what's next? So I suppose 'Convert-a-Pet' came out of that.

"I was particularly fond of penguins and little furry animals. John's favorite at one stage was ferrets. On the radio series *I'm Sorry, I'll Read That Again*, we even wrote a ferret song for that: *I've Got a Ferret Sticking Up My Nose*. It's a nice song. It was one of the closing numbers in . . . *the 1948 Show*, done on a grand scale, with cannons exploding, a fleet sailing by and all that, while John sang this rather weedy song about some man with a ferret up his nose."

Show 11—The Royal Philharmonic Orchestra Goes to the Bathroom

RECORDED AS SERIES 1, SHOW 11—PROD. #55375

The "It's" Man (MP) runs through traffic before gasping "It's"

Titles

Episode Two The Royal Philharmonic Orchestra Goes to the Bathroom

A Man (MP) knocks on the door impatiently, as the Warsaw Concerto by Rachmaninov is heard inside. A series of angry letters of objection follow; there is film of the orchestra playing as they flush, and a sequence of toilet-oriented animation follows as people leave the concert hall.

Prof. R.J. Canning (GC) hosts "The World of History," discussing the Black Death, but he is interrupted once too often by film of undertakers, including one scene where two hearses drag race past other undertakers having tea.

Meanwhile Inspector Tiger (JC) enters an English drawing room to investigate an apparent murder, but has trouble announcing to Colonel Pickering (GC) and his Wife (CC) that no one is to leave the room. After Tiger is taken away by nurses and receives a lobotomy, he returns to the scene, where the lights go out suddenly. When they come back on, Tiger is found with an arrow through his neck, a bullet through his forehead, and a bottle of poison beside him. Lookout of the Yard (EI), accompanied by a Constable (MP), arrives to investigate the murder of Tiger, but is himself shot when the lights go out. The next investigation is conducted by Assistant Chief Constable There's a Man Behind You (TJ), followed by Constable Fire (ID).

More film of the undertakers carrying a coffin down a road shows them dumping the corpse and dancing away with the empty box.

Intellectual sports analyst Brian (EI) inter-views the extremely stupid footballer Jimmy Buzzard (JC), who is only capable of three sentences. Another clip of undertakers follows, then a return to the murder scene (where the bodies are piling up), and more undertakers, as they become animated. The animation continues with two rather bitchy ladies, and escalates into warfare.

The host of "Interesting People" begins the show by interviewing Mr. Howard Stools, who is half an inch tall. This is followed by Ali Bayan of Egypt (TJ), who is stark raving mad; the Rachel Toovey Bicycle Bell Choir playing "Men of Harlech"; a man (JC) giving a cat influenza; Mr. Thomas Walters (EI), who becomes virtually invisible before our eyes; and a cricket match is held in a boxing ring. The show continues with Ken Dove (JC), who is interested in shouting, Don Savage (GC) and his cat, who is flung through the air into a bucket of water, and Keith Maniac of Guatemala (TJ), who puts bricks to sleep by hypnosis.

Back at the interview (after we see four tired undertakers), Jimmy Buzzard falls off his chair. The coffin then drives itself to the cemetery, as miners, surfers, and Orientals climb from the hole; there is animation of the coffins below ground.

This leads into a series of nude women, who introduce "The World of History," discussing eighteenth-century social legislation. A.J.P. Taylor (CC, with voice dubbed by JC) rolls around in bed wearing a negligee as she lectures, interrupted by a "bit of fun" (a quick striptease). Next is Professor Gert Van der Whoops (MP), of the Rejksmuseum in the Hague, trying to lecture in bed while being caressed by a blonde. A man wearing wings (TJ) is lowered to the ground to introduce R.J. Canning again, who discusses the Battle of Trafalgar. He introduces Professor R.J. Gumby (MP) and his friend (TJ), who claim the battle was fought on dry land near Cudworth in Yorkshire.

Short links follow with the Gumbys, then "The World of History" shifts to Mrs. Rita Fairbanks (EI) and her Townswomen's Guild, who reenact the Battle of Pearl Harbor in a muddy field. Canning is interrupted again by film of the undertakers, and a funeral in which the Vicar (JC) shoots into the grave after dirt is thrown back at his face. The undertakers all drive off in a brightly painted hearse. Canning begins a letter to Lord Hill, as the "It's" Man runs back across the street.

ALSO APPEARING: Carol Cleveland
Ian Davidson
Flanagan

☞ "Interesting People" was originally written for Show 9, presented as a sketch written by the Colonel. Cut from the scene is a bit with Herbert Arkwright, who eats herds of buffalo.

☞ Another sketch (originally following the "Agatha Christie" sketch) was apparently never used. It featured a punch-drunk interviewer talking with new British light-heavyweight prospect Henry Pratt, who combines a lack of ability with extreme physical cowardice.

☞ FUN ON LOCATION

"The attack on Pearl Harbor was the most painful thing we ever shot. Very unpleasant!" recalls Michael Palin. "It was a cold day, and we were filming up in North Yorkshire. It was really awful—we were just covered with filth, and there was nowhere to wash off, except for a little outhouse at a farm with cold water. It was very bizarre. We had all these people, soaked and covered with mud, peeling their stockings off and removing these mud-stained bras . . . "

Show 12—The Naked Ant

RECORDED AS SERIES 1, SHOW 12—PROD. #55628

The "It's" Man (MP) runs through a forest, bouncing off trees like a pinball, gasping "It's"
Titles
Episodes 17–26   The Naked Ant
A Signal Box Somewhere Near Hove. A Train Engineer (TJ) struggles with a polar bear (wrestling it for 3.48 seconds, according to the script).

But in an office off the Goswell Road:

Two executives (EI and JC) sit near a window working, as several men fall past their window. They argue about their identities and place bets on who will be next, realizing there is a board meeting in progress.

A letter of complaint is begun, but the author falls while writing. In the office, more people fall, then animated people fall sideways and bounce off the stomach of a woman. An animated magician conjures flowers, and eventually a globe, which begins:

"Spectrum," in which the Presenter (MP) talks about what it all means, why, and what the solution is. Alexander Hardacre (GC), of the Economic Affairs Bureau, speaks intensely and with great authority as he shows charts and graphs, while Professor Tiddles of Leeds University (JC) and pro cricketer (EI) are interviewed, and the Presenter begins talking increasingly rapidly.

There is more train film, and the Engineer is still fighting the polar bear.

At a small boarding house in Minehead, Somerset, a holidaying couple, Mr. (EI) and Mrs.

The group lines up in a display of upper-class fashion sensibilities. They enjoyed deflating such upper-class twits, though never with such pinpoint accuracy as in ''The Twit of the Year'' contest. **Photo copyright BBC and Python Productions**

Johnson visit a landlady (TJ), describing their journey and saying they are ready for tea. They are then introduced to Mr. and Mrs. Phillips (TG and CB), and Mr. Hilter (JC), Mr. Bimmler (MP), and Ron Viventroff (GC). Hilter gets a phone call from Mr. McGoering. He is a Bocialist candidate in the Minehead election. Film of their campaign rallies in Britain shows them riding through the streets, and Hilter gives a speech from a balcony to a Farmer (TJ) and some children, while the sounds of a crowd are played on a phonograph. Mr. Gumby and a conservative businessman give their views on Hilter.

''Spectrum'' sums up.

A Man (TJ) tries to report a burglary to a Police Sergeant (JC), who asks him to speak in a high, squeaky voice. Another Sergeant, Charlie (GC) replaces the first one and has him talk in a lower voice, followed by a Detective Sergeant (EI),

and the policemen try to talk to each other.

''Vox Pops'' follow, with an Upper-Class Twit saying ''Some people talk in the most extraordinary way'' leading to:

The 127th ''Upper-Class Twit of the Year Contest'' at Hurlingham Park, which includes such events as Walking a Straight Line, Jumping Three Rows of Matchboxes, Kicking the Beggar, Insulting the Waiter, Taking the Bras off the Debutantes, Waking the Neighbors, and eventually Shooting Themselves. Their coffins are decorated with ribbons, and a letter is read that tells how wonderful it is to be able to get rid of these people this way.

Animation sees a soldier fall apart, and then become stuffed in a pipe by Terry Jones. A balloon, a flea, and a humpback whale then escape from the bowl of the pipe.

Ken Shabby (MP), a filthy, disgusting man who cleans out public lavatories, asks a Father (GC) for permission to marry his lovely daughter (CB). The story so far is summed up, with a voice-over and peculiar pictures.

A corner of a bedsitter watches a party political broadcast by the Wood Party. In the middle of his speech, the Minister, the Rt. Hon. Lambert Warbeck (GC), falls, apparently through the earth's crust, according to a studio technician (EI). Another man, Tex (TG), throws him a rope; the Minister tries to continue his speech while dangling from the rope. He slips, but the picture is turned upside-down. Three Linkmen (TJ, EI and JC), all named Robert, discuss various aspects of the incident. One talks about the structure and heat of the layers of the earth, another analyzes distances fallen by politicians, while the third becomes so excited that he is set on fire.

Everyone on the show agrees that they don't have anything more to add, and a sixteen-ton weight is dropped on the Host of "Spectrum."

The "It's" Man runs back through the woods, as the credits roll.

ALSO APPEARING: Connie Booth
Flanagan

☞ The BBC rehearsal script reads "MONTY PYTHON'S FLYING CIRCUS STARRING ERIC IDLE with Graham Chapman, John Cleese, Terry Jones, Michael Palin and Terry Gilliam."

☞ The original script for this show did not include the Upper-Class Twit contest, which was an insert written in by hand; Ken Shabby was also not in the original script.

☞ The script for the Rt. Hon. Lambert Warbeck's speech reads as follows:

Good evening. We in the Wood Party feel very strongly about the weak drafting in the present Local Government Bill. And we intend to fight— (He thumps on his desk and he falls through the floor. Yes, Mr. Director, you did read that right. He fell through the floor and added a fortune to the budget.)

👉 COMEDY WITH A VENGEANCE

The "Upper-Class Twit of the Year Contest" was another sketch that was suggested by environment, according to Graham Chapman.

"John Cleese had an apartment on a street just behind Harrod's, not far from Sloane Square," he says. "There were a lot of Sloane Rangers* wandering around at night in the wine bars. As I remember, there was a wine bar just over the road from John's called "The Loose Box," where there were a lot of these chinless wonders with names like Nigel. They would indeed make braying noises, and generally behave like the twits in the sketch. They would, in fact, keep John awake quite late at night by banging car doors and so on. So that was our revenge on them!"

*British yuppies.

Show 13—Intermission

RECORDED AS SERIES 1, SHOW 13—PROD. #55997

Four undertakers carry a coffin; the "It's" Man (MP) emerges to say "It's"
A slide announcing a short intermission
Titles

Another slide announcing a medium-sized intermission
Animation in which a man in a bird's nest is fed the word "intermission"

Douglas (JC) and his wife Shirley (EI), who never stops talking, are seated in a restaurant by Hopkins, the maître d' (TJ), who then leaves to commit suicide. Thompson (MP), the Head Waiter, tells them that it's a vegetarian restaurant, of which they are not only proud but smug. They speak to the Headmaster (GC), and the now-nude Hopkins is wheeled by on a cart. He says he's the day's special, Hopkins au gratin à la chef, and advises them against eating the Vicar (EI), who has been there for two weeks.

Another intermission slide promises a whopping great intermission.

Pearls for Swine Presents: an ad for Soho Motors (on the second floor), and an ad for the La Gondola Restaurant, managed by Luigi Vercotti (MP), featuring a variety of Sicilian delicacies.

A salesgirl (JC) in the theater tries to sell an albatross to a customer (TJ).

A very short intermission follows, as does an announcement that there will be no feature film presented that evening, as it cuts into the profits.

The customer with the albatross introduces a Man (MP) reporting a stolen wallet to a Policeman (JC), with the Man eventually propositioning the Policeman. This is followed by the stock film of the Women's Institute applause.

Mr. Burtenshaw (TG) visits a doctor (EI) and nurses (CC and JC), and go through the "Me, doctor, she, nurse, he, Mr. Burtenshaw" confusion, again followed by stock film of Women's Institute applause.

Mr. Gumby asks to see John the Baptist's impersonation of Graham Hill, which leads into "Historical Impersonations," featuring host Wally Wiggins (MP). Cardinal Richelieu (MP) does his impression of Petula Clark, Julius Caesar (EI) impersonates Eddie Waring, followed by Florence Nightingale (GC) as Brian London, Ivan the Terrible (JC) as a shoe salesman, and W.G. Grace (animated) as a music box. Mr. Gumby makes his request again, with more Women's Institute applause. Napoleon (TJ) impersonates the R-101 disaster, and Marcel Marceau (GC) mimes a man walking into the wind, as well as a man being struck by a sixteen-ton weight.

A Man (JC) interviews two small Children (EI and MP) who would like to have Raquel Welch dropped on top of them. He then interviews two bussinessmen in the same condescending manner, including Trevor Atkinson (GC) of the Empire General Insurance Company and his Friend (MP).

Trevor requests more police fairy stories.

Another Policeman (TJ) pumps up an inflatable robber (EI), and a group of policemen give chase. An Officer in a tutu (MP) uses a magic wand on them.

"Probearound" looks at the Special Crimes Squad, with a Host (EI) who has just shot the First Host (JC). Inspector Harry "Snapper" Organs of H Division (MP) uses a voodoo doll, several policemen use an Ouija board, and other policemen use wands on illegally parked cars.

Attila the Hun (MP), the son of Mr. and Mrs. Norman Hun, wearing horn-rimmed glasses and a suit, turns himself in to police (TJ and JC) for looting, pillaging, and sacking a major city. The Sergeant (JC) brings in a breathalyzer, which shows he is actually Alexander the Great. Objecting letters are read, and there is animation featuring a police car.

Dr. Larch (JC), who wants it made clear that he is a psychiatrist, has his first patient (TJ, dressed as Napoleon) leave before he can give his first line. The next patient, Mr. Notlob (MP), hears guitars and people singing "We're All Going to the Zoo," and visits a Doctor Friend of Larch (GC) who operates on him. A Hippie (EI) and a Nude Woman (CC) are found living inside him as squatters. The Police (JC and MP) get a court order to go inside and drag them out.

Animation highlights the end of the series, and the "It's" Man runs from the undertakers as the credits roll.

ALSO APPEARING: David Ballantyne
Carol Cleveland

A final intermission slide appears, noting that when the series returns, it will be put out on Monday mornings as a test card, and will be described by *The Radio Times* as a *History of Irish Agriculture*.

☞ Several sketches here were not in the BBC rehearsal script for the show, including "Police/Come Back to my Place," "Historical Impersonations," "Children's/Stockbroker's Interviews," and "Magic Police."

☞ A one-page bit was cut from the "A.t. Hun" sketch, with the Police Constable solving crimes sent in by viewers.

HISTORY COMES ALIVE

Of all the historical characters in Python, John Cleese has his own favorite. "I love the impersonation I do of Ivan the Terrible as a shoe salesman. I've got that funny bent board that they use to put the foot on. So, when the guy sets his foot on it, I draw this *enormous* sword and *completely* bisect him! I loved that one . . ."

 ## POLICE FRIENDS

Of all the politicians and public figures that the Pythons took aim at, very few of their targets apparently responded to the group. Reginald Maudling, a frequent donee died not long after the Pythons featured him, though most of the other politicians are still around. Michael Palin is proud to point out that they were sending up Margaret Thatcher years ago, but admits that Thatcher doesn't speak to them much.

"On the whole, our targets haven't mixed with us that much—except for the police," Palin says. "We always used to get on about police corruption, and how thick the police were. Various police used to come and see the show, and they absolutely loved it.

"We could do the most obvious attacks on the police, suggesting bribery and corruption and all sorts of venality, and they thought it was absolutely wonderful! It just shows that satire doesn't really change people at all. They never believe they're the target, they always think it's somebody else. For some reason, John Cleese is very friendly with the police—we're not sure why. He used to invite them along." Palin laughs.

Cleese admits to the police charges leveled by Palin. "I've always been fascinated by the police. I think they do an extremely difficult job. Because I'm an introvert and a coward, I'm fascinated to know people who are extroverts and brave.

"I've always been intrigued by those guys. But of course, the Pythons, being basically left-wing, have the usual paranoid attitude that all policemen are bad persons, and that one should not associate with them for fear of becoming morally contaminated." Cleese smiles. "This is an argument which I do not accept, as can be seen from the curdling of my lip."

TEST YOUR PYTHON QUOTIENT

1. How did Mrs. G. Pinnet have to sign for her new gas cooker?
2. Why does the Minister of Silly Walks arrive at his office late?
3. What is the annual budget for the Ministry of Silly Walks?
4. What was the Piranha Brothers' prison sentence?
5. What was the occupation of Arthur Piranha, Doug and Dinsdale's father?
6. What happened the week Dinsdale did not nail Vince Snetterton Lewis's head to the floor?
7. For which surveillance role was Harry "Snapper" Organs of "Q" Division panned by critics?
8. What was the name of the giant hedgehog that followed the Piranha Brothers?
9. How large was the hedgehog?
10. What is pneumoconiosis?
11. In the Disgusting Objects International at Wembley, how did England defeat Spain?
12. What did the Chairman of the Board of Irresponsible People feed to his goldfish?
13. True or false: Goldfish are quite happy eating breadcrumbs, ants, eggs, and the occasional pheasant.
14. "Still no sign of land. How long is it?"

15. What three ways does the undertaker initially recommend to deal with stiffs?

16. What is the name of the man who has a "fifty-percent bonus in the region of what you said"?

17. What is the song attempted by Arthur Ewing and His Musical Mice?

18. What would members of the stock exchange do about the "Mouse Problem"?

19. What is the name of that most dangerous of animals, the clever sheep?

20. What are the only four phrases spoken by Jimmy Buzzard?

21. Why is Mr. Howard Stools particularly interesting?

22. What is the name of the flying cat that lands in a bucket of water (when she is flung)?

23. Don't you ever take the bones out?

24. What play did Leatherhead Rep do with the Redfoot Indian tribe?

25. Which two stars did Irving C. Saltzberg plan to star in his next film?

26. Why does the llama have a beak?

27. What does R.J. Gumby croon while hitting himself in the head with bricks?

28. What does the barber drink before cutting Terry Jones's hair?

29. Which Python is featured in the Stop the Film segment on "Blackmail"?

30. How many things did the Australasian branch of the Society for Putting Things on Top of Other Things put on top of things last year?

31. Name two methods for waking Ken Clean-Air System.

32. Which of his films does director Ellis Dibley call a "real failure"?

33. How many votes did Kevin Phillips Bong (the Slightly Silly candidate at Luton) receive?

34. "Do like all smart motorists—choose _____."

35. What is Archbishop Shabby doing for peace?

36. What is the first lesson in not being seen? The second?

37. Coventry City last won the F.A. Cup in what year?

38. The other works of art voted unanimously to support the strike by the paintings in the National Gallery. Which work abstained from voting?

39. What tool does Mr. Gumby use in flower arranging?

40. The "Black Eagle" was based on what novel?

41. What was the official slogan of the British Army?

42. What does the smuggler claim his watches are?

43. What is in the brown paper bag planted by Police Constable Henry Thatcher?

44. What is the secret of Charles Fatless?

45. What are the five chief weapons of the Spanish Inquisition?

46. What does the Gumby Brain Specialist want done to his patient?

47. What joke did Hitler come up with to challenge the Allied Killer Joke?

48. Who is high scorer in "Mozart's Famous Deaths"?
49. What is Whizzo Butter compared to in a TV commercial?
50. Who serves as a character witness for Harold Larch? How does Inspector Dim trip him up?
51. What would Dim like to be (if he were not in the CID)? And Bartlett?
52. Where are the numbers on a camel?
53. Why would men turn into Scotsmen?
54. In separate shows, which members of the group played Dracula and Frankenstein's monster?
55. Why was the Norwegian Blue sitting on its perch in the first place?
56. What does the bandit steal from the lingerie shop?
57. What program follows "It's a Tree" at 9:30?
58. What is the ideal job for Mr. Anchovy?
59. What are Mr. Anchovy's qualifications for lion taming?
60. What does Cardinal Richelieu perform on "Historical Impersonations"?
61. What message do the police get on their Ouija board?
62. What does the courteous hijacker call out as he is pushed from the jet?
63. What kind of car insurance policy does the Vicar have?
64. What is the main food that penguins eat?
65. Who sings a Jimmy Durante song?
66. What is the name of Rev. Arthur Belling's church?
67. How did Roy Spim lose his left arm?
68. What did Kemal Atatürk name his entire menagerie?
69. What was the first scene shot in "Scott of the Antarctic"?
70. What did the crew of "Scott of the Antarctic" use for snow?
71. What is Michael Norman Randall's sentence for the murder of twenty people?
72. How do you put budgies down, according to the book?
73. What do Mrs. Premise and Mrs. Conclusion sing while phoning Jean Paul Sartre?
74. Who is featured on "Farming Club"?
75. What was Brian Norris's first book?
76. What was the result of treating athlete's foot with explosives?
77. What is the jugged fish?
78. The Church Police conclude their arrest with what hymn?
79. What is Annie Elk's theory of the brontosaurus?
80. What does the Fire Brigade request to drink (in unison)?
81. What was Biggles writing thank-you notes to royalty for?
82. What do the men from the lifeboat order with their tea?
83. What is the name of the man who owns the Cheese Shop?
84. Why did Reg Pither crash his bicycle?
85. What does Eartha Kitt sing to the Central Committee?
86. The poster for the Moscow Praesidium advertises Eartha Kitt, Burgess and Maclean, Marshall Bulganin and "Charlie," and who else?
87. Where is the bomb (for a pound)?

88. Which two countries are in the finale of the Olympic Hide and Seek?

89. Where does Don Roberts hide?

90. Who is the author of "Gay Boys in Bondage"?

91. What is Dennis Moore's horse's name?

92. Which two shows feature animation that parodies *2001*?

Answers

1. Since the invoice was made out to Mrs. G. Crump, she was requested to sign it "Mrs. Crump-Pinnet."

2. "My walk has become rather sillier recently."

3. Three hundred and forty-eight million pounds a year.

4. Four hundred years' imprisonment for crimes of violence.

5. He was a scrap metal dealer and TV quizmaster (he married Kitty Malone, an up-and-coming East End boxer).

6. Dinsdale screwed his pelvis to a cake stand instead.

7. Sancho Panza in *Man of La Mancha*.

8. Spiny Norman plagued Dinsdale.

9. He ranged anywhere from twelve feet to eight hundred yards.

10. A disease miners get.

11. A plate of braised pus bested a putrid herring.

12. Cold consummé, sausages, greens, potatoes, bread, gravy, etc.

13. True (according to the Board of Irresponsible People).

14. Thirty-three days (a rather personal question).

15. Burning, burying, or dumping (in the Thames).

16. Arthur ("Is that chair comfortable?") Frampton.

17. The twenty-three white mice played "The Bells of St. Mary's."

18. Suck their brains out with a straw, sell the widows and orphans, and go into South American zinc.

19. Harold.

20. (1) Good evening, Brian; (2) I'm opening a boutique; (3) I hit the ball first time, and there it was in the back of the net; (4) I've fallen off my chair, Brian.

21. He is only half an inch tall.

22. Tibbles.

23. If we took the bones out, it [the frog] wouldn't be crunchy.

24. *Dial "M" for Murder.*
25. Doris Day and Rock Hudson.
26. For eating honey.
27. "It's Only Make Believe."
28. Red Eye.
29. Terry Jones.
30. Twenty-two.
31. Drive a steel peg into his skull with a mallet, or (when in a deep sleep), saw his head off.
32. *Finian's Rainbow* ("Ten seconds of solid boredom").
33. None.
34. Crelm Toothpaste.
35. Raising polecats.
36. (1) Not to stand up; (2) Not to choose a very obvious piece of cover.
37. This is a trick question. Coventry City have never won the F.A. Cup.
38. *Venus de Milo* (she didn't raise her hands).
39. A large wooden mallet.
40. *The Blue Eagle.*
41. "It's a Man's (Dog's) (Pig's) Life in the Modern Army."
42. Vests.
43. Sandwiches.
44. Dynamo Tension!
45. Fear, surprise, ruthless efficiency, an almost fanatical devotion to the Pope, and nice red uniforms.
46. He wants bits of Mr. Gumby's brain taken out.
47. "My dog's got no nose." "How does he smell?" "Awful!"
48. St. Stephen.
49. A dead crab.
50. Cardinal Richelieu; he reveals that the Cardinal died in 1642, and that he is actually Ron Higgins, an impersonator.
51. A window cleaner; an engine driver.
52. On the side of the engine, above the piston box.
53. Only because they have no control over their own destinies.
54. Graham Chapman played Dracula in "Oh, You're No Fun Anymore," and John Cleese played Frankenstein's monster in "The Dull Life of a City Stockbroker."
55. It had been nailed there.
56. A pair of knickers.
57. "Yes, It's the Sewage Farm Attendant," in which Dan falls into a vat of human dung, with hilarious consequences.
58. Chartered accountancy.
59. He has a lion-taming hat.
60. Petula Clark's "Don't Sleep in the Subway."
61. Up yours.
62. Thank you . . .
63. A "never-pay" policy.
64. Reginald Maudling is close enough; pork lunch and meat, Spam, themselves, horses, armchairs, pepperoni, lasagna, lobster thermidor, Brian Close, Henri Bergson, and a buffalo with an aqualung are all wrong.

65. Beethoven's mynah bird sings "I'm the Guy Who Found the Lost Chord."
66. St. Looney Up the Cream Bun and Jam.
67. In a battle with an ant.
68. Abdul.
69. Scene 1.
70. Twenty-eight thousand feet of Wintrex, a new, white foam rubber, plus sixteen thousand cubic U.S. furlongs of white paint with a special snow finish.
71. Six months, suspended.
72. Either hit them with the book, or shoot them just above the beak (although Mrs. Essence flushed hers down the loo).
73. "The Girl From Ipanema."
74. Tchaikovsky.
75. *A Short History of Motor Traffic Between Esher and Purley.*
76. Eighty-four dead, sixty-five severely wounded, twelve missing and believed lost.
77. Halibut.
78. "Jerusalem."
79. All brontosauruses are thin at one end, much, much thicker in the middle, and then thin again at the far end.
80. A drop of sherry.
81. Eels.
82. Two dozen fruitcakes and ten macaroons.
83. Henry Wensleydale.
84. His pump got caught in his trouser leg (badly crushing his sandwiches).
85. "Old-Fashioned Girl."
86. Peter Cook and Dudley Moore (Leningrad has never laughed so much).
87. The luggage compartment.
88. Paraguay and Britain.
89. A castle in Sardinia.
90. Shakespeare.
91. Concorde.
92. "A Book at Bedtime" (in which a bone becomes a space station, and falls on a caveman), and "Spam" (the titles to World Forum/Communist Quiz).

A LOOK FROM THE INSIDE

Of all the production and crew members that worked on *Monty Python's Flying Circus*, few served longer than Hazel Pethig, who was in charge of designing and procuring the costumes worn on the shows. In addition to working on the first thirty-nine shows—three seasons' worth—she also served on *Holy Grail* and *Life of Brian*, in addition to such individual Python projects as *Jabberwocky*. As an insider, Pethig had a unique opportunity to work with and observe Python from its beginnings, and agreed to share her thoughts in view of the twentieth anniversary of the group.

"I was initially told it was called *Owl-Stretching Time*," she recalls, "so I thought that was a hint as to its approach. I hadn't done a lot of work before, which was quite good, as I had to be extremely flexible. I can remember Eric asking me at 7:00 a.m., when we were about to set off filming, if he could dress up as a fairy in a tutu. I managed to do it, but I think a lot of people that were established wouldn't have enjoyed that. Not being a traditional costume lady, I was much more suitable for that kind of work—I enjoyed making something out of nothing."

Rounding all of them up for costume fittings proved to be more difficult than she had expected. "I could hardly ever get them for fittings because the shows happened very fast, and they weren't keen on fittings. I managed to get them all in one day for fittings in the stockroom, and they went riot! They were running around like schoolboys, playing around," she says.

The most uncooperative of an uncooperative group was John Cleese, but Pethig says she learned how to handle him. "Squeezing John into costume was difficult for me. He didn't like wearing costumes, and he didn't like wearing beards and moustaches. He used to puff himself up like a bullfrog so his costumes wouldn't fit. He'd say 'Look, I can't wear it, it doesn't fit.' I had to pummel him until he fit into the costume."

The group never hesitated to take on historical roles, as Eric Idle demonstrates here. Photo copyright BBC and Python Productions

Perhaps the most interesting aspect of her job was observing the interaction of the Pythons in their own environment, a vantage point available to few others.

"As a group, they're quite riotous. Individually, they were different people. John, in particular—he was the rebel of the group. Terry Jones and Mike were like old school buddies, Eric used to bury himself in a book, and Graham was just absolutely zany and adorable. The others were mainly verbal, [but] Terry Gilliam was the opposite. I felt a rapport with Terry, because he used to work alone, late at night, and had to be physically creative, which is what I had to do.

"They used to get into some nice little scraps. I used to enjoy it—they used to criticize one another without upsetting each other, so it was exciting to watch, to see a group that could all be honest to one another. I've always found it inspirational to see people having a go at one another, and still seem to care for each other. There were times when I thought they would fall apart, the group wouldn't survive it, but they have all stayed very close, especially Mike and Terry Jones.

"It's taken a long time, in a way, for those two to go off by themselves, to let each other go and do their own thing, especially Terry. Mike is a very popular guy, he's the most amiable and least cutting of the group, and that's very hard for Terry Jones. When Terry went to do his Chaucer book and Mike had *Ripping Yarns*, that was a very tricky time—the gradual separation of Terry and Michael was taking place. It was tricky because they were very close. And the same was true for Graham and John, because they used to be very close.

"They were all supportive of one another, but at the same time—being intelligent university people—they were taught that one had to be critical, to improve everybody," Pethig says.

"John was dominant and always easily recognizable on the street. He didn't wear costumes and wigs so much, so he was *always* recognizable. Terry J and Mike were always scurrying around, doing all of the dirty work, in a way. Eric was always more caustic, and Terry G worked a lot in isolation. It wasn't just the costumes that were interesting, it was the people."

In the early days, Pethig says she also had to contend with tiny budgets, and make the best of what she had. She often found herself scrounging things at the last minute, or taking extra costumes to be on the safe side. She became an expert on seeking out old clothing shops, and notes that few of them are still around today. "I was always trying to persuade people to let me have things at the last minute," she recalls. One incident in particular involved the "New Cooker" sketch, in which a long, long line of gas men wait in a street outside a house. "I had to find lots and lots of raincoats and spectacles for the queue of gas men. I managed to get hold of all these joke glasses, but I couldn't have gotten them nowadays."

She also worked with the special effects (SFX) people to achieve more elaborate costumes, rising to the challenges the group often presented. "I remember one odd little costume, in which Terry Jones had to be half a Frenchman and half an English businessman," for the Anglo-French Silly Walk. "On one side of the camera is an Englishman in a bowler hat; when he turns around, he's a Frenchman with a stupid shirt. That all had to work quite well—it was tricky! There would be all sorts of costumes that had to fall apart, like the nude organist who lost all his clothes, which meant working with the SFX guy. I once had to make a carrot costume for Graham that he wore to some university debates—the problem was mainly with the shoulders and the makeup."

The TV series gradually became more and more successful, but Pethig says their success didn't affect them adversely. "The changes came much later—they were pretty consistent through-

out. Now that I've worked with other groups, I think Python got along terribly well. John got disenchanted and separated from the rest, and Eric became a little more isolated, and they sometimes found Terry Jones and Michael Palin a little overenthusiastic, but I didn't really see them change.

"When they went to Canada to do the stage show, they could have changed and they didn't. I saw a little wave of it in North America, because they were engulfed with publicity, and parties, and women waiting outside the stage doors—their heads could have been turned, but they weren't. They survived that as well."

As time went on, Cleese in particular became tired of Python. When members of the public would shout at him to "Do the Silly Walk, John!", he found it increasingly irritating. "John *hates* being linked up with that, and sometimes with Python. He's never realized how brilliant 'Silly Walks' is. But there was never any strong resentment, or they wouldn't have kept together," says Pethig.

The tendency, particularly in Britain, to consider Cleese the "star" of Monty Python is inaccurate and unfair, says Pethig. "Sometimes I thought it was unfair the way the populace set

Cleese's aversion to costumes is seen in this **Life of Brian** *rehearsal shot; he preferred to work in his tunic as much as possible before donning armor for the actual takes.* **Photo copyright KHJ**

John off so much. They all contributed a lot to Python. When I went to the script meetings, they *all* put as much into the script. John *wasn't* Monty Python—Monty Python was the *team*. John was a strong voice, extremely intelligent, but the others put in just as much.

"We see rock groups that never manage to keep together. I remember making friends with some people in Dire Straits, and comparing them to Python—they had similar problems. They can go through a rough patch where they say it's the end, they get through it, and adjust accordingly for the future.

"I can understand the group members not wanting to get stuck with [the Python] identity as well. They have to progress. The public would love for them to do more Monty Python shows, but they've passed that stage—they don't need to do that anymore."

As strong as her admiration is for the Pythons and their work, the group feels the same about her, both personally and professionally.

"John used to say that they could phone me from fifteen hundred miles away, on a crackling line, and tell me what they wanted, and I'd come back with what they were trying to describe. I suppose that did happen."

Pethig was always a great admirer of the Python humor as well, and its legacy. "Python was always breaking down barriers that now people are benefiting from—not just in show business, either. They stood up for their ideas, and their vaguely anarchic, but still responsible attitudes.

"And it was great fun!"

THE SECOND SERIES

**AIRED SEPT. 15–29, 1970,
AND OCT. 20–DEC. 22, 1970**

*T*here was little doubt that *Monty Python's Flying Circus* would return for a second season. The show received a groundswell of support that built slowly but surely, so that the group was certain they would be renewed.

"By the time we'd gotten two-thirds of the way through the first series, there was a definite swell of opinion in our favor coming from all the newspapers, although for the first six shows, nobody could make head or tail of it," says John Cleese.

"All the critics did what they do when they're cowardly and don't know which way to jump, which is to describe in detail what was in the shows, without saying whether they were good, bad, or indifferent. Ever so slowly, about Show 6, there was very clearly opinion that began to form in favor of the show, which gathered strength a great deal."

The second series experienced both the advantages and disadvantages of familiarity. Most of the usable material the group had saved up going into the first series had been dealt with, and so there was not as comfortable a cushion of back-logged sketches to fall back on. But in other ways they were

hitting their stride, realizing the freedom of the format they had developed and attempting to take full advantage of it.

There were few changes in the look of the show itself. In fact, the only way to distinguish shows in the second series is by the lead-in to the opening titles. While the first series used a (sometimes lengthy) sequence with the "It's" Man, his part was considerably shortened in the buildups to the titles in the second series. After his initial "It's," he would be followed by John Cleese, in a dinner jacket and usually at a desk, in some peculiar location saying "And now for something completely different," which by now had become the group's catchphrase.

"I think we realized it maybe five or six shows in," Michael Palin recalls. "There was very little press coverage about Python to start with— it wasn't reviewed by the normal television critics. The *Washington Post* had one of the earliest articles about Python, by a journalist called Fred Friendly, who said 'This is an absolutely wonderful, amazing show, and it should come to America.' And everyone said no, of course it won't. He was really ahead of the day—that was 1969!

"But a lot of the newspaper articles would have the headline 'And Now For Something Completely Different,' which I think was John and Graham's catchphrase," says Palin. "The great thing was, it was said so often anyway, normally, on television, that we just found ourselves saying it. By that time, we'd identified it as a silly catchphrase, and now no one can say it without really being aware of Python."

The Silly Walk, in profile; Cleese excelled in his portrayals of mad authority figures. According to costumer Hazel Pethig, Cleese hated dressing up in strange and uncomfortable costumes, and would have been perfectly happy to perform all of his Python scenes in a coat and tie. **Photo copyright BBC and Python Productions**

As usual, Cleese's man in the dinner jacket sits at a desk located in the most incongruous locations available. **Photo copyright BBC and Python Productions**

Show 1—Dinsdale

RECORDED AS SERIES 2, SHOW 4—PROD. #60530

The Newsreader (JC) is in a cage at the zoo as he says "And now for something completely different"; the "'It's'" Man (MP) is in an adjacent cage as he announces "It's"

Titles

"Face the Press" features the Minister for Home Affairs (GC), whose pink tulle dress and accessories are described by the Interviewer (EI). The Minister is to debate a small patch of brown liquid (possibly creosote), and opts to answer his first question in both his real voice, and a silly high-pitched whine. The Interviewer talks on a TV monitor with Air Chief Marshall Sir Vincent "Kill the Japs" Forster, who is attired in outrageous drag.

The program is being watched at home by Mrs. G. Pinnet (TJ); she answers her front door to begin the "New Cooker" sketch. Two Gas Men (GC and MP), in caps and brown trenchcoats, have confused her with a Mrs. G. Crump.

After the Gas Men inform her that she is in the wrong house, *Mrs. G. Pinnet (Jones) is quick to oblige them.* **Photo copyright BBC and Python Productions**

She signs the receipt, at their insistence, as Mrs. Crump-Pinnet; after signing more invoices and installation forms, they find the connection order is also for a Mrs. Crump. She decides to submit to the gas fumes for faster service, and the crowd of Gas Men (all with caps and brown trenchcoats) form a long line down the street. They are all turning and muttering incomprehensible technicalities to each other, as the group eventually fades into animation.

More animation features vintage model European monarchs in flight, and an old man shaves his neck.

A lascivious, winking Customer with an evil eye (EI) tries to rent a small white pussycat, some chest of drawers, and a bit of pram, but is discouraged when the Shopowner (TJ) shows him the less-than-naughty items. Meanwhile, a gentleman buying a newspaper in the shop turns out to be Mr. Teabags of the Ministry of Silly Walks (JC) on his

The Silly Walk in action: one of the public's most-loved Python sketches, and one of Cleese's least favorites. **Photo copyright BBC and Python Productions**

Dinsdale. Interviews with a neighbor, April Simnel (MP), one of their teachers, Anthony Viney (GC), and Police Inspector Harry "Snapper" Organs (TJ) trace the careers of this violent, sarcastic pair.

Stig O'Tracy (EI) has had his head nailed to the floor, but doesn't have an unkind word for the brothers; neither does his wife (GC), whose head is still nailed to a coffee table. A Female Impersonator, Gloria (JC), tells of Dinsdale's fear of a giant, imaginary hedgehog called Spiny Norman. Luigi Vercotti (MP), who runs an escort service, talks about Doug's dreaded use of sarcasm.

The Piranha's atom-bombing of Luton Airport has finally caused the police to sit up and take notice. Supt. Harry "Snapper" Organs follows them disguised as various theatrical characters, though some critics have chided him for his abusive ad libs and unscheduled appearances on-stage.

As the closing credits roll, an animated Spiny Norman cries "Dinsdale!" as it peers over the city skyline. The Newsreader (JC) is still in his cage, while the adjacent cage is occupied by a skeleton looking like the "It's" Man.

ALSO APPEARING: David Ballantyne
John Hughman
Stanley Mason

Although one report claims this sequence with Michael Palin is part of the "Wacky Queen" sketch, it finally surfaced in the TV series as a segment in the "Vintage Silly Walk" film shown at the close of that sketch. Either way, it is extremely silly. **Photo copyright BBC and Python Productions**

way to work (where he passes the long line of gas men).

At the office, Mr. Putey (MP) demonstrates his own rather lame silly walk, and explains that he was hoping for a government grant to make it much sillier. His secretary, Miss Twolumps, makes a futile attempt to bring them coffee, and they screen footage of some vintage silly walks. Putey is offered a position to help develop the Anglo-French Silly Walk (La Marche Futile), unveiled by two Frenchmen (JC and MP) and demonstrated by their Anglo-French subject (TJ).

A BBC 1 announcer introduces "Ethel the Frog," which the Host (JC) explains will be looking at the violence of the Piranha Brothers, Doug and

- The title page of the script credits GC, JC, EI, TJ, and MP, "with prize-winning animations by Terry Gilliam." The unofficial title of the show is "Give Us Money, Not Awards."
- The group had hoped to open the show with a match featuring the Chelsea Football Team. The players would have kicked the ball down the field, running past John Cleese in dinner jacket at his usual desk. The original ending would then have occurred in the footballers' changing room. The script notes that Eric claimed he could get the entire team for the pre-credit sequence. Apparently, he couldn't.
- The "Timmy Williams Show" sketch had originally been intended for this show, to follow the "Ministry of Silly Walks"; it is now in Series 2, Show 6.
- Michael's Mr. Putey character, introduced in the "Silly Walks" sketch, was originally named Mr. Standford.

The live performance of "Silly Walks," including a silly walk-on by Carol Cleveland, sees Cleese giving his all. **Photo copyright KHJ**

 ## WALKING SILLY

"John Cleese and I were writing together one day, and John had been thinking of doing something about anger. He's very good at it, and he likes that emotion very much indeed. I'd been noticing that there were all sorts of ministries for strange things that were likely to distract people from the main issues of the day, and make it look like the government was doing something. A lot of attention would either go to a drought or flood that probably didn't exist anyway, and there seemed to be lots of useless ministries. I thought, why not a Ministry of Anger?

"It's difficult to remember whether it was John's or my idea, but I do know that the next stage was Silly Walks, which was more ludicrous and petty than an emotion like anger. My house was on a very steep hill, and we saw a man walk past, uphill, stooped very sharply backward, defying the laws of gravity! Well, we thought Silly Walks was a good idea, but we couldn't quite think how to develop it.

"As usual, we were supposed to be writing something else when this idea occurred —anything to prevent us from getting to that work! But we thought we'd better get on to writing what we were supposed to be writing. So we rang up Mike (Palin) and Terry (Jones)—to interrupt them from whatever they were supposed to be doing—and made them write the sketch."

"Silly Walks" is one of Cleese's most

dreaded sketches today, largely because of the fan reaction that has plagued him ever since. So he politely rebuffs any and all requests to perform it, up through his appearance on *Donahue* with the cast of *A Fish Called Wanda* in August 1988. Featured on a live video link to the N.Y. studio, with Jamie Lee Curtis in L.A., Cleese was badgered by virtually everyone to perform the walk, and appeared to relent. So he stood up, walked off-camera for a few moments, during which he claimed to do the Silly Walks, and returned to an enthusiastic ovation.

Show 2 — The Spanish Inquisition

RECORDED AS SERIES 2, SHOW 3—PROD. #60440

A man (JC) runs across a field, cranking a pair of mechanical wings. He appears to fly, but the camera tilts to show he is actually falling down a cliff, and crashes into the ground. At a nearby desk, the man in the dinner jacket (JC) says "And now for something completely different," and the "It's" Man (MP) says "It's"

Titles

Jarrow, New Year's Eve, 1911 is followed by Jarrow, 1912. Lady Mountback (CC) sits in a drawing room, when Reg (GC) bursts in to announce trouble at the mill, saying "One on't cross beams gone owt askew in treddle!"* When she questions him, he says he didn't expect a kind of Spanish Inquisition.

A trio of red-robed men from the Spanish Inquisition rush in, led by Cardinal Ximinez (MP). He triumphantly announces "No one escapes the Spanish Inquisition!" Unfortunately he keeps blowing his lines, and Cardinal Biggles (TJ) tries to help. They have to make several entrances before Biggles and Cardinal Fang (TG) apply the rack, which turns out to be a rack for dishwashing. They try to get Lady Mountback to confess to heresy. Captions describe their diabolical laughter, and their diabolical acting.

Reg sits calmly in the back, puffing on his pipe, when a BBC Man (JC) arrives, asking if he would answer a door in a sketch. He is driven across town to the house, and obligingly answers the door.

Johnson, a joke salesman (EI), describes his products for the BBC Man (a comedy hernia kit, a Wicked Willie with a life-sized winkle, guaranteed to break the ice at parties), but he is unable to give the punch line for the salesman. When Johnson protests that he wasn't told, the BBC man borrows his head for a bit of animation.

His now-animated head is wheeled in with an animated baby carriage; a can-can dancer passes through his eyes, and a pupil is shot out of a Civil War cannon, which rolls into photos of nude women covered by binoculars, faucets, etc.

The Head of a government commission (JC) on the fiscal deficit tries to find new methods of taxation. Reasoning that everything else pleasurable is taxed, one of the three civil servants (TJ) suggests they place a tax on . . . thingy. A series of "Vox Pops" on taxation follow, including a suggestion from Mr. Gumby.

A Dear Old Lady (MW) is showing some holiday snaps (to CC, who tears them up as she goes), when the Spanish Inquisition, complete with a lengthy historical introduction, bursts in. They pathetically attempt to torture her with the Soft Cushions, then resort to the Comfy Chair. An animated policeman confesses, followed by several other bits of "I confess" animation.

This leads into the beginning of 20th Century Vole's "Semaphore Version of Wuthering Heights," with CC as Catherine, EI as her husband and TJ as Heathcliff. The maid stutters, saying "Your fffather! He's fffallen ill with fffever!" Also shown are clips from "Julius Caesar on an Addis Lamp" (with GC as Caesar), "Gunfight at the OK Corral in Morse Code," and the "Smokesignal Version of Gentlemen Prefer Blondes."

In Central Criminal Court, the Jury Foreman

*One of the crossbeams has gone out of skew on the treadle.

(MP) gives the verdict in charades, and the Judge (GC) finds him not guilcup. He acts out "Call the next defendant," who is Judge Kilb (TJ). The first Judge announces that he is leaving for South Africa, where they still have the cat o' nine tails, four death sentences a week, cheap drinks, slave labor, and a booming stock market. His parting shot is sentencing the defendant to be burned at the stake. The defendant says he didn't expect a kind of Spanish Inquisition, and the Inquisition trio tries to rush over as fast as possible before the show ends.

The Spanish Inquisition is on a bus as the credits roll, but just as they burst into the courtroom, it's The End.

ALSO APPEARING:
Carol Cleveland
Marjorie Wilde

 "The Smoke-signal Version of Gentlemen Prefer Blondes" was originally followed by "the all-talking version of the 'Chemist Shop' sketch ('Who's got the pox?')." This version of "Chemist Shop," which is in Show 4, here uses "biscuit barrel" as the naughty words for toilet, instead of "Semprini." "Chemist Shop" is then supposed to be followed by a different courtroom scene, which still ends with the Spanish inquisition rushing to the courtroom as the credits roll. The courtroom scene in this show was actually intended to run after the final credits.

TAKEN BY SURPRISE

When Michael Palin is asked how he gets his ideas, he explains that he sits with a piece of

Outside his home office, Palin poses with a Mr. Gumby doll made by a fan. **Photo copyright KHJ**

paper, and lets something come into his head. "There's nothing odd about that. Sometimes in the morning, when I'm half awake, or just when I'm about to go to sleep, all sorts of strange thoughts will come into my mind," Palin says, laughing.

"There are moments when the mind drifts, and that's what happened with the Spanish Inquisition. There was all this stuff about 'trouble at t'mill,' and Carol saying she doesn't understand. Graham breaks out of his accent, still talking Northern, and says 'gone owt askew on treddle.' 'No, I still don't understand.' He says 'All I came in here was to tell you there was trouble at t'mill, I didn't expect a kind of Spanish Inquisition.'

"I wrote that line, just as it was, and I thought 'Great! What we must do here is bring the Spanish Inquisition into it!' So, the door opens, and in come these people saying 'Nobody expects the Spanish Inquisition!' That's really how it was written—it was just stream of consciousness."

MEET MR. GUMBY

The gum-booted, suspendered, handkerchief-hatted Gumbies were created gradually, but soon became favorites of the group and viewers. Though Michael Palin perfected the characters, it was John Cleese who made the initial appearance in Gumby uniform; he assembled the costume while the group was filming their "Vox Pops" (Voice of the People, man-in-the-street one-liners).

"Recording the 'Vox Pops' was as near as Python ever came to improvising," Palin explains, "because all the studio stuff and the longer film bits were clearly worked out. Many of these little 'Vox Pops' were just people putting on these silly costumes, and saying silly things like 'My brain hurts,' or 'Don't believe a word of it,' or 'It's not really changed my life.'

"John had to say something particularly imbecilic and said 'What should I wear? I've got to go stand in the middle of a stream.' He put on these gumboots and rolled up his trousers, and said 'I'd tax people who stand in water,' while he was standing in a stream.

"So that costume was sort of around, and the next time I did something where he became more of a character whose brain hurt. John had already gotten the costume and the complete mindlessness of the character."

Show 3—Show 5

RECORDED AS SERIES 2, SHOW 5—PROD. #60531

A woman begins undressing in the window of a high-rise, when the Man in the Dinner Jacket (JC) is pulled up on a window-washing platform. He says "And now for something completely different," and an elk explodes. Back on the window ledge, he says "And now for something more completely different," and the "It's" Man (MP) says "It's"

Titles

Another animal explodes in the woods, where Mr. Chigger (TJ) approaches a Cardinal (MP), who is rehearsing his lines for Show 8. Chigger asks him about flying lessons, but the Cardinal says he isn't in the present show. A Secretary (CC) leads him through the woods, wading in a stream past other business executives, through a field, in a cave, under a road, and they finally end up in an office, where a man is suspended in the air. Mr. Anemone (GC) tells him to fly by flapping his arms, but Chigger protests, pointing out that he is hanging from wires, which Anemone goes to great lengths to disprove.

Two years later (actually six years later, after a Balfour Airlines correction), Chigger and his Copilot (JC) are commercial pilots interrupted by a Spokesman (EI) for Balfour Airlines, who points out some mistakes in the previous sketch, as well as last week's "High Chapparal," and begins to wander as he discusses other mistakes. The pilots are interrupted by a pounding on the cockpit door. A Man (GC) enters who has mistaken the cabin for a bathroom. He apologizes, then steps out of the plane to land on a bale of hay just outside of a bathroom. A Stewardess (CC) enters the cabin followed by a Hijacker (MP) on the scheduled flight to Cuba, but he wants to go to Luton. They throw him out on a bale of hay and he catches a bus to Luton, which is suddenly hijacked to Cuba.

The works of Scottish poet Ewan McTeagle (TJ) are studied, including his poem *Will You Lend Us a Quid?* Lassie O'Shea (EI) reads a personal poem written for her by McTeagle. St. John Limbo, a poetry expert (JC), discusses how McTeagle widened his scope by asking for ever-increasing amounts, and a Shakespearean Actor (EI) reads his masterpiece, *Can I Have Fifty Pounds to Mend the Shed?* A Very Good Playwright (MP) analyzes his work, and McTeagle walks past an exploding animal. A Highland Spokesman (JC) in a kilt stands up to deliver corrections, and has a man under his kilt (MP) examining him.

Animation features dismemberment and other violence, including a garden of hands, and a cowboy riding a severed hand. His lasso is attached to knitting being done by Mrs. Ratbag (GC).

Mrs. Ratbag is examined by a Psychiatrist Milkman (EI). As he takes her to a dairy, they pass an exploding cat and the Gynecologist (MP) who was just examining the Scotsman. They are interrupted by another man who claims they are just making a pat diagnosis without knowing the complete medical history of the patient. This is followed by a complaint about the previous complaint, and still more complaints. Dr. Cream (TJ), another psychiatrist milkman, talks to a cow lying on his couch, and Mrs. Ratbag is led through the field by a milkmaid, following the same route as the walk taken by Chigger at the beginning of the show, but in reverse order.

"It's the Mind," hosted by Mr. Boniface (MP), says the program will look at "The strange phenomenon of déjà vu, that strange feeling we sometimes get that we've lived through something before." Déjà vu strikes him, and he goes through the opening of the show several times. Panicking, he catches a psychiatrist dairy bus and runs back into Dr. Cream's office, only to find himself back on the bus and running to the office again, etc., and the credits roll.

ALSO APPEARING: Carol Cleveland
Jeannette Wild

☞ "Election Night Special" was originally set to follow "It's the Mind," with a very brief déjà vu ending; it was moved to Show 6.
☞ In the middle of "Psychiatrist Dairies/Déjà Vu," Mrs. Ratbag's name mysteriously changes to Mrs. Pim.

☞ **AUDITIONS**

There was a general method followed in distributing roles in Python sketches, according to Eric Idle, and casting within the group was usually rather easy.

"We'd never cast until the end, because everything had to be written. Once we'd established what the show was, and what was going to be said and done, then we'd sit down and cast it. For TV, we'd cast several shows at once, so if somebody was light in one show, we could make it up in the next," Idle says.

"Basically, it was all done by consent. Clearly, if it was a John sketch, it would be insane not to cast John as the authoritarian figure. As I think about it now, we were pretty good at casting, because people were very British. They didn't say 'Oh, I want to play that!'," Idle says in a sharp American accent. "They'd say 'Oh, I wouldn't mind . . .' People might have their eye on a little piece, and the rest of it was done very quickly. 'Eric, Mike, Terry, you want to do that?' 'I'll do that.'

"There were never any big arguments. As a matter of fact, we operated in reverse—people actually got better and better at giving their stuff away! I remember Terry Jones in *Meaning of Life*, for example, gave me a little old lady part in the condoms sketch. He thought I should do it, which was very nice of him!

"I think we very rarely miscast," Idle continues. "By and large, a lot of parts were Eric or Mike. It was clear which parts were Terry Jones parts—the little ratbag ladies; Graham Chapman was always the Colonel, and John, the authoritarian figures. In the middle were a range of characters that could always be Eric or Mike, and they were often written down that way."

Show 4—The Buzz Aldrin Show

RECORDED AS SERIES 2, SHOW 8—PROD. #61964

An animated caterpillar/man crawls into a house, and turns into a butterfly/poof. The Man in the Dinner Jacket (JC), with propellers on his desk, flies up to say "And now for something completely different," and the "It's" Man says "It's"
Titles

The BBC apologizes for the next announcement, which is five Gumbies introducing "The Architect" sketch, pointing to an office above them.

In the office, Mr. Tid (GC) throws down water to silence the Gumbies below, who are shouting "Up there!" He introduces the designers of a residential block of flats. Mr. Wiggin (JC) has designed an abattoir* with which to slaughter the tenants, but he is rejected. His chief regret is that he could never join the Masons, and he begs them for a chance. The next architect is Mr. Wymiss (EI), whose model catches fire and falls apart. He does give the Masonic handshake, however. Several ways of recognizing Masons are shown, including their handshakes, hats with antlers, etc.

An animated Mason (GC) undergoes anti-Masonic therapy.

Another apology is issued as the Gumbies introduce the "Insurance" sketch. Mr. Devious (MP) tries to sell the Straight Man (GC) a policy that includes a nude lady. The Reverend Morrison (EI) enters as the Straight Man leaves, as the script shows he has no more lines. The Vicar's car was hit while parked in his garage, but he is found to have a "never-pay" policy; his policy mentions filling his mouth in with cement. He finally leaves with his nude lady, as a Bishop (TJ) steps into Devious's office.

"The Bishop" titles, complete with secret-agent music, follow the Bishop as he tries to stop an explosion at a baptism and other incidents, but arrives too late. As he walks down a street with

Always equipped with a delightfully absurd logic, Gilliam's animations retained the ability to surprise and sometimes shock. **Photo copyright Python Productions Ltd.**

*Slaughterhouse.

his entourage, the Reverend Morrison shouts from the office, and they rush upstairs to get Devious, as "The Bishop" titles roll again. In a theater, Mr. and Mrs. Potter (MP and GC) note that this was where they came in.

The Potters are living in the street, and a Man (EI) wants to feature them in a documentary on Britain's housing program. Mrs. Potter chases them off to do a documentary on the drug problem, and the Potters are revealed as having Alfred Lord Tennyson in the bath. The Sales Manager of the East Midlands Poet Board (JC) does a promo, including an animated jingle, for the Poet Board. Wombat Harness (MP), who goes door to door reading poets, is seduced by a Housewife (TJ) when he tries to read her Wordsworth (EI).

Derek Hart (JC) is the moderator of a panel on nudity, featuring a Nude Man (GC). The music and titles start to roll again for "The Bishop."

Animation features men bouncing on a nude woman, with Gumby and the Beanstalk. Animated frogs turn into live Gumbies, and introduce "The Chemist" sketch.

A Chemist (JC) dispenses drugs by asking customers who has the pox, a boil on the botty, and a chest rash. An apology is then issued for using such words as knockers, wee-wee, and semprini; the chemist is arrested (by GC) for a "boil on his semprini."

A Customer (EI) at a less-naughty Chemist (TJ) is taken away for his after-shave joke. A not-at-all naughty Chemist (MP) is visited by a Customer (EI) who wants halibut after-shave. The Chemist pretends to go off to the basement to look for some, and finally pretends to go to Kensington. A "Vox Pops" segment has other people tell what they use for after-shave.

Police Constable Pan Am (GC) runs into the Chemists, and as a fat man shoplifts, the innocent Customer is arrested. The Constable cracks up and calls to Buzz Aldrin; another apology is issued as the credits follow for "The Buzz Aldrin Show," with Buzz Aldrin in most of the credits.
ALSO APPEARING: Sandra Richards
Stanley Mason

The five Gumbies announce "And now for something completely different," as they change into women.

☞ The "Chemist" sketch was originally intended for Show 2.
☞ In the original script, when the Bishop and his crew try to break into Devious's office, the whole set shakes and starts to fall.

☞ **IMPROVISING ANIMATIONS**

As he would eventually do when he became a film director, Terry Gilliam looked for opportunities to improvise while creating his animations, changing direction when an interesting opportunity presented itself.

"My approach has always been to keep an eye open for lucky accidents or mistakes. That's the advantage of cutouts. I had all this material sitting around the place, so it could fall into any number of patterns and suggest ideas," Gilliam explains.

"Paper and I had a very good relationship, and inspired each other. Sometimes they would write things like 'Titles for "The Bishop," ' or something like that—a title sequence—okay, so I do a title sequence. I had a very clear idea of what I wanted; I would storyboard what I was doing, and spend a lot of time trying to find the bits of artwork or photos that I wanted. Because of time limitations, I wouldn't quite find what I was looking for, but find something else that was slightly different. Okay, so it was a bit different from what I planned . . ."

Show 5—Live from the Grillomat

Recorded as Series 2, Show 7—Prod. #61851

A BBC 1 world symbol slide announces that the show will be presented live from the Grillomat Snack Bar in Paignton. The Host in the Dinner Jacket (JC) is sitting at a table in the Grillomat calling for the Titles, which are preceded by the "It's" Man (MP).

The Host, still at a table, calls for the opening sketch, or the "hors d'oeuvres," which is the Blackmail quiz show, hosted by the cheery Wally Wiggins (MP). He demands fifteen pounds from Mrs. Betty Teal to stop him from revealing the name of her lover in Bolton. He promises to show more of a revealing photo, and introduces a Stop the Film segment, where the amount increases as the film continues. A Nude Organist (TG) plays a fanfare as they attempt to extort the various sums.

A Member (TJ) of the Society for Putting Things on Top of Other Things is late for their dinner meeting, as he has just phoned the Blackmail show. The Society's chairman, Sir William Gore Fisk (GC), gives an annual overview of the previous year's progress, and Cutler, the delegate from the Staffordshire branch (JC), is chastised. The meeting is adjourned, however, when everyone agrees that it's all very silly.

The chairman walks out the door to leave, but is startled to find that he's on film. He tries to escape through the other doors and windows, but when the group sees it is surrounded by film, the room becomes a POW camp, and they decide to tunnel their way out.

In an animated sequence, five of them exit into a stomach, and are expelled through the bowels.

Mr. Praline (JC), the Host of a new half-hour chat show, tries to discuss the population explosion, but his guest, Brookie (EI), only attempts to tell jokes. When the Director (TJ) tells them their bit has been cut from the show, they hear noises under their feet, and decide they may still make it into the show as a link.

Below the floorboards (Praline says it's due to color separation), the five animated men travel through pipes beneath them, until they are belched out. One of them lands in a painting of *The Last Supper*, and is taken up to a cloud with the other four; the crowd on the cloud below them urges them not to jump.

Back at the Grillomat, the Waitress (GC) is talking too loudly for the "main course" to be introduced, which is Prawn Salad Ltd., or "The Accident" sketch.

A Man (EI) is ushered into a drawing room by a Butler (GC). He waits alone for a Mr. Thompson, when a mirror suddenly falls. The Butler is skeptical, and after he leaves again, a china cabinet falls completely by itself, though the Butler assumes the Man did it. A Maid (CC) enters the room and falls on the Brazilian dagger she has asked him to hold, and an Older Man (TJ) and a Police Officer (MP) both die when they are left alone with the innocent Man. The ceiling suddenly falls on the Butler, and as the Man leaves, the mansion falls apart behind him and explodes.

The five formerly animated men walk past a Bishop (MP), who is rehearsing for next week's show (the man at the Grillomat sees no need to interrupt), and enter the school hall at the Dibley School for Boys, where they are presenting *Seven Brides for Seven Brothers*. Praline and Brookie sit at the piano as four boys (TJ, EI, TG, and JC) represent the seven brothers, while two girls are the seven brides. The Headmaster (GC) calls in the Padre (MP) to perform the ceremony.

The sheet music becomes animated, and turns into a piggy bank hunting sequence with Neddy and Teddy, ending up as a chart in a butcher shop.

The Butcher (EI) is alternately polite and insulting to a City Gent (MP), attitudes changing with each sentence.

Back at the Grillomat, the Host and Waitress get into a dispute over whether he has offered coffee or tea, which leads into the story of an almost totally stupid boxer.

Ken Clean-Air System (JC) rubs gravel in his hair every day for lunch, according to his manager, Englebert Humperdinck (GC). Interviews with his wife Mrs. Nellie Air-Vent (EI), his mother (TJ), and his Trainer (MP) show a typical day training for a big fight: He arrives at a hospital, thinking it is a gymnasium. His opponent is teen-aged Petulia Wilcox (CB), shown knitting in her bedroom at home; in the ring, he is shown giving her a senseless beating.

At the Grillomat, the Waitress reads a note from the now-departed Host, who is shown leaving the show on a bus. He apologizes and says he won't be back the next week, as some of the jokes weren't as funny as they might have been. As the credits roll, he explains that he's really more of a visual performer, and wishes that he had been able to do his funny walk.

ALSO APPEARING: Carol Cleveland
      Ian Davidson
      Connie Booth
      Mrs. Idle

☛ The title page of the script credits Terry Palin, Eric Jones, Michael Cleese, Graham Gilliam, Terry Chapman, and John Idle.

☛ A lengthy sequence was cut from the final show involving Praline and Brookie rambling on about phone service, while Brookie interjects homely Yorkshire aphorisms, just before the animations appear under the floor.

☛ Following the "Butcher Shop" sketch, a sequence was cut which featured the 1958 Cup Final discussing the implications of the previous sketch on a TV chat show.

☛ The "Dibley" name surfaces again here, as the name of the Boys' School.

☞ GWEN DIBLEY'S FLYING CIRCUS: DIBLEY NOTES

When the group was deciding on a name for the original TV series, among the bizarre suggestions—many of which were eventually used as titles for individual shows ("Owl-Stretching Time," "Bunn, Wackett, Buzzard, Stubble, and Boot," etc.)—Michael Palin favored naming the show after Gwen Dibley.

Who?

"There actually was a Gwen Dibley," Palin explains. "She seemed the sort of person who would be miles away from anyone who would ever watch a Python show. It was in one of my wife's mother's magazines, one of these Women's Institute's monthly gatherings, where someone talked about flower display. At the end it said 'And Gwen Dibley accompanied on the piano.'

"I just thought it was a nice idea to give someone their own show, even though they didn't know it. The satisfaction of someone getting their copy of *The Radio Times*, and the children of Gwen Dibley discovering it first—the sheer, stunned surprise that their mother had been given her own show without her knowing it, appealed to us greatly. We also liked the name 'Gwen Dibley.'

"But like a lot of our titles, they worked one afternoon, and the next morning people weren't quite so sure. I think we also thought we might get sued, quite rightly, by the Dibley family, if they didn't like it. It wasn't really fair to drag her into something that no one knew what it was going to be like. And so she lost her chance to be associated with one of the great comedy shows."

Actually, though, the group managed to work the Dibley name into several of the shows, sometimes in the most unlikely places. Among the various namesakes are the Dibley School for Boys, seen in this show as the place where *Seven Brides For Seven Brothers* is staged, director L.F. Dibley, and Dibley Road, the address of Earnest Scribbler, author of the funniest joke in the world.

As it turned out, the group's inability to decide on a title for the show actually forced the BBC's hand, according to producer Barry Took. "They couldn't think of a title. At one stage, they wanted to call it 'Whither Canada?' and all sorts of things like that. The BBC finally told them 'It doesn't matter what you call it as long as the words "flying circus" are in it,' because all the notes and memos going around internally at the BBC called it 'The Circus.' It would confuse the BBC if they called it anything else, so they went away and invented Monty Python."

Actually, some of the BBC personnel had a further nickname for it as well, but somehow, "Baron Von Took's Flying Circus" never seemed to catch on.

Show 6—School Prizes

RECORDED AS SERIES 2, SHOW 10—PROD. #61852

The Compère (EI) of "It's a Living" explains the game, the rules and fees received, thanks his guests, and promises to come back next week.

A BBC 1 world symbol announces the time, but the animation following can't find the lights in time for the opening
Titles

The Man in the Dinner Jacket (JC) sits at a desk in a blacksmith's shop, explaining that he didn't say "And now for something completely different" because he isn't in this week's show.

A Man (TJ) looks into the camera, complaining about his toothache, and a Nabarro figure (GC) interrupts to introduce the School Prize Awards.

The Bishop of East Anglia (MP) is dragged under the table and is attacked by Another Man (EI), who emerges and claims to be the Bishop of East Anglia. He declines to give out any of the silver trophies, and puts them all in his sack, until an Oriental Man (GC) says he is the Bishop of East Anglia, and claims the school prizes for the People's Republic of China. Inspector Elizabeth Bradshaw (TJ) and the Leader of a commando squad (JC) also try to claim the trophies, as gunshots erupt.

This is all being viewed on television as the latest film by director L.F. Dibley (TJ). An Interviewer (GC) talks with the director, who has made lesser-known versions of *If . . ., 2001: A Space Odyssey, Midnight Cowboy,* as well as ten-second versions of *Rear Window* and *Finian's Rainbow,* which are shown.

The Interviewer introduces the Foreign Secretary (just returned from the bitter fighting in the Gulf of Ammah) on canoeing, and his craft is thrown into a lake by two Arabs as he sits in it. Three other politicians form a human pyramid before each of them is thrown in the lake, and the president of the Board of Trade is placed in a hamper and then thrown in the lake. Leaving the discussion of problems of Britain's industrial reorganization, other public figures are thrown into the lake, concluding with Dame Irene Stoat (MP) reading one of her poems before being shoved in by a samurai warrior.

Two couples at a dinner party are interrupted by a Man (JC) delivering their free dung from the Book of the Month Club. Host Mr. Forbes (MP) tries to refuse it, and another deliveryman (GC)

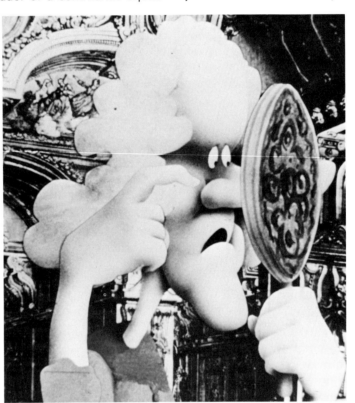

The animated Prince first discovers the Black Spot that will kill him and drive the censors insane. Photo copyright Python Productions Ltd.

brings them a free dead Indian, and the couple wins the M-4 Motorway. The couple then find they are the prizes in a police raffle, and a Policeman (TJ) describes some of the other prizes.

An animated sequence follows, with a samurai slicing everything—including himself—in two, and the parts are used in a cooking demonstration.

Nigel Watt (TJ), whose wife has just died, is joined at a restaurant by the wonderfully David Frost-ish Timmy Williams (EI). His attempts at a heart-to-heart chat are futile, as Timmy's writers, photographers, and hangers-on are everywhere. Nigel finally shoots himself, and the "Timmy Williams' Coffee Time" credits roll, crediting Timmy for everything.

An Interviewer (MP) talks to one of the country's leading skin specialists, Raymond Luxury-Yacht (GC), whose name is actually pronounced "throat-wobbler mangrove"; his extraordinarily large nose proves to be false, and he is thrown off the show.

Animation of sexual athletes follows, with a nude woman and a topless Mona Lisa.

At a marriage-license bureau, a Man (TJ) tells Henry, the registrar (EI), that he wants to get married. He is joined by two other men with the same request (MP and GC), but the registrar agrees to marry all of them, until his Wife (JC) finds him out.

Animation of a woman applying lipstick becomes the story of an enchanted prince who discovers a spot on his face, and dies three years later, although the spot flourishes.

"Election Night Special" features the entire

group with the results of the Silly Party, the Slightly Silly Party, the Sensible Party, and the independent Very Silly candidates. The politicians include Jethroe Q. Walrustitty, Arthur J. Smith, and Tarquin Fintimlinbinwhinbimlimbus-stop F'Tang-F'Tang-Ole-Biscuit-Barrel. Analyses follow, as do the credits, then "Monty Python has held the critics!"

ALSO APPEARING: Rita Davies
Ian Davidson

 "Timmy Williams" had originally been intended for Series 2, Show 1; "Election Night Special" was intended for Series 2, Show 3.

 The group uses the name of Ray Millichope, film editor of the first three series, as one of the politicians who forms a human pyramid by the lake ("Ray Millichope, leader of Allied Technician's Union").

Cleese and Cleveland as Mr. and Mrs. Attila the Hun, stars of their own sitcom. **Photo copyright BBC and Python Productions**

THE BLACK SPOT

Even Terry Gilliam's animations were not immune to the BBC censors, though the inanity of one instance still irritates Gilliam. In the original version of "The Prince and the Black Spot" (and the version still shown in the feature-length *And Now For Something Completely Different*), the Prince ignores the black spot and dies of cancer. However, in all subsequent repeats, another voice is dubbed over the word "cancer," and the word "gangrene" inserted.

"That's the most bizarre, silly, stupid thing, because it went out, millions of people watched it, and the world didn't change—so, I don't know why one changes it on the repeats," says a still-irritated Gilliam.

"It's just crazy. Who's protecting who from what? I don't know. I didn't think it was dangerous to mention the word 'cancer,' but it obviously touched a fear that a lot of people didn't want to deal with."

CHINAMAN'S CHANCE

The individual members of Python tended to specialize in their own characterizations as the show developed. For no apparent reason, Graham Chapman seemed to end up playing Chinese and other Oriental characters. "There is no known reason for that. I had a lot of Chinese friends at the time, so perhaps that's why I tended to get Chinese parts handed to me on a plate. Maybe the lads thought I would like them. I didn't mind."

THE WONDERFUL DAVID FROST

At various times, the individual Pythons have all been involved with the ubiquitous David Frost, either writing or performing for him early in their careers. Although they all enjoyed taking a few jabs at their one-time mentor, it was usually Eric Idle who ended up portraying the various incarnations of Frost, whether as a straightforward interviewer or as Arthur Tree, a tree hosting his own talk show.

According to Idle, however, his impersonation of Frost got no feedback from the target himself until long after the Python TV shows. "Actually, I talked to him after I did the Nixon interviews on *Saturday Night Live*—Danny Ackroyd played Nixon, and I played him.

"I saw Frost about two weeks later when I came back to London. He came up to me and said 'I loved your Frost'—as though it wasn't him, but somebody else that I was doing!" Idle laughs. " 'Loved your Frost' . . . But we all used to work for him, writing ad libs for him in the '60s. He gave us our big breaks, though we would never admit that in public."

The most obvious assault on Frost was

"Timmy Williams' Coffee Time." Idle and the Pythons got back at him in numerous ways, including closing credits that include dozens of writers' names.

"That used to be David. His shows would say 'Written by David Frost, Contributions by—' and then three hundred names would roll by, the names of the people who actually wrote the show," Idle says. "He always took a nice big script credit, and I don't think he ever wrote a joke."

Show 7—The Attila the Hun Show

RECORDED AS SERIES 2, SHOW 11—PROD. #62572

A filmed introduction of the Romans fighting ancient barbarians leads into "The Attila the Hun Show," a cute situation comedy with Attila (JC), Mrs. Hun (CC), Robin and Jennie (MP and GC), his children, and Uncle Tom (EI), their black butler. The theme song and opening credits closely copy *The Debbie Reynolds Show*, and the laugh track blares loudly.

The Man in the Dinner Jacket says "And now for something completely different," the "It's" Man (MP) says "It's"

Titles

Atilla the Nun is in a hospital room; at the other end, Miss Norris (CC) is going to be

Shooting the filmed opening to "The Attila the Hun Show" on location, as Chapman gets into his costume as teenaged Jennie Hun. **Photo copyright BBC and Python Productions**

examined by Charles Crompton, the stripping doctor (GC), in a room with mood lighting and music, while several shabby men in filthy macs (students) look on.

The Compère (EI) at the Peephole Club applauds, and introduces the Secretary of State for Commonwealth Affairs (TJ), who does a striptease as he delivers a speech on agricultural subsidies and their effects on commonwealth relationships. Next is the Minister of Pensions and Social Securities (GC), who does a belly dance.

"Vox Pops" follows with political groupies.

Mr. and Mrs.

Concrete (TJ and MP) are visited by Leslie Ames (GC), the Council Ratcatcher. He finds that they have sheep instead of mice. He enters a large hole in the wainscoting, but the sheep have guns; killer sheep terrorize the countryside. A Professor (EI) and his assistant, Miss Garter Oil (CC), attempt to handle the problem; they investigate the wolf's clothing worn by the killer sheep. They are interrupted by cricketers looking for the third test match, and are attacked by some animated sheep, who later rob the Westminster Bank, riding off in cars and on horseback, accompanied by "Foggy Mountain Breakdown"* as they head into the hills.

A Newsreader (MP) gives the news for parrots, and Part 3 of *A Tale of Two Cities*, adapted by Joey Boy, is featured (starring GC). This is followed by the news for gibbons, with "Today in Parliament" (read by EI) after that. Seven hours later, news for wombats leads into the animated Attila the Bun.

Arthur Figgis (JC), village idiot, explains why the idiot is necessary to rural society (in between spasms and drooling). He is shown working out on training equipment designed to keep him silly, and works on his personal appearance. Bank president Marlon Brando (GC) tells how idioting is profitable, and graduation from the University of East Anglia Idioting School is shown. The Urban Idiots Headquarters is shown at St. John's Wood, at Lord's Cricket Ground.

Three Cricket Announcers (JC, GC, and EI) on the second day of the first test against Iceland, all drinking heavily, see a green Chesterfield sofa batting, while a spin dryer bowls against it; various pieces of furniture play the outfield. Following that is the Epsom furniture race.

A Bishop (MP) and some priests are seen in the audience of "Spot the Brain Cell," hosted by a Michael Miles grinning-type monster (JC). Mrs. Scum (TJ) is the contestant who tries for a blow on the head.

License fees† for January 1969 are shown, as the credits roll.

ALSO APPEARING: Carol Cleveland
　　　　　　　　　Ian Davidson

 ## SPOT THE BRAIN CELL

" 'Spot the Brain Cell' was a sketch that I originally did with Marty Feldman for *At Last, the 1948 Show*, which I'm sure has been wiped out, lost to posterity. It was based on a man called Michael Miles, who had a terrible quiz show in which he treated the contestants—who were almost all brain-damaged old ladies—with a contempt that had to be *seen* to be *believed!*" says John Cleese, laughing. "It was appropriate, but it was still over the top!

"I brought this sketch up again, played it for Terry Jones, and rewrote it completely. It got much, much madder, but I was almost enormously fond of it. It always struck me as being genuinely funny."

When Cleese and Jones were involved in one of the Secret Policeman's Amnesty International Shows, the sketch was rewritten again to add another dimension, and to allow for celebrity guests.

"I incorporated into it an idea that was sent to me by this famous, very straight Scottish singer, Kenneth McKellar. He suggested we have a television show in which a well-known television celebrity turned up and beat up a blindfolded guest, who, while being beaten up, had to identify the celebrity," Cleese says.

"I always thought it was a great idea, and very funny, and I asked Kenneth if he'd come on the show and be the celebrity. I think he felt a little uncomfortable about it. We used it anyway, and incorporated that into the end of this sketch from the . . . *1948 Show*. It's a very funny piece."

*Flatt and Scruggs's *Bonnie and Clyde* theme.
†The annual British tax on TV sets.

Show 8—Archeology Today

BBC 1 previews its new fall shows, including *Rain Stopped Play*, the Classics Series presents *Snooker My Way, Owzat*, and of course there's sport; the Voice-over Man (EI) adds "And now for something completely different: sport."

Titles

At the end of the animated title sequence, the foot crumbles. A town springs up and falls, and as luxury flats are constructed, the toe is found and an elephant is reconstructed; this serves as an opening for

"Archeology Today," in which the Interviewer (MP) quizzes his guests, the 5 foot 10 inch Professor Lucien Kastner of Oslo (TJ) and the 6 foot 5 inch Sir Robert Eversley (JC), about their respective heights; he is very impressed by tall persons. Kastner leaves angrily, and Eversley strikes the Interviewer, who swears revenge.

"Flaming Star," with western-style titles, is the story of one man's search for vengeance in the raw and violent world of international archeology. At a dig in Egypt, 1920, Eversley discovers Hittite baking dishes from the Fifth Dynasty, and sings his happiness with Danielle (CC), his assistant. He is tracked down by the Interviewer (MP) and challenges him. Kastner leaps onto his shoulders, and Danielle leaps onto Eversley's shoulders; when several people are stacked up, they battle fiercely, to end "Archeology Today."

Rev. Arthur Belling (GC) delivers an appeal for sanity, wearing a hatchet in his head; he demonstrates what can be done about it.

An appeal on behalf of the National Truss is delivered by a Woman (EI) who can't remember her correct name; when she is eventually knocked down by a Prizefighter (TG), there is stock film of Women's Institute applause.

Eggs Diamond and his gang, courtesy of Terry Gilliam. **Photo copyright Python Productions Ltd.**

A Man (EI) visits a Marriage Registrar (TJ) to trade in his wife for a different woman, until an Official (JC) blows a whistle to stop and resume the action. Dr. Watson (GC) begins a sketch with another Doctor (MP), but that one is also abandoned when the Official blows his whistle.

An animated soccer match begins the day for Eggs Diamond, leader of the notorious chicken gang, and an appearance by Spiny Norman. An animated book ad for Raising Gangsters for Fun and Profit leads into a party.

John Stokes (MP) is introduced to Snivelling Little Rat-Faced Git (TJ) and his wife, Mrs. Dreary Fat Boring Old Git (JC). Nora Stokes (CC) is aghast, and Mrs. Git vomits in her purse.

A nice version of the same sketch follows, and a nun who liked the dirty version is knocked out by the Prizefighter, to the stock film of Women's Institute applause.

Roy and Hank Spim (EI and GC) are Australians who go hunting mosquito with bazookas, machine guns, and tanks. They later hunt moth with air-to-air missiles, and go fishing with dynamite.

Two Judges (EI and MP) coming from court discuss their day as they undress, and reveal themselves to be transvestites.

Mrs. Thing (GC) and Mrs. Entity (EI) complain about their day, and discuss the wives of government officials and Beethoven; a flashback follows.

Beethoven (JC) is bothered by a mynah bird taunting him about his upcoming deafness, and his Wife (GC) annoys him as she looks for a sugar bowl and jam spoon, and runs the sweeper while he tries to compose his Fifth Symphony. Shakespeare (EI) and Michelangelo (TJ) discuss their similar problems; Mozart (MP) wants his son to be a ratcatcher. Colin "Chopper" Mozart (MP) is seen calling on the Beethovens, where rats are everywhere; he machine-guns all the rodents.

The two camp Judges are heard again, as the credits roll.

ALSO APPEARING: Carol Cleveland

The Judges say they like the butch voices of BBC announcers who talk after programs are over.

☞ THE MUSIC MAN

John Cleese has always taken a certain glee in referring to himself as "the most unmusical man in Europe," and his Python musical appearances have been almost nonexistent (except for his performance of "Eric the Half a Bee" on *Monty Python's Previous Record*). In fact, when Cleese's archeologist character is required to sing in this show, a bit of trickery was used.

"Terry Jones actually dubbed me in 'Archeology Today.' I can't remember singing on any other occasions," Cleese says. "I'm appalling. I can't sing at all! I can *just* sing badly. On . . . *the 1948 Show*, I sang 'The Rhubarb Tart Song,' and someday, in an Amnesty show, I want very much to sing 'I've Got a Ferret Sticking Up My Nose.'"

Show 9 — How to Recognize Different Parts of the Body

RECORDED AS SERIES 2, SHOW 9 — PROD. #62027

Several bikini-clad women pose sexily, as does the man (JC) at the desk, posing in a bikini on top of his desk as he says "And now for something completely different," and the "It's" Man, also in bikini, says "It's"

Titles

"How to Recognize Different Parts of the Body" begins with 1. The Foot, which is the animated foot from the titles. It is followed by 2. The Shoulder, 3. The Other Foot, 4. The Bridge of the Nose, 5. Naughty Bits, 6. Just Above the Elbow, 7. Two Inches to the Right of a Very Naughty Bit, Indeed.

Eight. The Kneecap leads into the Australian University of Woolamaloo, in which all of the. faculty wear khaki shorts, bush shirts, and Aussie hats. They drink heavily and are all named Bruce. They are introduced to a new instructor, Michael Baldwin (TJ), a chap from Pommie Land new to the Philosophy Department. They explain their rules, emphasizing "No pooftahs," and tell him they don't like stuck-up sticky beaks there.

Nine. The Ear, 10. The Big Toe, 11. More Naughty Bits, 12. The Naughty Bits of

Before there was Crocodile Dundee, there were the Bruces. In the stage show, Idle, Innes, and Palin (with animated cutouts in the background) slug down Fosters and pelt the audience with their beer cans, before leading the crowd in "The Bruces' Philosophers' Song." **Photo copyright KHJ**

a Lady, 13. Naughty Bits of a Horse, 14. Naughty Bits of an Ant, 15. Naughty Bits of Reginald Maudling.

Sixteen. The Hand, which is pulled off to start the next sketch. An Interviewer (MP) talks to Norman St. John Polevaulter (TJ), who contradicts people. The Man in the Dinner Jacket (JC) is at his desk holding a pig, as more parts of the body are featured: 17. The Top of the Head (the Pope is shown), 18. The Feather (rare).

Nineteen. The Nose starts with Raymond Luxury-Yacht (GC), who still wants his name pronounced "throat-wobbler mangrove." He enters an office in which the nameplate extends throughout the room. He wants Professor Sir Sir Adrian Furrows (JC), a specialist, to perform surgery on his huge nose, even after Furrows pulls it off and tells him it is polystyrene. Furrows agrees to do it if he will come on a camping holiday with him.

The men of the Second Battalion of the Derbyshire Light Infantry put on a precision display of bad temper, followed by close order swanning about when their Leader (MP) orders "Squad! Camp it . . . up!"

Animated military leaders perform the Dance of the Sugar Plum Fairies, and an animated eyeball leads into the Menace of the Killer Cars, which are disposed of by the gigantic Killer Cats. The huge felines prove to be an even greater threat, however, as they gobble down skyscrapers.

Mr. and Mrs. Irrelevant (GC and CC) visit the office of the Verri-fast Plaine Company, Ltd., which seems to use a rubber band-operated plane and a Kamikaze pilot.

At the beach, a Man (JC) introduces Mrs. Rita Fairbanks (EI) of the Batley Townswomen's Guild, and she introduces their reenactment of the first heart transplant. Also shown are the underwater versions of *Measure for Measure, Hello, Dolly!* and animated Formula 2 car racing.

More parts of the body are shown, up to 22. The Nipple, shown as a radio dial. Two Pepperpots (JC and GC) listen to the Death of Mary, Queen of Scots, until the radio explodes. They notice a penguin on top of the television set, and then a television announcer tells them the penguin is going to explode—which it does.

Twenty-six is Margaret Thatcher's Brain (an arrow points to her knee), and 29. is the Interior of a Country House. Two men (JC and GC) and a woman are questioned by an amateur investigator, Inspector Muffin, the Mule (MP), who is not sure whether a burglary or murder was committed. Sergeant Duckie (TJ) arrives with more policemen, and he sings his entry in the Eurovision Song

Contest.* It is announced as the final entry of the contest (by EI in drag), and Chief Inspector Zatapatique (GC) sings the winning entry, "Bing Tiddle Tiddle Bong," as the credits roll.

ALSO APPEARING: Carol Cleveland
The Fred Tomlinson Singers
Vincent Wong
Roy Gunson
Alexander Curry
Ralph Wood
John Clement

☞ The animated titles were to have included the "little chicken man who drags across a banner reading 'How to Recognize Different Parts of the Body.'"

☞ The film of the first heart transplant is actually the same film used for the battle of Pearl Harbor in the first series.

☞ **TAKE 14**

The film portions of the TV shows were usually shot far in advance of broadcast, but the group had a rather limited amount of time for shooting the live action in the BBC studio. Though they managed to make it through, there were few opportunities for retakes—which was often a problem.

"Most of the retakes were little bits, just going back to pick up something because the camera hadn't been on the right person, or somebody had forgotten something minor; but, they usually went through fairly smoothly," explains Graham Chapman.

"Some retakes were for other reasons. The worst occasion was a complete lack of responsibility on the part of John and myself, when we were playing the Pepperpots discussing the penguins on top of the television set. That took us about fourteen takes because of our very naughty laughing at each other. Eventually, we did come to our senses, and got through it all right. But it

*A real, annual, pan-European popular-song contest.

took us a *long* time, because it got so irresponsible. We took no notice of the screaming producer, and that made it worse!"

☞ **SAY G'DAY, BRUCE!**

The Pythons' tribute to the Land Down Under was based on their own personal observations, and the Australian image in Britain at the time, long before Crocodile Dundee. Still, the group's portrait of Aussies is the one most fondly remembered by Python fans.

"It's really a traditional English view of Australians, and one of the few sketches John Cleese and I wrote together," says Eric Idle. "Barry Humphries was always claiming that we nicked it off him. I don't think we actually did. He used to have a comic strip with a hero called Bruce, but I knew some Australians in the early '60s—they were always called Bruce, and they were always in films. In fact, I based it on a now-famous film director called Bruce, who's done a lot of American films—he always seemed to be around. We just based it on my Australian friends who always seemed to be called Bruce . . . "

☞ **THE KILLER ANIMATION**

The Invasion of the Killer Cars, followed by the Killer Cats, is the stuff of grade-B monster movies, which is exactly what Terry Gilliam intended for the animated sequence.

"It's 1950s science fiction, like *The Worm That Ate New York*, a lot of silly things like *Them*," Gilliam explains. "There's a lot of *2001* influence in the cartoons. It's just taking something monumental and quite serious, and making jokes about it. It's easy to make jokes out of something that serious and on that scale. It's easy pickings—but it's also some wonderful stuff."

Show 10—Scott of the Antarctic

A clip is shown from "La Fromage Grand," which takes place on a rubbish dump. Brianette Jatabatique (CC) sits alone, holding a cabbage, and Brian Distel (TJ) comes up and talks with her (their French is translated with English subtitles). Phil (EI), a snobbish, sniffing film critic, explains the subtext of the previous scene. Another clip is shown, with the two of them again on the rubbish dump, intercut with stock shots of war and violence. She is holding a Webb's Wonder lettuce this time, which explodes to end the film, and the critic analyzes the film before a special report on the filming of "Scott of the Antarctic."

Chris Conger (GC) reports from the film set, where Paignton Pier has been transformed into the South Pole. He interviews producer Gerry Schlick (EI), who explains that they are using twenty-eight thousand cubic feet of Wintrex, a new white foam rubber, as a substitute for real snow, along with sixteen thousand cubic U.S. furlongs of white paint with a special snow finish.

Director James McRettin (JC), drinking heavily, has trouble remembering which scene is being shot first; Kirk Vilb (MP) is starring as Lieu-tenant Scott, Terence Lemming (TJ) plays Ensign Oates, and Bowers is Scott's other assistant. Vanilla Hoare (CC) plays Miss Evans, but has trouble remembering her lines; she plays a scene in a trench while Vilb acts on boxes. She quits when they ask her to act out of the trench, and the director passes out drunk.

Gilliam found the scenes with the giant among the easiest to shoot in his own **Time Bandits,** *using a normal-sized actor and filming from very low camera angles.* **Photo copyright Handmade Films/Time Bandits**

Vilb wants to fight a lion, even though there are no lions in the Antarctic, so the film becomes "Scott of the Sahara," and he is pulled across the sand on a dogsled.

Coming attractions show Vilb fighting a "lion," a fight between Oates and a twenty-foot-high electric penguin with tentacles, and Vanilla's clothes are torn off as she runs from a giant set of teeth pursuing her across the sand. She passes the Man with the Din-ner Jacket (JC) at his desk, who says "And now for something completely different," and the "It's" Man says "It's"

Titles

Animation shows the foot stepping on several figures, leading up to Conrad Poohs and his Dancing Teeth. Conrad later opens a letter which travels backward to its sender (TJ).

As he leaves the post office, Eric Praline (JC) walks in to buy a fish license for his pet fish Eric from Mr. Last (MP). When he is turned down, he demands a statement from the Lord Mayor that he needs no such license, and the impossibly tall Mayor enters for the traditional signing of the exemption from the fish license.

The Mayor and his retinue then run onto a soccer field to play against a pro team. A Linkman (MP) interviews Cliff (GC) on sports, and the talk turns to China. This is followed by a match between the Bournemouth Gynecologists and the Watford Long John Silver Impersonators. The Linkman is struck by a sixteen-ton weight, and scenes of destruction are seen as the credits roll.

ALSO APPEARING: Carol Cleveland
Mrs. Idle

☞ Several changes were made in "Scott of the Antarctic"; a lunchtime interview with Gerry Schlick, in which he discusses making Evans a girl, was cut, and Lemming discusses Oates. Evans was originally to be pursued by a roll-top writing desk, rather than the set of teeth. Also cut was a scene where Bowers fights a dreaded Congolese ringing tarantula in the desert. From twenty feet away, it rings like a telephone and leaps up to his face. Bowers shoots it and it stops ringing.

☞ The twenty-foot penguin with tentacles was actually a model, about one foot high, that would light up and look electric. It was kept close to the camera in the foreground to appear huge; it was intercut with a lot of phony reverses.

☞ The football match originally involved the Bournemouth Automobile Association (with breeches, boots, and yellow crash helmets), rather than the Gynecologists.

☞ TAKE TWO

Shooting "Scott of the Sahara" had its share of good times, according to costumer Hazel Pethig, who had to help stage the fight with the lion. "We had footage of a real lion, we had somebody dressed up as a lion, and we had a stuffed lion. Getting a lion's costume wasn't too easy—I remember being totally dismayed! Very often, the costumes that they wore had to be ruined, by

going into the sea, or whatever, so I had to talk them into letting me use stuff, or find a way around it.

" 'Scott of the Sahara' was wonderful to do. I remember Carol losing her coat and her bra on a cactus; I rushed in to cover her up and ruined the shot! Everybody shrieked with laughter, and found it very funny—partly because they had to redo it. So, they got to see Carol losing her clothes all over again!"

☞ TO BEE OR NOT TO BEE

The "Fish License" sketch also has a song that was not performed in the TV show, involving the philosophical implications of half a bee. It is heard on *Monty Python's Previous Record*, and is the only solo John Cleese musical performance in all of Python. Cleese says he is actually quite proud of the song.

"I started to sing 'Eric the Half a Bee' in the stage show, when we did our British tour, because I was bored stiff with the stupid 'Silly Walk' sketch. They made me do that, and I lost 'Eric the Half a Bee,' which I love doing!" Cleese enthuses.

"It's a funny little sad song with Eric, about this bee that had been bisected. It was a little philosophical song about whether half a bee can be, or philosophically can not be.

"Eric and I had a couple of characters we liked—mine was called Praline. He was the guy who went into the Whizzo Chocolate Company. We got fascinated by Praline when we did the parrot sketch—it was the same character. Eric had a strange man called Badger. We had an interminable sketch we did. I can never remember if it got in one of the shows or not. We thought it was funny, but we didn't think the audience was very interested." He laughs.

☞ INSIDE SPORTS

Filming sketches on location always drew interesting reactions—or lack of reactions—sparked by costumes or props.

"The great one was when we were doing the Long John Silver Impersonators football match against the Gynecologists," Michael Palin recalls.

"In those days, of course, the BBC had no buses, let alone limousines, to take us to the filming—we just got there any way we could. John and Graham never had a car, so I was always giving lifts to Graham, and sometimes to John.

"I had a Mini, which is about the smallest car made, and John and Graham are two of the largest people made. So, there were four of us squashed in there, complete with Long John Silver outfits, because we'd been to Television Centre and gotten dressed for the filming.

"As we passed a bank, I thought I should go in and cash a check—when I'm filming, I never have any time for mundane things like that. So I went to the bank, and they came along as well.

"So, these four Long John Silvers came up to the girl at the counter, and she looked up. I said 'Can I cash a check?' She said 'Yes, if you've got a credit card.' Not a single mention of the fact that we all had parrots on our shoulders and one leg!"

 FX

His solo films have given Terry Gilliam more than a nodding acquaintance with special effects; work on *Baron Munchausen*, *Brazil*, and *Time Bandits* have all involved some rather heavy FX sequences.

Although the Python TV shows seldom required much in the way of FX, occasional elements like a twenty-foot electric penguin with tentacles gave Gilliam a taste of what he would eventually be contending with, keeping an eye on the budget while being creative.

"It's all in the *way* the effects are done," Gilliam explains. "Whatever we're doing, I always try to decide whether we can afford it. If we can't, I try to think of a way to avoid the problem. When we write the effects, we have to be naive enough to think it's all quite easy.

"It's odd, but the effects that are usually the most difficult to do tend to look the most ordinary, while the ones that look the most spectacular are often the easiest. Depending on what the special effect is, sometimes we can achieve it with just the right sound effect, as opposed to an elaborate visual.

"The easiest thing in *Time Bandits* was the giant, because there was nothing special about it," Gilliam says, explaining that they just placed a camera on the ground and aimed it upwards at the normal-sized actor. "We just had to choose the right angle and lens, and shoot it at the right speed. Other shots, like Kevin jumping into the time holes, were extremely complicated shots that look quite ordinary."

Show 11—How Not to Be Seen

RECORDED AS SERIES 2, SHOW 6—PROD. #60528

An Advertising Director (JC) is reading *Chinese for Advertising Men* as Mr. S. Frog (EI) enters his office through a window. The Director is disturbed about his new campaign for Conquistador Coffee; he has used the word "leprosy" instead of "coffee" as part of a joke/sales campaign. He has come up with "Conquistador Coffee brings a new meaning to the word 'vomit,'" and the introduc-tory offer of a free dead dog with every jar. Although sales have plummeted, people remember the name.

A seaside scene is shown while lush music plays, but a phonograph record playing the music sticks. The Man in the Dinner Jacket (JC) also becomes stuck on "And now for something completely—pletely—pletely different"; the "It's"

Man (MP) says "It's" as the Titles roll, though they become struck as well.

Nineteen twenty-nine. British Prime Minister Ramsey MacDonald (MP) enters his office, exclaiming, "My, it's hot in here," and takes off his clothes, under which he wears a bra and panties.

Exchange and Mart editor Mr. Glans (JC) is visited by Mr. Bee (TJ), who is applying for a job as assistant editor. Glans tries to bargain for his briefcase, umbrella, and chair in exchange for the job, though Bee initially resists, to Glans's bewilderment ("Not for sale? What does that mean?"). He finally trades everything, and bargains with his animated secretary, Miss Johnson, for two coffees and a biscuit.

Unfortunately, the animated secretary falls victim to the International Chinese Communist Conspiracy. The red hordes fill her office, but she is saved by Uncle Sam, who does a commercial for American defense. Animated commercials follow for Crelm Toothpaste, using two cars, and another ad for Shrill petrol.

John and Jasmina (JC and CC) enter a room to discover her father, Sir Horace Partridge, dead. They discuss repercussions of the local train schedules on the crime, and Lady Partridge (GC) arrives, equally concerned about the murder and the trains. Police Inspector Davis (TJ) and young Tony (MP) both enter, discussing train schedules. Tony is tripped up by his confusion over the details of the schedules, and is forced to confess to the murder for the old man's seat reservations. It is all revealed as an exerpt from a West End play, "It All Happened on the 11:20 from Hainault" by railroad playwright Neville Shunt (TJ); his play expresses the human condition in terms of British Rail. His works are analyzed by Gavin Millarrrrrrrr (JC): "The point is frozen, the beast is dead . . ."

An Interviewer (MP) then discusses the works of and introduces a chat with writer/dentist Martin Curry (GC), conducted by Matthew Padget (TJ). He tries not to mention Curry's enormous incisors, for all of Curry's actors have foot-long front teeth, as shown in clips from his productions of *The Twelve Caesars* and *Trafalgar*. Curry tries futilely to drink a glass of water.

Arthur Crackpot (EI) is President and God of Crackpot Religions, Ltd., the first religion with free gifts, such as tea trolleys, a three-piece lounge suite, and a luxury caravan; a Nude Organist (TG) plays a fanfare.

A Priest (JC) oversees Mrs. Collins (MP) choose the correct hymn number, and she wins the entire Norwich City Council. Modern methods of conversion are shown. Archbishop Gumby (MP) bashes bricks together, while Archbishop Shabby raises polecats. Also shown are Archbishop Nudge (EI), Naughty Religions, Ltd. (JC), the Popular Religions, Ltd. (GC), the No Questions Asked Religion (MP), the Lunatic Religion (TJ), and Cartoon Religions, Ltd. Religious animation follows.

Next is H.M. Government Public Service Film 42, Para 6: "How Not to Be Seen." Although the participants are usually hidden, most of them are found through a liberal use of explosives. Back in a studio, a Presenter (MP) talks with Ludovic Grayson (TJ), who is inside a filing cabinet so that he cannot be seen. He is eventually blown up as well.

Jackie Charleton and the Tonettes sing "Yummy, Yummy, Yummy, I've Got Love in My Tummy" from inside crates and boxes, though the lights and camerawork continue normally, as in *Top of the Pops*,* and the credits roll.

Following the credits, a BBC 1 slide is shown, and an announcer says that for those persons who have just missed Monty Python, here it is again—and the entire show is recapped with scores of clips shown in about thirty seconds.

ALSO APPEARING: Carol Cleveland

☞ The show was originally to start with a strip by Stanley Baldwin (instead of Ramsay MacDonald) immediately following the titles.
☞ The rehearsal script lists the song to be performed by Jackie Charleton and the Tonettes as "Don't Treat Me Like a Child."
☞ The quick reprise of the entire show was in the script of Show 6.
☞ Cut from the show was the Arthur Crackpot Handbook, with such entries as "Blessed are the wealthy, for they have the earth," "It is as easy for a rich man to enter heaven as anybody—if not easier," and "Sell all you have and give it to the rich."

*A British version of *American Bandstand*.

111

MORE FROST REVENGE

Although none of them claim responsibility for it, the Pythons admit to an interesting stunt that apparently actually happened. Due to a still-unexplained mixup, David Frost's home telephone number was used in a sketch, and Frost was soon troubled by numerous phone calls from Python viewers.

"We did it because, when we started, Frost had John under contract to do a TV show, as he had Ronnie Corbett and Ronnie Barker, because they were all on *The Frost Report*," says Eric Idle. "Because he had John under contract, there had to be some sort of agreement to allow him to do Python. I don't know what they agreed, but obviously a contract like that isn't worth very much if somebody doesn't want to appear—it can't be enforced. I think Frost just took a wider view, that John was in his own area now."

Michael Palin claims he doesn't actually remember the circumstances behind the Frost phone number, but doesn't deny that it happened. "I think it was outside a church, when we did Crackpot Religions. 'If you're tired of life, come in here, if you're not, ring ***-****.' It was a Frost joke, he used to use that a lot on his show: 'I was passing a church the other day, had a wonderful sign, "If you're tired of sin, come in here." Somebody had written underneath "If you're not, ring Blackman 4271." ' There it is. Somebody put his number there when we did it, but I didn't know it was his. I'm certain. I promise I didn't."

Strangely enough, there was an effort to include Frost as a seventh Python—an effort instigated by Frost that went no further. "Frost seriously, tried to get himself into Python. We'd started writing, and he rang up and said 'Can I be in it?' We said 'No, piss off!' " Idle laughs. " 'No, seriously, I could just do jokes, I could link it, it'd be wonderful!' 'No, no, piss off David, you're not in this.' "

Show 12—Spam

RECORDED AS SERIES 2, SHOW 1—PROD. #60129

Opening titles and credits are shown for *The Black Eagle*, a swashbuckling pirate adventure that begins with "In 1742, the Spanish Empire lay in ruins . . ." As pirates pull their lifeboat onto the beach, they drag it past the Man in the Dinner Jacket (JC) at his desk as he says "And now for something completely different." The "It's" Man adds "It's"

Titles

Beginning with the caption "In 1970, the British Empire lay in ruins," a Hungarian Gentleman (JC) visits a Tobacconist (TJ), and attempts to use a phrasebook in which phrases asking for cigarettes and matches come out as "I will not buy this record, it is scratched," and "My hover-craft is full of eels," as well as several naughtier phrases. The Tobacconist tries out a phrase on the Hungarian, and is punched out. When a Policeman (GC) runs through town to the shop, the Hungarian tells him "You have beautiful thighs," "Drop your panties, Sir William, I cannot wait until lunchtime," and "My nipples explode with delight."

Alexander Yahlt (MP), publisher of the English-Hungarian phrasebook, is put on trial. The Prosecutor (EI) explains that the phrase "Can you direct me to the station?" is translated as "Please fondle my bum." Yahlt pleads incompetence, and a Police Constable (GC) asks for an adjournment, followed by stock film of Women's Institute applause. Testimony is heard from a Page Three girl* cutout, Abigail Tesler, along with newspaper photo blowups of Judge Maltravers (TJ) and Q.C.† Nelson Bedowes (JC).

Animation follows in which a protest against the Judge turns into a student demonstration, and a large police helmet turns into a planet for a *2001* parody. The planet turns into a soccer ball for the next sketch.

"World Forum" sees the unctuous Presenter (EI) greet guests

The Pythons themselves played all the parts in "World Forum/Communist Quiz" when it was presented live onstage. From the left: Gilliam as Mao Tse-tung, Palin as Che Guevara, Idle as the presenter, Cleese as Lenin, and Jones as Karl Marx, the lucky contestant. In the background of this dress rehearsal, a portion of the lyrics to the "Bruces Philosophers' Song" can be seen. Photo copyright KHJ

Karl Marx (TJ), Che Guevara, Lenin, and Mao Tse-tung; they are all questioned on English football. Karl Marx plays in the final round for a lounge suite.

Ypres, 1914. "In 1914, the Balance of Power lay in ruins . . ." leads to a World War I trench, where Jenkins (EI) talks to Sergeant Jackson (MP) about his family, but the floor manager (TJ) has to clear the set of unnecessary actors, which include a Viking, male mermaid, Greek Orthodox priest, a sheikh, milkman, and a nun. The next caption reads "Knickers 1914," and the director also removes an astronaut from the set before restarting the sketch.

In a museum, a sign identifies "Italian Masters of the Renaissance." As two Art Critics (EI and MP) wander through the gallery, the Bumpkin (TJ) from Constable's *Hay Wain* talks to the figures in a six foot by ten foot Titian canvas, including a Cherub (TG) and Solomon (GC), who reports a walkout by the Impressionists. The animated characters from various works go out on strike and picket, while an Auctioneer from Sotheby's (JC) auctions off the works without their famous figures, including Vermeer's *Lady Who Used to Be*

at a Window and *Nothing at Bay* by Landseer.

The "Ypres" sketch resumes as a Major (GC) interrupts Jenkins, the Sarge, Kipper (TG), and the armless Padre (JC). He says there are only provisions for four, and they must choose the one who is to die. After drawing straws, doing "dip, dip, dip, my little ship," and scissors-paper-stone and choosing the Major each time, the Padre is forced to volunteer. He gives a long, patriotic speech before he is rushed to the Royal Hospital for Overacting. A Doctor (GC) tours the hospital, where there are several King Rats in Casualty Pantomime, and the crowded Richard the Third Ward, along with several animated Hamlets.

Animated bombs and flowers lead into "Flower Arrangement" with D.P. Gumby (MP), who suggests arranging begonias, tulips, irises, and freesias.

As a Man and his Wife (EI and GC) are lowered by wires into a cafe, the Waitress (TJ) reads a menu that consists almost entirely of Spam dishes. Groups of Vikings scattered around the cafe sing about Spam and the Hungarian enters, but is quickly thrown out.

In a studio, a Historian (MP) discusses Vikings, and back in the cafe they are singing about Spam. The closing caption reads "In 1970, *Monty Python's Flying Circus* lay in ruins, and then the words on the screen said: The End."

---

*A photo of a scantily clad or topless girl that appears on page three of London's tabloid newspapers.
†Queen's counsel.

The closing credits all involve Spam and/or other breakfast foods, and a quick shot is seen of Marx and Lenin in bed together.
ALSO APPEARING: The Fred Tomlinson Singers

☛ The title page of the script credits the show to "Alfie Bass, Lew Hoard, and Deidre Sinclair."

☛ The rehearsal script shows very different material intended for the show. "Gumby Flower Arranging" was to lead into "Herbert Mental/ Birdwatchers Eggs" and "Pigeon Fancier Racing" (from Show 13), then "Page Three Newspaper Photo Blowups" (Show 11), then into a much longer Sergeant Duckie and "Bing Tiddle Tiddle Bong" (show 9). "Spam" was not originally intended for this show.

☛ NOTES: INSTRUCTIONS FOR TERRY GILLIAM'S ANIMATIONS

Terry was given a rather free hand, with the script often just noting which bits were to be linked. Below is an example of the script directions given to him to link the "Overacting" sketch to "Gumby Flower Arranging":

He opens door; from here Gilliam's fevered, not to say feverish, imagination leads us into the whacky world of award-winning graphic humor, where comedy is king in a no-holds-barred joke jamboree that'll have you throwing yourself into the Thames.

"But even this jolly jokesmith from Oriental (sic) College must control himself and provide us with a link into "Flower Arrangement."

Delicate music. Studio set. Flowers in vases, etc. Super caption "Flower Arrangement" then another caption "Introduced by D.P. Gumby".

☛ THE BLACK EAGLE

Starting the show with a fictitious historical film, *The Black Eagle*, the Pythons apparently managed to fool audiences who had tuned in expecting to see *Monty Python's Flying Circus*—which was, of course, the idea. As the series continued, the opening titles were often shown later and later (and in at least one show, they weren't included at all).

"Anything to confuse and mislead, really, with the eventual notion that it made things more interesting, and that we weren't starting in the same old way," Chapman recalls. "To actually do almost an entire program where nothing had been announced—that would have been an aim, I suppose.

"Certainly, we took it quite a long way with the smuggling sequence. I even had one or two writing friends changing channels, just to see whether they were on the right channel—that was nice! Of course, it was obvious when they saw John at the desk."

Show 13 — Royal Episode 13

RECORDED AS SERIES 2, SHOW 13—PROD. #67550

The Man in the Dinner Jacket (JC) stands, announcing that he won't be saying "And now for something completely different" this week because the Queen would be tuning in sometime during the show. However, he emphasizes that everything else will remain the same.

A new set of regal Titles are used, and "God Save the Queen" is substituted for the usual theme.

Royal Episode Thirteen. First Spoof: A coal

mine in Llandarog Carmarthen sees Welsh coal miners argue violently and brawl over such historical trivia as the date of the Treaty of Utrecht (ratified in 1713), Greek architecture, and the Treaty of Westphalia. The arrival of a Frightfully Important Person (JC) is of no help, while a Newsreader (MP) reports on other miners' disputes across the nation, as well as the Disgusting Objects International at Wembley.

The "Toad Elevating Moment" features the Host (TJ) interviewing Mr. Pudifoot (GC), who says things in a very roundabout way. After he leaves indignantly, the next three guests include Mr. . . . Ohn . . . Ith (EI), who speaks only the endings of words, Mr. J . . . Sm . . . (JC), who speaks only the beginnings of words, and . . . Oh . . . . . . I . . . (MP), who speaks only the middles of words. Together, the three of them say "Good evening."

Commercials feature two animated dragons demonstrating the maiden-attracting power of Crelm toothpaste; Fibro-Val detergent is used on furniture in a washing machine (by EI); and a young couple romp through a beautiful, animated, Disney-like forest while wearing surgical garments, and it becomes a truss commercial.

"Fish Club" begins, with its Host (MP) demonstrating how to feed a goldfish, based on the recommendations of the Board of Irresponsible People. As sausages, soup, and such are dropped into the fishbowl, he is dragged offstage, and a

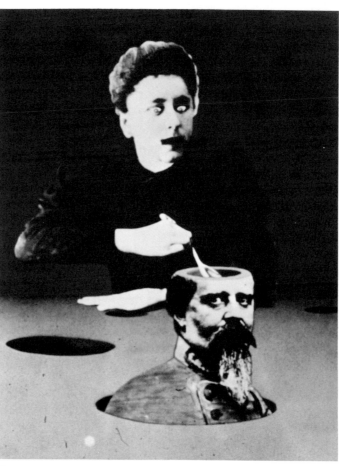

Everyone wanted to get into the act when the Pythons set their sights on cannibalism; Terry Gilliam was quite happy to tackle the subject with accompanying animation. Copyright Python Productions Ltd.

disclaimer is read.

As sounds of young lovers are heard in the woods, a Birdwatcher (MP) has his eggs stolen by Herbert Mental (TJ), who collects birdwatchers' eggs. Interviewing himself in front of his collection, he explains that he also collects butterfly hunters, and likes to race pigeon fanciers. He is shown racing the latter through a field, while a whole flock of pigeon fanciers (all in trenchcoats and caps) wander through Trafalgar Square.

A series of brief animations follow, including Spiny Norman, plus elaborate titles for the "Insurance" sketch. Martin (EI), a man interested in buying life insurance, has collected twelve gallons of urine to conform with their requirements, but Feldman (JC), the insurance agent, is less than impressed.

Suddenly the Queen tunes in and the actors and audience stand, but before they can deliver the first royal joke, she quickly switches over to the *News at Ten*, where the actual newsreader, Reg Bosanquet,* stands.

At St. Pooves Hospital, the heavily bandaged, crippled patients are called into formation by a Drill Instructor/Doctor (JC) and given a rigorous workout. Another Doctor (EI) explains their system of A.R.T., or Active Recuperation Techniques, in which the patients are there to serve the doctors—although the seriously ill do sport. Brief looks at other

*A newscaster on the *News at Ten*.

115

hospitals where doctors' conditions are improving follow, including St. Nathan's Hospital for Young Attractive Girls Who Aren't Particularly Ill, and a Hospital for Linkmen that introduces a very brief mountaineering sketch.

Next is the "Exploding Version of the Blue Danube."

In the darkness of a dormitory at a girls' public school, a man searches for Agnes, though the dorm is entirely occupied by men. A still follows promoting "The Naughtiest Girl in the School," starring the men of the 14th Marine Command.

Via stock World War II footage, the girls of Oakdean High School reenact the Battle of Normandy. Then, inside a modern-day submarine, a group of Pepperpots, including Capt. Mrs. Spimm (GC) and Mrs. Lt. Edale (JC), give orders to put the kettle on, feed the cat, and fire Mrs. Midshipman Nesbit. An animated Nesbit is fired through the torpedo tube. A link shows a Man (TG) with a stoat through his head, stock footage of Women's Institute applause, and a Newsreader (MP).

The "Lifeboat" sketch features five men (GC, JC, EI, TJ, and MP) adrift, reverting to cannibalism, and giving their dinner orders to a passing Waitress (CC). Animated cannibals follow, along with a letter of complaint from Captain B.J. Smethwick in a white wine sauce, with shallots, mushrooms, and garlic, before the action shifts to a mortuary.

A Man (JC) whose mother has just died visits an Undertaker (GC), who convinces the Man they should eat her as his Assistant (EI) lights the oven. The disgusted audience boos, hisses, and rushes the stage to attack them. They are saved when the credits roll to "God Save the Queen," and everyone stands at attention.

ALSO APPEARING: Carol Cleveland
Ian Davidson

☞ "International Chess" and "Life-Saving" was to follow the "Exploding Blue Danube," which then turns into a "Critic" sketch before returning to the "Girls Dormitory."

☞ This is the only one of the forty-five programs that was never rerun in its entirety in England, though not entirely because of the rampant cannibalism toward the end of the show. In fact, it was reportedly the royalty theme that influenced the BBC's decision.

The cannibalism material, particularly the "Undertaker" sketch, caused its share of controversy at the BBC, however. In fact, as Graham Chapman recalls, the only way they were permitted to perform the sketch was if they allowed the audience to charge onstage and attack them at the end—which they did.

☞ **EXPLOSIVE HUMOR**

One of the trademarks of Python seems to combine comedy and explosions. The group has blown up all sorts of animals, buildings, and people, but one bit of blasting stands out for Eric Idle.

"The best was the 'Exploding Version of the Blue Danube'—I liked that a lot. They absolutely had to do it live. It was spot on, and brilliant! We did it in one take, which was great, because we couldn't afford another one," Idle says, laughing.

☞ **CENSORED**

An entire book could be devoted to Monty Python's battles with the censors—and indeed, one has, the excellent *Monty Python: the Case Against*, by Robert Hewison.

During the first part of the first series, the group escaped detection by the BBC, for the most part. In fact, the only BBC reaction to the first shows came from Tom Sloane, then head of light entertainment.

"His first comments to me, after seeing the first two shows, were 'Does John Cleese have to say "bastard" twice?'" recalls BBC producer Barry Took. "I said 'Well, yes, if he chooses to. That's the whole nature of this program. He's such an intelligent man, he would not have said it had he not thought it artistically correct.' He said 'Oh, that's fine,' and that was the only true criticism I'd had at the beginning.

"They were much, much enjoyed by the very top people at the BBC, they thought it was a terrific show. Even though it wasn't immediately popular, particularly amongst the lower ranks of the hierarchy, they persisted with it and booked a new series, because they thought it was really enchanting comedy, just the sort of thing they thought the BBC should be doing around that time."

In general, however, by the second season of Python, things were heating up, because the group was taking more chances, and because the BBC was starting to pay attention to them.

"By the second or third season, the BBC had seen much more, and were a little vigilant," says Michael Palin. "But at the start, we could virtually do almost anything. We were on late Saturdays, and also things were fairly easygoing then. Television had not been taken by the scruff of the neck and made to perform like it is at the moment. Hugh Carlton-Greene was the director-general of the BBC, and had a very artistic view of things—creative people were always right. So, it was very good!"

THE PYTHONIC VERSES:

MONTY PYTHON'S GUIDE TO LIFE

ACCOUNTING
"Well, it'd certainly make chartered accountancy a much more interesting job."

> Government spokesman, on a proposal to tax sex (EI)

AMBITION
"He was such a pretty baby, always so kind and gentle . . . really considerate to his mother. Not at all the kind of person you'd expect to pulverize their opponent into a bloody mass of flesh and raw bone, spitting teeth and fragments of gum into a ring which had become one man's hell and Ken's glory."

> Mrs. Nellie Air-Vent (TJ), mother of boxer
> Ken Clean-Air System

ANALYSIS (political)
"This is largely as I predicted, except that the Silly Party won. I think this is mainly due to the number of votes cast."

> Norman, TV Commentator (MP)

APTITUDE
"Our experts describe you as an appallingly dull fellow, unimaginative, timid, lacking in initiative, spineless, easily dominated, no sense of humor, tedious company, and irrepressibly drab and

awful; and whereas in most professions, these would be considerable drawbacks, in chartered accountancy, they're a positive boon!"

Vocational Guidance Counselor (JC)

ATTITUDES (societal)
"What a lot of people don't realize is that a mouse, once accepted, can fulfill a useful role in society. Indeed, there are examples throughout history of famous men known to have been mice."

Linkman (MP), "The World Around Us"

ATTITUDES (sociological)
"The whole problem of these senile delinquents lies in their complete rejection of the values of contemporary society. They've seen their children grow up to become accountants, stockbrokers, and sociologists, and they begin to wonder—is it really AAAGGHH . . ."

Sociologist as he falls through a manhole (EI)

BBC
"I'm mainly in comedy. I'd like to be in program planning, but unfortunately, I've got a degree."

BBC employee (JC)

BELIEF
"I believe in peace and bashing two bricks together."

Archbishop Gumby (MP)

BRAINS (size):
"If we increase the size of the penguin until it is the same height as the man, and then compare the relative brain sizes, we now find that the penguin's brain is still smaller. But—and this is the point—it is larger than it was!"

Prof. Ken Rosewall (GC)

BREATH
"I use a body rub called halitosis. It makes my breath seem sweet."

Mr. Gumby (MP)

BRITISH NAVAL ENCOUNTERS
"They was too clever for the German fleet."

Prof. R. J. Gumby (MP),
on why he thinks the Battle of Trafalgar was fought near Yorkshire

BRITISH NAVY
"There is no cannibalism in the British Navy, absolutely none, and when I say none, I mean there is a certain amount."

Sir John Cunningham (GC)

BULLFIGHTING

"A bull is heavy, violent, abusive, and aggressive, with four legs and great sharp teeth—whereas a bullfighter is only a small greasy Spaniard."

Narrator of "Probe" (EI)

BUSINESS PRACTICES (sound)

"If that idea of yours isn't worth a pound, I'd like to know what is! The only trouble is, you gave me the idea before I'd given you the pound, and that's not good business!"

Merchant Banker (JC)

CAMEL-SPOTTING

"The dromedary has one hump, and a camel has a refreshment car, buffet, and ticket collector."

A Camel/Train-Spotter (EI)

CELEBRITY

"Why is it the world never remembers the name of Johann Gambolputty de von Ausfernschpledenschlittcras-screnbonfriediggerdingledangledonglebursteinvonknackerthrash-erapplebangerhorowitzticolensicgranderknottyspelltinklegrand-lichgrumbelmeyerspellerwasserkurstlichhimbleeisenbahnwagen-gutenabenabendbitteeinnurnburgebratwurstlegerspurtenmitzwei-macheluberhundsfutgumberaberschonendankerkalbsfleisch-mittleraucher Von Hauptkopt of Ulm?"

Arthur Figgis (GC)

CEMENT

"I think cement is more interesting than people think."

Prof. Enid Gumby (JC)

CHOICES

"Your Life or your lupines!"

Dennis Moore (JC)

CITIZENS (senior)

"We have a lot of trouble with these oldies. Pension day's the worst—they go mad! As soon as they get their hands on their money, they blow it all on milk, bread, tea, a tin of meat for the cat . . ."

Policeman (GC)

CLASS STRUGGLE

"They should attack the lower classes, first with bombs and rockets to destroy their homes, and then when they run helpless into the street, mow them down with machine guns. And then, of course, release the vultures. I know these views aren't popular, but I have never thought of popularity."

Stockbroker (JC)

COMMUNIST SUBVERSION

"Using this diagram of a tooth to represent any small country, we can see how international communism works, by eroding away from the inside. When one country or tooth falls victim to international communism, the others soon follow. In dentistry, this is known as the Domino Theory."

Uncle Sam (ANIMATED)

CONSUMER EDUCATION

"If only the general public would take more care when buying sweeties, it would reduce the number of man-hours lost to the nation, and they would spend less time having their stomachs pumped and sitting around in public lavatories."

Police Supt. Parrot (GC)

CONVALESCENCE

"I know some hospitals where you get the patients lying around in bed, sleeping, resting, recuperating, convalescing. Well, that's not the way we do things here! If you fracture your tibia here, you keep quiet about it!"

Sgt. Doctor, St. Pooves (JC)

CRIME (statistics)

"If there were fewer robbers, there wouldn't be so many of them."

Anonymous Vicar (JC)

CRIMINOLOGY

"It's easy for us to judge Dinsdale Piranha too harshly. After all, he only did what most of us simply dream of doing. A murderer is only an extroverted suicide."

Criminologist (GC)

CULINARY EXPERIENCES

"When people place a nice choc-y in their mouth, they don't want their cheeks pierced."

Police Inspector (JC)

CULTURE

"One day you'll realize there's more to life than culture! There's dirt, and smoke, and good honest sweat!"

Ken (EI) to his playwright/father

DANGER

"There's nothing more dangerous than a wounded mosquito."

Roy Spim (EI)

DEFINITIONS

"Your cat is suffering from what we vets haven't found a word for yet."

Veterinarian (GC)

DIAGNOSIS

"There's nothing wrong with you that an expensive operation can't prolong."

Surgeon (GC) to Mr. Notlob

EXPLOSIONS

"Exploding is a perfectly normal medical phenomenon. In many fields of medicine nowadays, a dose of dynamite can do a world of good."

Doctor (GC)

FLUTES

"You blow there, and move your fingers up and down here."

Alan (GC), on how to play the flute

HEROES (identification of)

"Is it a stockbroker?" "Is it a quantity surveyor?" "Is it a church-warden?" "No! It's Bicycle Repair Man!"

Three Passersby (TJ, GC, JC)

HOUSEHOLD HINTS

"Now here is a reminder about leaving your radio on during the night: leave your radio on during the night."

Voiceover Announcer (EI)

ICHTHYOLOGY

"Contrary to what most people think, the goldfish has a ravenous appetite . . . So, once a week, give your goldfish a really good meal. Here's one specially recommended by the Board of Irresponsible People. First, some cold consommé or gazpacho, then some sausages, greens, potatoes, bread, gravy . . ."

Chairman, Board of Irresponsible People (MP)

IMAGE (political)

"I don't want you to think of the Wood Party as a lot of middle-aged men who like hanging around on ropes."

Rt. Hon. Lambert Warbeck (GC)

INGRATITUDE

"When you're walking home tonight and some homicidal maniac comes after you with a bunch of loganberries, don't come crying to me."

Sgt. Major (JC)

INSURANCE

"We can guarantee you that not a single armored division will get done over for, say, fifteen bob a week."

Vercotti Bros. (TJ and MP) to the Colonel

INTELLIGENCE

"Would Albert Einstein ever have hit on the theory of relativity if he hadn't of been clever?"

Host (JC), "Frontiers of Medicine"

INTERRUPTIONS

"We interrupt this program to annoy you and generally irritate you."

Adrian Voiceover, BBC Announcer

INVESTMENTS

"I would bring back hanging, and go into rope."

Merchant Banker (JC)

IRONY

"It's funny, isn't it, how I can go through life, as I have, disliking bananas and being indifferent to cheese, but still be able to eat and enjoy a banana and cheese sandwich like that?"

Mr. Pither (MP)

ISOLATION

"That's the trouble with living halfway up a cliff—you feel so cut off . . ."

Frank, a Hermit (EI)

JUSTICE (dental)

"Funny, isn't it, how naughty dentists always make that one fatal mistake?"

Arthur Lemming, British Dental Assoc. (EI)

JUSTICE (traffic)

"Parking offense, schmarking offense—we must leave no stone unturned!"

Mr. Bartlett, Solicitor (JC)

LAW AND ORDER

"Customs men should be armed, so they can kill people carrying more than two hundred cigarettes."

Housewife (EI)

LOBBYING

"We're in it for the lobbying, you know . . . We love lobbying."

Political Groupie (EI)

LOGIC

"The point is frozen, the beast is dead, what is the difference?"

Gavin Millarrrrrrrrr (JC)

MACHISMO

"A man can run and run for year after year, till he realizes that what he's runnin' from is hisself. A man's gotta do what a man's gotta do, and there ain't no sense in runnin'. Now, you gotta turn, and you gotta fight, and you gotta hold your head up high. Now you go back in there, son, and be a man. Walk tall."

Cowboy in Black (JC) to Arthur Putey

MARKSMANSHIP

"An entirely new strain of sheep! Killer sheep, that can not only hold a rifle, but is also a first-class shot!"

Professor (EI)

MEDIA

"I object to all this sex on the television. I mean, I keep falling off!"

Anonymous Woman (GC)

MEDICINE (preventive)

"Flu? Perhaps they've eaten too much fresh fruit."

Sgt. Major (JC)

MIME

"When Beethoven went deaf, the mynah bird just used to mime."

Mrs. Thing (GC)

MOLLUSKS

"The randiest of the gastropods is the limpet. This hot-blooded little beast, with its tent-like shell, is always on the job. Its extramarital activities are something startling. Frankly, I don't see how the female limpet finds time to adhere to the rock face."

Mollusk Documentary Producer (JC)

MONTY PYTHON

"It's all a bit zany, a bit madcap . . . Frankly, I don't fully understand it myself. The kids seem to like it . . ."

BBC Employee (JC)

MORALE

"I abhor the implication that the Royal Navy is a haven for cannibalism. It is well known that we now have the problem relatively under control, and that it is the RAF who now suffer the most casualties in this area."

Letter from Capt. B. J. Smeth-
icke in a white wine sauce,
with shallots, mushrooms, and
garlic

MOUNTAINEERING

"Kilimanjaro is a pretty tricky climb. Most of it's up, until you reach the very, very top, and then it tends to slope away rather sharply."

Sir George Head, OBE (JC)

NATURE

"I always preferred the outdoor life . . . hunting . . . shooting . . . fishing . . . getting out there with a gun and slaughtering a few of God's creatures."

Bevis the Barber (MP)

NOSTALGIA

"Kids were very different then. They didn't have their heads filled with all this Cartesian Dualism . . ."

April Simnel, Piranha Bros. Neighbor (MP)

OPPORTUNITY

"Nowadays, the really blithering idiot can make anything up to ten thousand pounds a year if he's the head of some big industrial combine."

M. Brando, Bank Manager (GC)

PERIPATEIA

"The thing about saying the wrong words is that A, I don't notice it, and B, sometimes orange water gibbon bucket and plastic."

Mr. Burrows (MP)

PILOTAGE

"I wouldn't fancy flying one of these sitting on the toilet. I mean, it'd take all the glamour out of being a pilot, wouldn't it? Flying around the world sitting on the toilet?"

Man in cockpit of Balpa Jet (GC)

POETRY

"A poet is essential for complete home comfort and all-year-round reliability at low cost."

Sales Manager, East Midlands Poet Board (JC)

POLICY (culinary)

"Never kill a customer."

Head Waiter (MP) to the Cook

PRINCIPLE

"I would only perform a scene in which there was full frontal nudity."

Vicar (JC)

PROFESSIONALISM

"I thought it better to consult a man of some professional qualifications rather than rely on the possibly confused testimony of some passerby."

Reg Pither (MP), asking doctor for directions

PROUST

"I don't think any of our contestants this evening have succeeded in encapsulating the intricacies of Proust's masterwork, so I'm going to award the first prize this evening to the girl with the biggest tits."

Arthur Me (TJ)

PUNCTUALITY

"I met my second wife at a second-wife swapping party. Trust me to arrive late."

Thompson (MP), Headwaiter

PURPOSE

"We must never forget that, if there was not one thing that was not on top of another thing, our society would be nothing more than a meaningless body of men gathered together for no good purpose."

President, Society for Putting Things on Top of Other Things (GC)

RESPONSIBILITY (fiscal)

"Last year the government spent less on the Ministry of Silly Walks than it did on National Defense!"

Mr. Teabags (JC), Minister of Silly Walks

RESPONSIBILITY (of News Media)

"It's perfectly easy for someone just to come along here to the BBC and simply claim they have a bit to spare in the botty department. The point is, our viewers need proof!"

Interviewer (JC) to Arthur Frampton

RHYMES

"He seeks them here, he seeks them there,
He seeks those lupines everywhere."

Lord of Buckingham (TJ) on Dennis Moore

ROMANCE

"Please excuse my wife. She may not be very beautiful, and she may have no money, and she may be talentless, boring, and dull, but on the other hand . . . Sorry, I can't think of anything."

Douglas (JC), Restaurant Patron

SANITATION

"To me, it's like a mountain—a vast bowl of pus!"

Restaurant Manager (EI), on a dirty fork received by a customer

SANITY

"There are a great many people in the country today who, through no fault of their own, are sane."

Rev. Arthur Belling (GC)

SARTRE (Jean Paul)

"I personally think that Jean Paul's masterwork, *Rues à Liberté,* is an allegory of our search for commitment."

Mrs. Premise (JC)

SCIENCE (library)

"I don't believe that libraries should be drab places, where people sit in silence, and that's been the main reason for our policy of employing wild animals as librarians."

Library Board Member (GC)

SELF-IMPROVEMENT

"Are you nervous? Irritable? Depressed? Tired of life? Keep it up!"

Enterprising Undertaker (TJ)

SHAKESPEARE (William)

"*Toledo Tit Parade?* What sort of play is that?"

Sir Phillip Sydney (MP)

SLOGANS

"Adopt, adapt, and improve—motto of the Round Table."

Bandit at lingerie shop (JC)

TAXATION

"I would tax Raquel Welch . . . and I've a feeling she'd tax me."

The "It's" Man (MP)

TACTICS (police)

"We at the Special Crimes Squad have been using wands for almost a year. You can make yourself invisible, you can defy time and space, and you can turn violent criminals into frogs—things you could never do with the old truncheons."

Policeman (MP)

TCHAIKOVSKY

"His head was about the same size as that of an extremely large dog, that is to say, two very small dogs, or four very large hamsters, or one medium-sized rabbit, if you count the whole of the body and not just the head."

Tchaikovsky Expert (GC)

TELEVISION

"It's not your bleeding high-browed plays that pull in the viewers, you know."

Mr. Birchenhall, BBC Spokesman (GC)

TENACITY

"Sheep are very dim. Once they get an idea into their head, there's no shifting it!"

Farmer (GC) to city neighbor

TOASTS

"Buttocks up!"

Mr. Atkinson (GC)

TRACKING

"A mosquito is a clever little bastard. You can track him for days and days, until you really get to know him like a friend."

Roy Spim (EI)

UNEMPLOYMENT

"Here we see a pantomime horse. It is engaged in a life or death struggle for a job at the merchant bank."

Voiceover for Nature Documentary (JC)

UNREST (labor)

"There's been a walkout in the Impressionists . . . Gaines' *Blue Boy* has brought out the eighteenth-century English portraits, the Flemish School is solid, and German woodcuts are at a meeting now."

Farmer (TJ) from Constable's *Hay Wain*

URINE

"No, you may not give urine instead of blood . . . We have quite enough of it without volunteers coming in donating it."

Doctor (JC)

WIT (failed)

"What's brown and sounds like a bell? Dung!"

Arthur Name (EI)

THE THIRD SERIES

*AIRED OCT. 19–DEC. 21, 1972,
AND JAN. 4–JAN. 18, 1973*

"**I** always say Graham and I really only wrote two totally original things in the whole third series. One was the 'Cleese Shop,' and the other was 'Dennis Moore,' " says John Cleese.

Easily bored, Cleese was already tiring of the TV show, and his enthusiasm was rapidly diminishing by the time of the third series.

"I wasn't even that keen to do the second half of the second season," he admits. "I felt we were repeating ourselves. But in retrospect, I think the others rather felt I was a troublemaker, that I wasn't a good member of the team. But I always said I wanted to do shows with 'em, I didn't want to marry 'em! I felt we were repeating our material, and had lost most of our originality. I slightly resisted the second half of the second series, I resisted the third series a bit, I resisted the second half of the third series even more, but I felt a bit steam-rollered by the others. I suppose they wanted to do it, and they felt it was five to one."

Regardless, some of the finest moments in Python are in

the third series, with their experience making up for any lack of initial enthusiasm. Terry Gilliam created a new set of opening titles, and the bits leading into the openings were also altered.

"The titles always got a bit longer in each series," notes Terry Jones, who was noted for playing an organ fanfare, while completely nude, in unlikely locations. "In the first one, it was just Mike as the 'It's' Man; in the second series, we had John saying 'And now for something completely different,' followed by 'It's.' Then, only in the third series, we had the nude organist."

The nude man at the organ was originally seen in earlier shows—notably "Blackmail"—usually played by Terry Gilliam. It was Jones, complete with fright wig, that claimed the role for his own, however.

"We lost a lot of our inhibitions by dressing up and being silly in the street. But Terry Jones had very few inhibitions to start with," says Michael Palin. "When he played the nude organist, he was stark naked in these nice, decorous little country towns—places like Norwich, which is very nice and smart. And there was Terry, sitting on top of the hill by the castle, stark naked, playing his organ. It does wonders for the inhibitions."

Show 1—Njorl's Saga

RECORDED AS SERIES 3, SHOW 5—PROD. #75749

"Njorl's Saga" (Iceland 1126) begins over an organ fanfare by a nude organist (TJ); the Man in the Dinner Jacket (JC) says "And now," the "It's" Man (MP) says "It's"

Titles

Michael Norman Randall (EI), a defendant in a murder trial accused of killing twenty different people on or about the morning of December 19, 1971, apologizes to the Judge (TJ), Prosecuting Attorney (JC), and Foreman of the Jury (MP) for dragging them in day after day to hear the private details of his petty atrocities. Several bandaged-up policemen sit by; they all cheer when the polite multiple murderer is given a suspended sentence, and all sing "For he's a jolly good felon."

An animated man in a cell sings ". . . Which nobody can deny," and vibrates until he falls apart. Animated detectives enter his body, travel throughout it, checking the spleen, trying to get out through the neck until food starts falling in on them.

"Njorl's Saga," Part II, is followed by a long introduction, and the exciting Icelandic Saga can't get started. Erik Njorl (TJ) rides twelve days to modern North Malden, which turns into a promotional film for the North Malden Icelandic Saga Society, as explained by the Mayor (MP). The next voiceover promises to conform more closely to twelfth-century Iceland. Njorl battles knights with letters on their chest spelling "Malden," while subliminal and overt messages advise "Invest in Malden," until the film is stopped.

"Njorl's Saga," Part III: In the earlier courtroom, everyone begins reading the "Call Erik Njorl" intro at the same time after a brief tirade about comedy shows by a BBC entertainment spokesman, Mr. Birchenall (GC). The defendant is brought in wearing a body cast, and Supt. Lufthansa (GC) reads the charges against him. Police Constable Pan Am (MP) testifies that Njorl assaulted him (MP's billy club breaks as he testifies); Njorl's head is taken off, and the animated detectives are still inside.

This turns into the "Stock Market Report." The Host (EI) slips into gibberish and non sequiturs until he is doused with water by the animated Mrs. Cutout.

Mrs. Cutout enters a launderette, where Beulah Premise (JC) and Mrs. Conclusion (GC) discuss burying the cat and putting budgies down.

They discuss the Sartres and decide to phone them, looking up their number in the phone book and traveling to North Malden by raft (a sign reads "North Malden Welcomes Careful Coastal Craft"), and Whicker (EI) talks about North Malden.

"Njorl's Saga," Part IV: Mrs. Premise and Mrs. Conclusion search for Paris and meet Mrs. Betty-Muriel Sartre (MP) to ask the meaning of *Rues à Liberté;* a goat is there to eat his papers and keep the place straightened up.

"Whicker's World" features an island inhabited entirely by exinternational interviewers in pursuit of the impossible dream. They compete for the camera as the credits roll, with all of the names including the word "Whicker."

ALSO APPEARING: Mrs. Idle
Connie Booth
Rita Davies
Nigel Jones
Frank Williams

☞ The title page reads "Starring Victor A. Lowndes and Alan A. Dale and introducing MIES VAN DER ROHE, the whacky architect who can't keep his hands off prestressed concrete."

☞ The original script includes trailers for upcoming BBC shows used in Show 12, intended to follow the Whicker credits. The show was to end with a brief "Njorl's Saga" in which Njorl throws a pie in his horse's face.

☞ RIDE 'EM, NJORL!

Playing Erik Njorl proved to be less than fun, as Terry Jones discovered while filming the sequences on location. The trickiest part of the role involved the horseback riding. Although he had ridden once before in *The Complete and Utter History of Britain,* he hadn't considered the costume he would be wearing.

Jones notes that he did ride his own horse for the show, "and I fell off it, too! The bloody thing kept on bolting every time I'd get on it! I couldn't bend my legs in my boots, and I was wearing an incredible amount of fur, so I was top-heavy!

"At the time I volunteered to do the part, I didn't think what it meant, that I was going to have all these furs on with this horse. And, I was

allergic to horses as well. It was a *very* unpleasant day of filming."

☞ A PRETTY GIRL IS LIKE A PEPPERPOT

Drag humor has long been a staple in British comedy, dating back before Shakespearean days, and the Pythons were quick to climb into dresses and wigs when the occasion demanded it. Depending on the types of women necessary, the group would recruit Carol Cleveland, Connie Booth, or other female supporting players ". . . when we wanted *real* tits! I suppose I could put it as bluntly as that," Michael Palin laughs.

"There were certain times when, if we wanted a grotesque woman, we'd use a Python. And if we wanted a real woman, we'd use one of the real women that we knew. And sometimes, I'm afraid it would be because they looked sexy, blonde, nice and curvy . . . Other times, we couldn't actually get the same humor out of it by having one of us play the woman.

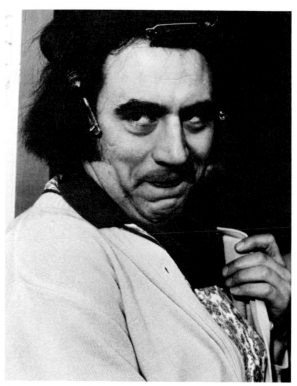

In a characteristic pose, Jones here takes on the attributes of a middle-aged Pepperpot. **Copyright BBC and Python Productions**

"Similarly, if we tried to use a middle-aged housewife to play the kind of parts that Terry Jones played, it would just never work. People say 'Oohh, you were really nasty about women then,' except it was actually a caricature of a certain type of woman, a caricature that had to be done with great gusto and panache. It couldn't be done half-way.

"Women become defeminized when we're doing terrible women in a supermarket," Palin says, and demonstrates with the typical screechy voice of a Python in drag. "We just used to screech at each other. Well, we can do that much better, really, for our purposes, than women ever could."

The Pythons referred to their old ladies as Pepperpots, named by Graham Chapman by their perceived resemblance to real pepperpots. And, Chapman says, most of the group enjoyed playing the absurd roles.

"The Pepperpots were favorite recurring characters—favorites to write for, because they had their own idiot logic, or lack of it, and also because of the effect it had on a person. Such a complete transformation of personality by means of costume and makeup meant that we could really behave like something else, instead of worrying about ourselves at all, which was quite liberating. There's something about being in that weird, elderly makeup that was so far removed from my own persona that it freed the mind quite a lot. I'd be able to ad lib as a Pepperpot more easily than anything else.

"They were also great fun to do because there was another person with a similarly outrageous costume and makeup, who frequently would have gone just a little too far, so that when I turned to look at him, I would be thrown. In working with Terry Jones on the stage show, his lipstick eventually took over half his face! It was really very, very, very gross! Wonderful, in that it just looked absolutely awful and slovenly to begin with, but then it really did get rather over the top," Chapman says, laughing.

Jones, a veteran at drag, is able to break down and analyze the female roles in which each of them specialized. "I quite liked the middle-aged, suburban, mumsy figures—I looked like my mum when I was doing it!" Jones laughs. "It seemed to be a character I could easily fit into.

"Eric made a wonderful woman as well. He used to do these slightly racier, younger women. Mike's got a great woman. I think his best one was in *Meaning of Life,* as the American lady who says 'I didn't even eat the salmon mousse!' It seems like everybody's got a female character that fits their personality. The middle-aged suburban woman suited me best."

*Show 2 — Mr. and Mrs. Brian Norris' Ford Popular**

RECORDED AS SERIES 3, SHOW 7—PROD. #76672

In the tradition of "The Kon-Tiki," "Ra 1," and "Ra 2" is "Mr. and Mrs. Brian Norris' Ford Popular," in which Norris (MP) tries to prove that the people living in Hounslow may have originally emigrated from Surbiton. His evidence includes identical houses, costumes, and most important of all, the lawn mower. Norris and wife Betty (GC) attempt to motor between Hounslow and Surbiton to prove it could have been done. They are held up by the Thames, but end up taking the railway. Ultimately, "Wrong-Way" Norris accidently discovers that the inhabitants of Hounslow had actually

*The cheapest Ford in Britain.

Middle-period generic group shot (left to right: Gilliam, Jones, Cleese, Idle, Chapman, and Palin). Photo copyright Python Productions, Ltd.

made the trek to Surbiton, and not vice versa.

A fanfare by the Nude Organist (TJ), the Man (JC) saying "And now," and the "It's" Man (MP) lead into the

Titles

A Headmaster (MP) calls in some students, Tidwell (TJ), Stebbins (EI), and Balderston (TG), to admonish them for running a unit trust-linked insurance scheme. He insists that such massive stock exchange deals must not happen in big schools. He's actually called them in to have Tidwell examine his wife, until he sees Stebbins is a gynecologist.

"How to Do It" features Alan (JC), Jackie (EI) and Noel (GC) as hosts of a children's show. They teach viewers how to cure all diseases, how to play the flute ("just blow in this end and move your fingers along here"), etc.

Mrs. Nigger-Baiter (MP) tells Mrs. Shazam (TJ) about her Son (JC), talking to him in baby talk even though he's Minister of Overseas Development. They shake a rattle at him, until Mrs. Nigger-Baiter explodes. A Vicar (EI) comes to the door and tries to sell them souvenirs, badges, and little naughty dogs for the backs of cars. A Doctor (GC) appears, discussing the use of explosives to cure such ills as athlete's foot, and the Vicar tries selling to him. An animated man from his anatomy chart falls out of the chart, and out of the edge of the cartoon frame.

In "Farming Club," the Presenter (EI) introduces the life of Tchaikovsky. An Expert (JC) appears, along with a famous Music Critic and Hairdresser (MP) and two Sports Commentators (GC and TJ). They have a three-stage model of Tchaikovsky's body, where they discuss the relative size of his body parts. Sviato Slav Richter (TJ) plays the First Piano Concerto in B-Flat Minor on piano while escaping from a large canvas sack.

Jean Wennerstrom (GC) and two Assistants

(EI and MP) discuss weight loss through slenderizing suits and theater. Trim-Jeans Theater Presents shows a before-and-after Kevin Francis (TJ) as Trigorin in *The Seagull,* where he lost over thirty-three inches. A season of classic plays and rapid slenderizing is promoted, including the Trim-Jeans version of *The Great Escape,* with a cast of thousands losing over fifteen hundred inches.

An animated compère follows, but he keeps losing his mouth before he can introduce the next sketch.

The "Fish-Slapping Dance" sees a Man (MP) dancing around Another Man (JC) and slapping him on the cheeks with two tiny fish, before he is knocked into the water himself. Underwater animation follows with a Nazi fish, and a British fish and Red Chinese fish swallowing him and each other.

Film of the *Titanic* sinking is shown, while the Ship's Captain (TJ) cries "Women and children first." The crew begins changing into drag, children's costumes, Indians, period clothing, etc. The shout is changed to "Women, children, Red Indians, and spacemen first," while crew members argue over whether one costume is the idealized version of the complete Renaissance man, or a Flemish merchant.

In a barren room, a BBC Spokesman (EI) denies that the BBC is going broke, as he shivers in a blanket.

The British Naval Officers have escaped from the ship, and the Police Chief of Venezuela (JC) interrogates them. The interrogation room becomes a pantomime, as Puss in Boots enters. The Captain explains that they are from the SS *Mother Goose,* but an attempt at a flashback fails. Scene shifters start removing the set, and an Old Lady (MP) chases them from her kitchen so she can use it for BBC 2. The closing credits appear written on real scraps of paper, and a real Foot (MP) steps down on them at the end.

ALSO APPEARING: Julia Breck

A talk show follows featuring Lulu and Ringo, and the "It's" Man (MP) comes onstage as the host. However, as he says "It's" the opening titles start to roll over the picture. The guests start to fight with him and leave.

☛ The title page lists the show as "DO NOT ADJUST YOUR SET (WHAT SORT OF TALK IS THAT?)" instead of MPFC.

☛ The script calls for "four extraordinarily famous guests (John and Yoko)" for the "It's" Man chat show.

☛ MEET THE BEATLE

The "It's" Man chat show had intended to use, as the script reads, "four extraordinarily famous guests." The script actually suggests John Lennon and Yoko Ono. The group ended up with Lulu and Ringo, for reasons unclear to Michael Palin.

"Ringo was the most extroverted of the Beatles, other than Lennon—he's just that sort of guy. He'll do anything that's a bit silly and mad. He's very nice and uncomplicated and easygoing. We wanted someone incredibly famous, and to get a Beatle at that time—we couldn't get much higher than that. The others were all going through various sorts of withdrawals after the Beatles split up, and had their own particular egos, whereas Ringo just used to knock about. Graham got to know him, and asked him along," Palin says.

"God knows where we got Lulu."

☛ FISH-SLAPPING

One of the shortest, silliest Python bits is Michael Palin's personal favorite. The "Fish-Slapping Dance" is twenty seconds of absurdity, which sees Palin slapping Cleese with tiny fish, until Cleese knocks him into the canal with a larger fish.

"It's my favorite of all time," Palin says. "One can analyze things until one is blue in the face, although in comedy, I don't think that one really should, as there's so little to analyze in that!

"There's a very spontaneous, instinctive reaction, the purest sort of laugh one can get, because there's a lot of silliness, and a real pratfall at the end when I get knocked into the canal. I'm just really glad it looked as good as it did, because it was quite painful to do! I got to the canal side, and there was much less water in it than I had imagined, so it was quite a long drop! There really was no question of jumping off feet-first—I just had to do a free fall, just had to go. I must say, I did a rather good fall. I was quite pleased. I just went flat down and into the water. It was very unpleasant and cold. Luckily, it worked as well as it did.

"Of all the Python stuff, that is something I would show people to determine whether they have any detectable sense of humor at all. That's something one could show to a person who is devoid of a sense of humor, and they might just begin to smile. And if they didn't, there would be no hope for them at all."

Palin says the brief sketch seems to crystalize Python attitudes in just twenty seconds. "There is a little bit of absurdity in the costumes we're wearing, and the fact that I'm slapping John with very little pilchards. I quite like that. I think John was breaking up at the time—John is the easiest person in the world to make laugh in a sketch. Well, me, too. I go terribly easy, and have since school . . ."

Show 3—The Money Programme

RECORDED AS SERIES 3, SHOW 1—PROD. #75516

The "Money Programme" features a money-loving Host (EI) who gets carried away talking about it. He bursts into a song about money and is joined by a chorus for a production number.

The fanfare by the Nude Organist (TJ), the Man in the Dinner Jacket (JC), and the "It's" Man (MP) lead into

Titles

Erisabeth L Episode Thlee The Almada A messenger (MP) brings a dispatch "flom Sil Flancis Dlake" in the New World to the Queen (GC); he and most of the court are riding mopeds, and everyone speaks with a Chinese accent. The Director (TJ), interrupts them and claims to be Visconti. He is ar-

Palin, Cleese, and Innes watch from backstage at the Hollywood Bowl, preparing to walk onstage and disrupt the proceedings as the "Church Fuzz." **Photo copyright KHJ**

rested for his impersonation by Inspector Leopard (JC, with TG) of Scotland Yard's Special Fraud Film Director's Squad, who is actually Japanese director Yakamoto. Leopard encapsulates Visconti's career and summarizes his films as he reads the charges.

Animated police look for the false Visconti, and a holdup man goes into action.

A radio program asks the panel what they would do if they were Hitler, while an Old Lady (TJ) fixes her Husband (EI) a dead unjugged rabbit fish for supper; all of her desserts have rat in them. Their Son (GC) reports a dead bishop on the landing, so they call the Church Police.

An Official (MP) arrives to investigate and a large hand accuses the Husband, followed by heavenly animation that evolves into women bouncing through a jungle.

Explorers Arthur and Betty Bailey (JC and CC), Charles Faquarsen (GC), and Mr. Spare-Buttons-Supplied-With-the-Shirt (EI) are led to a restaurant in the middle of the jungle. The guests are sometimes attacked by wild animals, and the owner, Mr. Akwekwe (MP) battles with a gorilla trying to do just that. A BBC slide appears over the next attack, describing it in detail and saying it's unsuitable for audiences, so it is replaced by a scene from *Ken Russell's Garden Club—1958,* in which a crowd of people rush into flower beds, including a Gumby, a nude woman, and a pantomime goose.

Back in the jungle, they are still trying to escape, as they spot the Sacred Volcano of Andu and the Forbidden Plateau of Roirama. A Black Native (TJ) has to borrow their script to carry on.

At the British Explorer's Club in London, Our Hero (TJ) and Hargreaves (MP) discuss the fate of the expedition and also have trouble with their scripts, and check their lines, but the hero resolves to go after them. In the jungle, the expedition realizes it can't be lost, because there is a camera crew filming them. They join the crew and realize they're being filmed by a second crew, etc. Before they sort it out, Inspector Baboon of Scotland Yard (EI) arrests one of the first crew (TJ) as an Antonioni impersonator; he is actually Ngumba Kwego Akarumba. As the Inspector starts to review Antonioni's career, the credits roll.

ALSO APPEARING: Rita Davies
Carol Cleveland
The Fred Tomlinson Singers

A BBC slide announces another six minutes of *MPFC.*

The Argument Clinic begins as Mr. Print (MP) asks a secretary, Miss Cyst (RD), for an argument. She directs him initially to Prescriber (GC), who is in charge of abuse, and then he goes on to Mr. Barnard-Vibrator (JC) for an unsatisfying, costly argument. He goes to Monday (EI) to complain, but instead, Monday does all the complaining. He is hit on the head by Spreaders (TJ), who gives lessons on the art before both of them are hit by Inspector Fox of the Light Entertainment Police, Comedy Division, Spec. Flying Squad (GC), who arrests and charges them under the Strange

Sketch Act. Another policeman, Inspector Thompson's Gazelle of the Yard (EI), arrests them, and another policeman (JC) enters at
"The End"
A BBC 1 slide promises one more minute of *MPFC.*

☞ "Salvation Fuzz" is not in the original script for this show, though it is noted in its correct position.
☞ The original "Money" song is as follows:

Money! Wonderful money,
Money Money Money Money!
Wonderful money! Give me
Money-money-money-money Money!
It's money money money money money! etc.

☞ LOSING IT

"One of the most enjoyable, but by *no* means one of the better sketches, is the 'Church Fuzz,' which we did at the Hollywood Bowl," recalls Graham Chapman. "I don't think we *ever* did the whole sketch completely properly, even then. On the stage, and in the studio, I remember I felt a certain irresponsibility about it. For one thing, all of us were in it, and when all of us are in something, it's always nice to be a bit naughty, and make one of the others laugh, or be a bit irresponsible, and do something one wasn't expected to do. It's nice to see that look of alarm on the faces of the others." He laughs.

"There's a certain group naughtiness, when one knows the others are in a similar frame of mind. It always occurred in that particular sketch whenever it was performed. Because it wasn't particularly consequential, each of us had no great problems. It wasn't a difficult thing to perform in any way, so we could let ourselves go."

☞ NO, IT ISN'T

"Argument Clinic" is a favorite of the group, though Michael Palin says it isn't the sort of sketch he and Terry Jones could have ever written. "It's a lovely thing, really marvelous, and very well worked out. John Cleese was much more assiduous and concentrated in his writing, more than Terry or myself. He'd work things out. I think Terry and my minds would have gone on to something else too quickly, but John was very good—he saw that one all the way through, and worked it out very thoroughly."

Show 4—Blood, Devastation, Death, War, and Horror

RECORDED AS SERIES 3, SHOW 2—PROD. #75517

The stock film at the beginning of "Blood, Devastation, Death, War, and Horror" features the Interviewer (MP) and his guest Graham (EI), who speaks only in anagrams. He is working on an anagram version of Shakespeare, but walks off, irate, when the interviewer catches him in a Spoonerism.

The fanfare by the Nude Organist (TJ), the Man in the Dinner Jacket (JC) and the "It's" Man (MP) lead into the

Titles, featuring "Tony M. Nyphot's Flying Risccu"

"Beat the Clock" features Mrs. Scum (TJ) trying to unscramble letters to spell out "merchant bank." When she succeeds, she is bludgeoned by a huge hammer.

A Merchant Banker (JC) is on the telephone setting the terms for a loan (a relative's house, children, etc.) when Mr. Ford tries to collect money for the Orphan's Home. The Banker can't understand the meaning of "gift," however. He decides to try to collect money himself, and drops Ford through a trap door. Two pantomime horses, Champion and Trigger, are then sent in. The Banker must fire one of them, so he orders the pair to fight to the death.

Nature films show sea lions fighting to the death, as well as limpets, an ant fighting a wolf, two men in a life-and-death struggle (joined by an enraged Jacques Cousteau), and a pantomime norse getting a sixteen-ton weight dropped on him. A pantomime goose engages in a life-and-death struggle with Terence Rattigan (JC), and an enraged pantomime Princess Margaret is in a life-and-death struggle with her breakfast.

An animated man and woman feed themselves to rooms in their house. The "Househunters" features men who destroy houses too dangerous to live in; they are hired by NCP Carparks. They hang a "condemned" sign on their prey, and the house becomes a car park.

At a "Mary Recruitment Office," a RSM (GC) hangs up a sign noting that an actor is wanted for a sketch that is just starting. A Man (EI) enters who wants to join either the Women's Army, or else a more effeminate regiment, so the recruiter suggests a particular infantry. The man is angry because he has had no funny lines, so they become a Bus Conductor (GC) and a Funny Passenger (EI), but the man still has no funny lines.

Mr. Horton (TJ), a dull, boring businessman, finds that people laugh at everything he says. His Boss (MP) has to sack him for disrupting his coworkers, and can't help laughing as Horton gives him a sob story.

Meanwhile, the Man (EI) is still unhappy that the RSM, now wearing a silly costume, still has all the funny lines. The RSM puts a fish down his trousers, splashes whitewash over him, and throws a pie in his face, to stock film of Women's Institute applause.

The "Bols Story" (about Holland's most famous aperitif) is a talk show in which Mr. Orbiter-5 (MP) gestures while talking to let people know whether he is pausing or finished. A BBC 1 slide interrupts to annoy viewers, and Orbiter-5 continues. Another BBC interruption explains that

Author Kim "Howard" Johnson backstage at the Hollywood Bowl in Pantomime Goose uniform. Photo copyright KHJ

they are also supplying work for one of their announcers.

The announcer in question, Jack (JC), says he is grateful and starts talking about his troubles; his wife and an announcer friend, Dick (MP), support him as he introduces the news. BBC Newsreader Richard Baker* is seen reading the news, though the announcers are heard. Strange visuals, including Nixon, breasts, and a man with a stoat through his head are seen, and the Newsreader uses the same gestures used by Orbiter-5.

A James Bond-ish opening for "The Pantomime Horse is a Secret Agent" features a Bond parody with credits, etc. The Horse is with a Woman (CC) in a rowboat when he is attacked by a Russian pantomime horse. A chase scene involves cars, bicycles, and rickshaws. The chase passes the "Mary Recruiting Office," where the

*The genuine article.

nuns outside are being solicited by the Merchant Banker.

The credits are all in anagrams.
ALSO APPEARING: Carol Cleveland

☛ The opening caption reads "Loretta Returns to Whitemead College" by Some People and their Brains, then "Blood, Devastation," etc.

☛ ANAGRAMS

Most of the Pythons seem to enjoy word games. In Tunisia, the group would often sit around the *Life of Brian* set passing the time with various brainteasers, and Graham Chapman is devoted to *The Times* crossword puzzle. Eric Idle is a big fan of anagrams, which he was able to use in his Python writing.

"I have one of those creative dyslexic brains which tends to look at a word, and break it up, and look at it backwards," Idle says. "I look at 'lager' and see 'regal,' I look at 'Evian' and see 'naive.' It's one of those minds that looks for hidden messages. I guess it comes from English literature. Most people in England start the day by doing the crossword puzzle in the paper—it's part of commuting and goes with the train ride. People do *The Times* crossword puzzle in eighteen minutes. It's very English . . ."

☛ ANIMATED AMNESIA

Terry Gilliam tends to dismiss much of his Python animation, claiming he has never been particularly interested in watching his footage; he is reluctant to name any of his favorite bits, in part for that reason.

"I don't remember anything," Gilliam jokes. "The easy answer to that is, my most favorite bit is the one that (director) Ian MacNaughton cut out when Terry Jones's back was turned. I can't remember what the point of the sequence was, but it involved trees that started growing. They somehow grew beyond the stratosphere, and eventually bumped into some invisible barrier in the middle of space, where they started growing sideways. When Terry wasn't looking and when I wasn't there, Ian, in one of his less-inspired moments, cut out this bit, and chopped out the whole interesting part of the sequence. We ended up with things starting and ending, but without things in the middle. That was one of my big irritations . . .

"There was always a lot I liked about the 'Househunters,' but I never watch the stuff. I just *never* look at the stuff. I don't know why—if it doesn't interest me, or if it frightens me . . . We'd watch it when it came out, and all I could see were the mistakes. I couldn't see any of the good stuff. It was the nature of being supercritical—which has its uses, but is terribly frustrating, so I actually can't enjoy the stuff. My theory was always to stay away from it, and then watch it years later, as an outsider. I've done that at different points, and thought it was rather good," Gilliam says, laughing.

 PANTOMIME CRITTERS

Several strange pantomime creatures made their appearance in Python. Graham Chapman says he has to take his share of the blame for many of them. "I don't know quite how, but the pantomime Princess Margaret fell into my consciousness one day . . . There were several pantomimatic items, really, the pantomime goose, Princess Margaret; there was the flag-seller who goes in to see the merchant banker, who has to have the meaning of the word 'gift' explained to him, and then in came the pantomime horses. That led into the pantomime horse as a secret agent," Chapman says.

"In pantomime, there is usually a pantomime horse or cow or cat, something fairly run of the mill. The idea of having a pantomime Princess Margaret—a huge dummy inside of which would ideally be two other people—would have been nice, but we had to make do with just the one. Still, quite a formidable spectacle."

Show 5—"The All-England Summarize Proust Competition"

RECORDED AS SERIES 3, SHOW 9—PROD. #78491

A fanfare by a Nude Organist (TJ), the Man in the Dinner Jacket (JC), and the "It's" Man (MP) lead into the

Titles

The "All England Summarize Proust Competition" includes evening gown and swimsuit competitions. Host Arthur Mee (TJ) requires contestants to give a brief summary of *A La Recherche Du Temps Perdu,* and the judges are all cardboard cutout figures of the Surrey Cricket Club. First contestant is Harry Bagot (GC), who

must summarize his first book in fifteen seconds. Failing that, the second contestant, Ronald Rutherford (MP), does even worse. The third contestant, the Bolton Choral Society, led by Supt. McGough (the Fred Tomlinson Singers), tries to summarize his books as a madrigal. Since no one has done well enough, the prize is given to the girl with the biggest tits; she is brought out and congratulated over the closing credits.
ALSO APPEARING: Carol Cleveland
The Fred Tomlinson Singers

Stock film of Mt. Everest (the mountain with the biggest tits in the world) begins the story of the International Hairdresser's Expedition on Everest. Leader of the expedition is Col. Sir John Teasy Weasy Butler (GC), who describes the assault. Patrice (EI) explains that they couldn't go outside during monsoons because he and Ricky had just had a blow dry and rinse. They receive competition from a team of French chiropodists and thirteen other expeditions. They decide to open their own salon on the side of the mountain, "Ricky Pule's Hairdressing Salon."

There is a cinema ad for "Ricky's" on a mountainside, plus coming attractions for *A Magnificent Festering* (an animated short in which Beatrice makes a fool of herself for James in three different scenes).

Idle as Mr. Smoketoomuch is led offstage by Cleese as he continues his oration against travel agents and package tours, to continue it throughout the audience. **Photo copyright KHJ**

Mrs. Little (TJ) calls the fire brigade (led by MP), but they are too busy doing needlepoint and cooking to answer the phone. Son Mervyn (JC) calls them for their hamster, telling his mother to go play her cello. He eventually takes off his shoe and tells them his size after answering "Yes . . . yes . . . yes . . ." while Mrs. Little takes the call after the hamster dies. She tells them her shoe size. Her son Eamonn (GC), carrying a spear and shield and dressed as a headhunter, arrives home from Dublin. The fire brigade eventually comes around on Friday night and she has a party for them, as Mrs. Little talks about her favorite TV show.

"Party Hints by Veronica Smalls" follows, in which Veronica (EI) tells how to deal with an armed communist uprising during a party.

Animated communists hide under a woman's bed, and they go door to door selling communist revolutions. LBJ laughs at communist revolutions, until he falls victim to the Puking Peter

doll.

Mr. Tick (JC) is taken through a language lab (by GC), where students are studying tapes on bigotry, politics, effeminate tapes, etc. Tick wants to be likeable, and asks for the "Life and Soul of the Party" tape; the students go into a '30s routine, wearing earphones and kicking their legs to Sandy Wilson's version of "The Devils," but the Proust choral madrigal cuts off their song.

Another shot of Mt. Everest becomes a poster in a travel agency, where Mr. Smoketoomuch (EI), who is fed up with packaged tours, begins a long tirade on them before the travel agent, Mr. Bounder (MP) and his Secretary (CC). The travel agent can't shut him up and calls the fire brigade, but they don't answer. He tries the police but begins answering "Yes . . . yes . . . yes . . ." The Secretary leads viewers to another room.

"Thrust" sees the host, Chris (GC) speak with Anne Elk (JC) on her theory of the brontosaurus. At the end of the interview the phone rings, and Chris answers "Yes . . . yes . . . yes . . ." They leave through the travel agency as the fire brigade arrives, and the Proust madrigal begins.

☞ The script has the show opening with a boy and girl meeting the Rev. Arthur Belling, the looney Vicar (now in Show 10), and then the titles.

☞ Anne Elk's second theory is: The Fire Brigade Chorus never sings songs about Monsieur Marcel Proust.

☛ PROUST HOBBIES

One of the better-known cases of censorship of the Python TV show involved Graham Chapman's character in "The All-England Summarize Proust Competition"; he gives his hobbies as golf, strangling animals, and masturbation. The BBC cut the audio track from the final word, although it has been broadcast with "masturbation" intact in America. The BBC version showed audiences breaking up with laughter at "strangling animals," and only lip-readers were able to get the real joke.

Chapman was unhappy that his line was lost: "Golf isn't very popular around here. And, 'masturbation' was cut or changed—we weren't allowed to say that. Ridiculous, isn't it—some safe pastime like that?"

"The whole Summarize Proust sketch was actually the product of Michael Palin and Terry Jones," says Chapman. "How they got that into their heads, I don't know. Of course, if one is thinking of having a 'summarize' something, that *would* be pretty tricky."

 **GOING PLACES**

The "Travel Agent" sketch, in which Eric Idle delivers a lengthy diatribe against package tours, is one of the highlights of the stage shows. As Mr. Smoketoomuch, Idle is led offstage (usually escorted by John Cleese) as he rants, only to reappear, breaking away from his captor and continuing his spiel as he walks through the delighted audience, often more than once. The live version of the speech runs several minutes longer than the original TV version, thanks to Idle.

"That sketch was actually written by John and Graham," Idle explains, "and it was funny enough when we were rehearsing it. But, it wasn't long enough. So, at some point, I took it over and wrote more, in that style; I wrote a couple of extra pages for the stage show. It's basically their sketch, but nobody else wanted to learn it!"

Show 6—The War Against Pornography

RECORDED AS SERIES 3, SHOW 6—PROD. #76570

Newsreel footage is shown of Pepperpots with gray hair and Mary Whitehouse glasses attacking the permissive society. They assault striking workers on picket lines, cover nude statues and attack smut (including Desdemona onstage with Othello), burn books, and wage war against porn.

A fanfare by the Nude Organist (TJ), the Man in the Dinner Jacket (JC), and the "It's" Man (MP) lead into the
    Titles
"Harley Street." Mr. T. F. Gumby (MP) enters a doctor's office calling for the doctor, trashing the room in the process, and a Gumby Brain Specialist (JC) decides to take out his brain. The

Chief Surgeon (GC) calls for his glasses, moustache, and handkerchief as he leads the Gumby surgical team.

An animated man attempting to study art finds the lights keep going out. The frame adjustment is also off, so he is upside down, sideways, etc.

On TV, the *Nine O'Clock News* is cancelled for the finals of the All-Essex Badminton championships, so Georges Jalin (TJ) and Cladees Jalin (GC) let a man at the door, Mr. Zorba (JC), do a live TV special on mollusks in their living room, with a cardboard TV screen all around him. They are about to switch it off because it's too dull, until he starts talking about the sexual perversions of various mollusks; he is followed by a Newsreader (TG) and other "Vox Pops."

During animation of people tickling a baby, a man becomes part of "Today in Parliament." The Newsreader (MP) talks about developments in strange government departments, until the show transforms into a classic serial, and then into "The Tuesday Documentary" (with EI). It becomes a children's story with animation, briefly returns to "The Tuesday Documentary," turns into a party political broadcast (with TJ), then changes into "Religion Today" before settling on "Match of the Day." The soccer players, in slow motion, all hug each other and dance about the field, as romantic music plays.

"Politicians—an Apology" asks forgiveness for the way the show depicts politicians as crabby, ulcerous, self-seeking little vermin.

An Interviewer (JC) reports on a British Naval expedition to explore Lake Pahoe, and talks with Rear Admiral Sir Jane Russell (MP) and Lt. Commander Dorothy Lamour (EI) (all the officers have the names of female film stars of the '40s). The Interviewer slowly transforms into Long John Silver, and an animated, psychedelic Royal Navy recruiting film is shown. Another Interviewer (TJ) apologizes for the first one, and talks to Vice Admiral Sir John Cunningham (GC), who maintains that there is absolutely no cannibalism in the Royal Navy. Their expedition is intended to cover up cannibalism and necrophilia, though they claim to be going to Lake Pahoe, which is located in a residential home at 22A Runcorn Avenue. They ask the Woman living there (EI) and her Husband (MP) where the lake is at, and are told to look in the basement flat, where they find a couple (MP and TJ) living in scuba gear, complaining about the dampness.

The host of a focus on the Magna Carta talks with Mr. Badger (EI) on his theories, and is answered in mime. They agree to have dinner together; later, Badger orders whiskeys and a bottle of wine as his dinner from the Waiter (MP). They all decide this is the silliest sketch they've ever been in, and decide to stop, and the closing credits roll.

ALSO APPEARING: Mrs. Idle

☛ In the original script, "Gumby Surgery" ends with the doctor pounding on his stomach with a mallet, shouting "Get better, brain!" while GC does not get into his gear.

☛ GUMBY SURGERY

The Gumbies were favorites of most of the Pythons, and Michael Palin is quick to cite his most memorable Gumby appearance. "The Gumby brain surgeon is still one of my favorite things to watch. I love that!

"It's got one of my favorite Python lines, when I say 'My brain, my brain hurts.' John, also a Gumby, comes up to me and starts loosening my trousers. I say 'No, no, my brain in my head!' I think that might have been an ad lib at the time. I just love 'My brain in my head!', suggesting there might be two."

☛ LAKE PAHOE

During the expedition to Lake Pahoe, a suburban couple, played by Terry Jones and Michael Palin, were found to be living underwater, in a lake beneath someone's house. Devoted to the cause, Graham Chapman says they used no doubles for the sketch, in which they had to wear aqualungs.

"Mike and Terry actually did go down in all the apparatus. It was very brave of them, I thought," says Chapman. "They spent quite a bit of time learning to breathe underwater. And they seemed to enjoy it, too. Jolly good!

"I did like the idea of a house with a huge lake underneath—not just a lake of the sort that one could accommodate inside a house, but something that was obviously far too big for most countries."

A set was built at the deep end of a swimming pool, according to Jones, and he and Palin were given brief, perfunctory lessons just prior to the filming.

"Some instructor showed up. He gave us these horror stories about 'You have to breathe out when you come to the surface, otherwise you'll be dead.' We were a bit worried about it." Jones laughs. "That was the first time I'd actually used an aqualung—the *only* time I've ever used an aqualung, come to think of it."

Show 7—Salad Days

RECORDED AS SERIES 3, SHOW 4—PROD. #75606

The clothes fly off the Organist (TJ) as he plays a fanfare, there is a nude string quartet, the Man in the Dinner Jacket (JC), and the "It's" Man (MP) lead into the

Titles

The "Adventures of Biggles," Part One: Biggles Dictates a Letter is seen over stock film of World War I planes dogfighting. Biggles (GC) dictates letters to King Haakon of Norway and the real Princess Margaret; he wears antlers whenever he's not dictating to Miss Bladder (NH), his secretary. Algy is called in, and when he says he's gay, Biggles shoots him. A pantomime Princess Margaret walks out of the cupboard, and the closing is shown over film of World War I dogfights.

Animated planes lead into a flying sheep being shot down, which knocks a nude woman out of a nest. When she lands, she causes traffic accidents, and buildings topple over like dominoes.

Not far away, on the Uxbridge Road, a Man (JC) interviews Bert Tagg (GC), leader of a mountain-climbing expedition that is scaling the north face of the Uxbridge Road. Another Man (MP) dressed in furs asks "Lemon curry?" and the climbers all fall down the road.

At Newhaven Lifeboat on 24 Parker Street, Mrs. Neves (TJ) is stuffing a turkey when a Man (MP) enters the house and tells her it's a lifeboat. Other men, also in raingear, find it's not a lifeboat, and go below for tea. In a neighboring house, Gladys (JC) and Enid (EI) stand in the midst of naval equipment, scopes, monitors, and tapes, spying on their neighbors. Gladys leaves her flat and finds herself on a lifeboat, where she tries to get ingredients for a fruitcake from Mrs. Edwards (GC).

The Host (EI) of "Storage Jars" presents a news report on those items. Reporter Ronald Rodgers (TJ) reports from La Paz, Bolivia, on the use of storage jars there, dodging bullets and bombs.

An animated TV viewer, Henry, has his eyeballs taken out, cleaned, and polished by a machine that comes out of his TV. A Good Fairy from Program Control releases Henry from the evil spell he's been under, and becomes a frog.

On "The Show So Far," Mr. Tussaud (TJ) does a recap of the show up to the point where he is hit on the head by a large hammer—and he is.

Mr. Mousebender (JC) enters a cheese shop, where he eventually finds out from the proprietor, Mr. Wensleydale (MP), that they have no cheese at all, so he shoots Wensleydale through the head. He is revealed as Rogue Cheddar, and "The End" appears.

Phillip Jenkinson (EI), a sniffing critic, discusses cheese westerns, and a clip is shown from *Sam Peckinpah's Salad Days,* in which arms and legs fall off freely in a bloodbath shot in slow motion. Blood spurts everywhere, and it is replayed several times. Jenkinson is shot in slow motion as are the credits, and there is stock film of Women's Institute applause.

ALSO APPEARING: Nicki Howorth

An apology is read to everyone in the world for the last scene, admitting it was in poor taste, and asking viewers not to write in as the BBC is going through an unhappy time now.

The BBC denies the previous apology, claiming that it is actually very happy.

A real newsreader reports that several storage jars were destroyed in a local explosion.

"Interlude" features shots of a seascape, and a man in a conquistador costume (JC) says that the show is shorter than usual this week. He leaves, then returns, saying there aren't any more jokes or anything, and then walks off as the scene eventually fades out.

 The newsreader part at the end of the show is not in the BBC rehearsal script, nor is the final "Interlude."

 BIGGLES

"Biggles is very much the archetypal Englishman, an aviator in the First World War, and the star of a lot of books primarily for boys—they were quite sexist about it," explains Graham Chapman about the character, created by Capt. W. E. Johns, who is unknown to most Americans.

"They were about airplanes and fighting one another, all very brave and stiff upper lips and no dirty tricks—one had to fight fair. Very character forming! It was rather nice to use that in a more familiar way—have Biggles be worried about whether his friends Algy and Ginger might, in fact, be gay. I think he discovered that Ginger was—I'm not sure. He probably shot him, because he was very English. He wouldn't understand anything about anything at all, but knows when he's being fair."

ON THE ROAD AGAIN

The British public proved to be unflappable when the Pythons walked among them. The group didn't always travel very far, however. "A lot of it was done in Acton, which was just around behind the BBC—the cheapest place to film, around those

"Sam Peckinpah's Salad Says," just before the carnage and blood begin; the crew began filming the idyllic day in the country during the daytime, but finally had to finish in complete darkness with the aid of huge lights. By that time, the cast was covered with artificial blood. **Photo copyright BBC and Python Productions**

little two-story working-class houses from Edwardian times. We used those streets quite a lot," says Michael Palin.

"It's amazing what one can do without people noticing. I remember when we were climbing the Uxbridge Road; that required us to actually lie flat on the road, dressed in mountaineering gear, and pull ourselves along. People just walked past us. One or two stopped and asked what was going on, but most people just carried on with their normal business."

👉 SHIP AHOY

Although there may have been more unpleasant filming days, Graham Chapman and Terry Jones say the queasiest day of Python shooting was undoubtedly the sequence shot on a real lifeboat.

"It was quite rough to do. They didn't take us out into the very high seas for long—they did a bit—but it wasn't too calm in the mouth of the harbor where we did most of the filming. Poor John Cleese had to be underneath the front hatch, the worst place to be, bouncing around in the dark like that. He just had one line to say, which he bravely did. Of course, there were times when we'd just get ready to shoot, say 'Action!', and John would come up and just go 'Ooooaagghh!', I'm afraid. It was just one of those things." Chapman laughs.

"Poor man—he really went through it! Almost everyone was sick on that afternoon's filming. I was relatively unscathed, largely as a result of a bottle of Glenfiddich . . . I was glad to get off the thing, too, but it wasn't quite so bad for me."

As Terry Jones remembers it, about half the group escaped seasickness; unfortunately, he was in the unlucky half, along with Cleese.

"John and I got *incredibly* seasick!" Jones recalls. "It was the first time in my life that I just didn't care *at all* what we were filming. I just wanted to get back on shore.

"The rushes were funny. We saw the cameras roll, and then we saw me throwing up over the side. We hear 'Action!', and then I get up and wipe my face, and stagger through the shot. When I get to the other end, I puke again." He laughs. "At that stage, I was *not* giving a performance."

👉 CHEESE SHOP

"Any sketch that involved a lot of shouting was always quite good fun, but I also liked playing most of the shop assistants that I'd be doing with John, because they were usually class sketches, and John was great to play against," says Michael Palin.

"John and I could never, ever play the 'Cheese Shop' in rehearsal without laughing at some point. It just got to both of us, and so there was this pitch of tension, this excruciating fear that we were going to laugh at any moment, which really helped us along. I don't think we've ever done it, *ever*, without laughing at some point, sometimes for quite long periods . . ."

👉 SALAD DAYS

The most bloodletting in a Python show probably occurred in "Sam Peckinpah's *Salad Days*," an affair which required tubes for blood, dismembered limbs, and other bits of gross, exaggerated violence. The shooting proved to be a more ambitious project than the group had realized, and they had trouble wrapping it all up in time. Of course, the scene all started benignly enough, with an innocent little party in the country.

"We really made a mess of this nice little bit of heartland. There were huge cylinders of blood, enormous great things! And it all had to be shot in one day," says Michael Palin. "In fact, if one looks at *Salad Days*, it suddenly gets very dark at one point; we were shooting with artificial light by the end. It started as a nice concert party on the lawn, and ended up being shot in the middle of the night."

👉 SELF-INFLATION

As Hazel Pethig says, John Cleese hated wearing costumes, and did what he could to get out of them. Fortunately, Pethig knew how to deal with him, as when they were shooting the "Interlude" sequence.

"In Jersey, he didn't want to dress up as a Spaniard," says Pethig. "He didn't want to put on the helmet and tunic and codpiece. He was *determined* not to get into it. So I punched him into it! He literally puffed himself up so that he'd be too big for the costume—'Look, I'm too big, I'm too big!' Anyone who wasn't used to him or was frightened of him would have thought 'Oh, what am I going to do? How am I going to get him into costume?' I had to pummel him into it! John loves to abuse people to see how they react, and if they answer back, he loves it. He would have loved to have been able to get me all flustered with a costume."

Show 8—The Cycling Tour

RECORDED AS SERIES 3, SHOW 10—PROD. #78642

Reg Pither (MP) rides through the countryside on his bicycle. He crashes his bicycle when the pump gets caught in his trouser leg, and his sandwiches are smashed; he goes to a diner for a banana and cheese sandwich and explains his difficulties (to EI), before resuming his cycling tour of North Cornwall.

Pither falls off again—an animated monster peers from beyond a hill—and he explains his troubles to an Indifferent Woman (JC) who does her gardening and ignores him completely. Resuming his cycling tour, he falls off several more times, due to his too-large pump. A Woman (EI) gives him directions to a Bicycle Pump Center, which specializes in shorter bicycle pumps. Pither then visits a Doctor (EI) to ask him for directions to Iddesley. He is uninjured, but wants the advice of a professional man. The doctor gives him a note to take to the chemist.

Pither interrupts a very personal discussion between James (JC) and Lucille (CC), who is urging him to leave his wife. Pither's interruptions cause her to leave him, and James throws him out of the pub.

Pither is picked up by Mr. Gulliver (TJ) in his car. They discuss damaged lunches and safer foods, then Gulliver's car crashes. Pither gives him a ride to the hospital on his bicycle when he loses his memory and believes he is Clodagh Rogers.*

*A late-'60s pop star.

Pither proves to be a jinx at the hospital's Casualty Department; the Nurse (GC) takes the particulars, and Gulliver is examined by Dr. Chang (JC) as the hospital collapses around them, and begins another personality change.

When Pither and Gulliver pitch camp that night, they are questioned by a French couple, M. Brun (JC) and Mme. Brun (EI). Gulliver signs autographs for their children as "Trotsky," and there is a quick clip of Lenin singing "If I Ruled the World."

Pither and Gulliver team up again at Smolensk and register with the Desk Clerk (TG) at the young Men's Anti-Christian Association. Pither then visits the British Consulate in Smolensk, which is decorated in Oriental furnishings. The British consul, Mr. Atkinson (GC), is Chinese, and offers Pither a drink or a game of bingo. His Chinese assistant, Mr. Lovington (JC), leads groups of Orientals that burst out of closets to shout "Bingo!"

The Desk Clerk tells Pither that Trotsky has gone to Moscow (to reunite with the Central Committee). Three secret policemen, Grip (EI), Bag (JC), and Wallet (GC), take him to Moscow.

At the U.S.S.R. 42nd International Clambake, a Soviet Official (JC), in gibberish Russian, introduces Trotsky. Gulliver begins to address the crowd as Trotsky, but changes to Eartha Kitt, complete with feather boa, and removes his facial hair as he sings "Old-Fashioned Girl."

Pither is thrown in a Russian cell and faces

a firing squad. An Officer (GC) runs up to the squad with a note, which reads "Carry on with the execution." The firing squad misses. They throw him back against the wall, and they miss a second time. Back in his cell, he dissolves back home, where his Mother (EI) tells him that he is in a dream, and is actually back in the cell.

At the Committee Meeting, Marshal Bulganin and "Charlie" finish their ventriloquism act, as the Russian compère (EI) tells a few jokes, and introduces Eartha Kitt. Unfortunately, Gulliver has now become Edward Heath, and delivers a speech to trade union leaders. He is hit by a tomato and becomes Mr. Gulliver again, the audience riots and chases him through the streets. He finds Pither by the firing squad, and they escape with the help of a "scene missing" card. They finally part company as Pither resumes his cycling tour, and the credits roll.

ALSO APPEARING: Carol Cleveland

Maurice and Kevin, the animated monsters from the beginning, sing the Clodagh Rogers song "Jack in the Box."

☞ Cut from the final show was a Gilliam animation of a record ad for "Lenin's Chartbusters, Volume III—twenty-six solid gold tracks, including 'If I Ruled the World,' 'Maybe It's Because I'm a Londoner,' 'Chirpy Chirpy Cheep Cheep,' and many others. Out now on the Bolshevik Label."

☞ A MIKE AND TERRY EXTRAVAGANZA

"If it's long, it's usually by Mike and Terry.

" 'Cycling Tour' was a complete half hour; it was actually complete and put up. What happened—and it was the only time we ever did it—we rewrote it," explains Eric Idle. "It was taken on as a sort of script dare: it had a beginning, middle, and end. We didn't like the ending, so we altered it, and added some input. So it's really a Mike and Terry thing, rewritten by the rest of us."

In fact, "Cycling Tour" was presented as a show of its own, rather than as *Monty Python's Flying Circus*—the opening titles never appeared in the show at all. In addition, it is the only Python TV show that tells one complete story from start to finish, although the "Michael Ellis" and "Mr. Neutron" shows in the fourth season are also quite linear.

Interestingly, this was one show that failed miserably when the group performed it in the studio, according to Jones. "It was strange what shows worked on the recording. The 'Cycling Tour' was very disappointing when we recorded it; people came out saying they didn't like it. Ian MacNaughton and I had a *really* heavy editing session on that, and the show was really made in the editing room. We really cut it around *hugely*. It was a lot longer to begin with, and things weren't working.

"It was shot in a very fragmented way, it wasn't in order; it was different from most shows because it was telling a story. For example, in the scene where Mr. Pither goes into the hospital casualty ward, the casualty ward sign falls down, the board falls on John's fingers, and so on—they had all been shot separately and didn't flow together. It was only in the editing, when we put them all together, that we could get the rhythm going. It was bang. Bang. Bang! And then suddenly we could see what it was meant to be. It was something that we *had* to do in the editing."

Show 9 — The Nude Man

RECORDED AS SERIES 3, SHOW 11—PROD. #78735

Captain MacPherson (MP) of East Scottish Airways and his Copilot (JC) are flying when Scottish Mr. Badger (EI) enters the cockpit and demands one thousand pounds to reveal where he has hidden a bomb, though he eventually lowers his demands. The Director (GC) evicts Badger from the sketch.

The Man at the Organ (TJ) is surrounded by paparazzi as he discusses the symbolism of "The Nude Man," the Man in the Dinner Jacket (JC) discusses the Bergsonian theory of laughter as a social sanction against inflexible behavior, when he must say "And now," and the "It's" Man says "It's"

Titles

Ten seconds of sex, accompanied by a blank screen, is interrupted by a Man (GC) who links it to "New Housing Developments."

A housing project built entirely by characters from nineteenth-century English literature is shown by a Commentator (MP). Little Nell from Dickens's *Old Curiosity Shop* and Arthur Huntingdon (EI) of Anne Bronte's *The Tenant of Wildfell*

A television panel with Chapman and Palin, with a nameplate inexplicably reading "The Amazing Kargol and Janet." Terry Jones and Carol Cleveland were supposed to portray Kargol and Janet, a psychiatrist/conjuring act, in Series 1, Show #1, but the sketch did not appear; it was Series 3, Show #9 that saw the pair appear in very similar roles as "The Amazing Mystico and Janet," who erect buildings by hypnosis. **Photo copyright BBC and Python Productions**

Hall work on the ducts and electrical system. A crowd of farmhands from *Tess of the D'Urbervilles* is supervised by Mrs. Jupp (GC), the genial landlady from Samuel Butler's *Way of All Flesh.* Meanwhile, character's from Milton's *Paradise Lost* are working on a motorway interchange.

The Amazing Mystico (TJ) and Janet put up buildings by hypnosis. Ken Very Big Liar (MP) explains the advantages of the system, and Clement Onan (GC), architect to the council, claims they're safe as long as people believe in them. A tenant couple (EI and GC) is interviewed, and cease believing for a moment. A biography of Janet follows, and Supt. Harry "Boot In" Swalk (TJ) discusses the recent outbreak of hangings, as the police radio broadcasts conversations and policemen singing "Jack in the Box."

Two mortuary workers (TG and TJ) eat lunch and listen to the *Mortuary Hour* on the radio. Their supervisor, Mr. Wong (JC), comes in to warn them, and a Senile Old Lord (MP) is wheeled in by the Lord Mayor (GC) and given a tour, but his brain becomes dislodged. The Scotsman (EI) appears again, and says he won't interrupt the sketch for a pound.

The Animator (TG) is caught explaining how he does his cartoons, followed by an animation which sees flying saucers become soldiers.

The Olympic Finals of the Men's Hide and Seek features a Commentator (EI) describing the match between Paraguayan Francisco Huron (TJ), the seeker, and Don Roberts of Britain (GC). Roberts takes a taxi to the airport and hides in a castle in Sardinia. Another Commentator (MP) interrupts for updated results six years later, and the field reporter (EI) is on the scene when he is found in eleven years, two months, twenty-six days, nine hours, three minutes, and twenty-seven point four seconds. A tie is declared, and they must begin the replay the next day.

An Unctuous, Red-jacketed Compère (MP) stands at the seaside, as donkey rides go on behind him. He tries to introduce a sitting-room sketch when he is hit with a rubber chicken by a Man (JC), who then gives it back to the knight. The Scotsman then volunteers a totally free interruption.

The man, Roger Robinson (JC), then arrives home, where his wife Beatrice (CC) has prepared dinner, and she tells him the Cheap Laughs from next door (TJ and GC) will be dropping in. One Evening with the Cheap Laughs Later, their house has been trashed. His wife asks why they have to buy everything just because the Cheap Laughs have one (whoopee cushions, hand buzzers, etc.). A sixteen-ton weight falls on Roger, and later that night when they're sitting in bed, the bed folds up to show "Probe."

The Narrator (EI) discusses the unfairness of bullfighting, and Brigadier Arthur Farquhar Smith (JC) gives his advice on how to make bullfighting safer, until he starts mincing and is hit by a hammer. The Scotsman turns out the lights and demands to be paid to switch them back on.

Animation features the turning on of the lights, and increasingly cosmic trees that lead to the planet Algon (the instrumental music is to the "Yangtse Song"), and Hitler makes an appearance.

A focus on Algon, with a satellite probe, reveals that an ordinary cup of drinking chocolate costs four million pounds, and everything else is extremely expensive. James M. Burke (MP) shows live film from the planet, and reveals that the price of split-crotch panties makes them virtually unattainable. Prof. Herman Khan (EI), Director of the Institute of Split-Crotch Panties, talks about naughty underwear. They locate a girl on the planet but lose contact with the Algon 1 probe.

The closing credits are then read by the Scotsman, who is being paid by the BBC to do so.
ALSO APPEARING: Carol Cleveland
Marie Anderson
Mrs. Idle

A sixteen-ton weight drops on top of the Scotsman.

LIVE FROM ALGON

The "Algon" sketch was something "slightly wild" written by Michael Palin and Terry Jones, taking aim at news reports, according to Palin. "That was a parody of the instant communication linkups in various areas, and the television presentation of an extraordinary event. The contrast was the discovery of this amazing, wonderful planet, with everyday worries like price inflation, which preoccupies the minds of those that study this planet far more than anything else.

"The American moon landings were wonderful feats, but I'm sure people were more interested in how they got on in their spaceships—wherever did they put their leftovers? The technology is going off into the future, but it's basically operated by humans. And as long as there are humans, there are human trivialities.

"It's wonderment reduced to the banality of humans, bringing this wonderful planet down to everyday life. It's like going to the sun and saying 'Where do we sit?'"

SIXTEEN-TON WEIGHT

The Pythons had a number of recurring characters and props; one of the most difficult to ignore was the huge sixteen-ton weight. "That came out of the mind somewhere or another," says Graham Chapman. "I believe it came from not knowing how to end a revue. We were thinking that this enormous boot must come down and crush everyone—and I suppose that's how the sixteen-ton weight came into the picture . . ."

Various construction crews erect housing projects. Clockwise from upper left: Jones as the Amazing Mystico puts up buildings by hypnosis, while Idle as Arthur Huntingdom from The Tenant of Wildfell Hall, *Chapman as Mrs. Jupp from* The Way of All Flesh, *and Palin as Heathcliffe from* Wuthering Heights *toil at a construction project built by characters from nineteenth-century English literature.* **Photo copyright BBC and Python Productions**

The weight, the knight with the chicken, the giant foot (used in the opening titles), and the frequent Python explosions were all useful ways to get rid of characters.

"They were convenient ways of getting rid of characters, and they livened up the shows a bit. It was the slightly destructive side of Python, getting rid of characters as they would in a cartoon, but doing it live," says Michael Palin. "Having a sixteen-ton weight coming down on people: Splosh!

"Television has so many people going on and on, and all we wanted to do was shoot them—nicely, obviously, but just shut them up. The explosions, the sixteen-ton weight, and the man in the suit of armor hitting people with the chicken are our little protests against the way people go on and on."

Show 10—E. Henry Thripshaw's Disease

RECORDED AS SERIES 3, SHOW 13—PROD. #78968

The Proprietor of the Tudor Job Agency (TJ), wearing a Tudor costume, is approached by a customer (GC) who wants a part-time job. All they offer are Tudor jobs: the Proprietor tries to interest him in sailing to Virginia with Walter Raleigh, but the Customer is more interested in dirty books, and is led to the back room, which is the interior of a Soho dirty book shop.

Another Customer (JC) asks the other Tudor Proprietor in the back (EI) for specific titles, but is shown *Bridgette, Queen of the Whip, Naughty Nora,* and *Sister Theresa, the Spanking Nun.* The Customer wants *Devonshire County Churches,* while the Proprietor suggests *Bum Bites.* The Customer is looking for general surveys of English church architecture, but settles for *The Lord Lieutenant in Nylons.*

Suddenly Supt. Inspector Henry Gaskell (MP), in Tudor costume, tries to raid the place. He goes out the back door to a Tudor estate with a woman and becomes Sir Phillip Sydney.

In "The Life of Sir Phillip Sydney," he is summoned from a pub to the coast, to stop Spanish porn merchants who are burying porn books. A swordfight follows, and he stems the tide of Spanish porn, stopping six thousand copies of *Tits and Bums* from entering the country. Sydney returns home to his wife in 1583 London, who is reading Shakespeare's *Gay Boys in Bondage.* He has her start reading it to him, but they are arrested by Sgt. Maddox, a modern-day policeman (GC).

Animation features Shakespeare's "Gay Boys in Bondage," a man falls through a pipe into an organ, and there is a fanfare played by the Nude Organist (TJ).

A Couple (JC and CC) are talking when a Vicar (MP) asks to join them if he won't be disturbing them. He proceeds to break plates, play with rubber animals, spray shaving cream on himself, etc. The Rev. Arthur Belling changes their life, and the entire congregation at St. Looney Up the Cream Bun and Jam acts like Belling.

The organ fanfare (by TJ) is followed by the Man in the Dinner Jacket (JC), and the "It's" Man (MP) says "It's"

Titles

An animated shooting gallery features men and animals, with dead animals dropped into a meat grinder.

"The Free Repetition of Doubtful Words, Skits, Spoofs, Japes, and Vignettes by a Very

Underrated Writer'' has Mr. Peepee (EI) visit a shop to ask the Telegram Inquiry Man (TJ) about a telegram from his wife. An animated telegram is unrolled to begin

"Is There?" in which Roger Last (JC) introduces a discussion on life after death, with three dead bodies.

In the "Peripeteia" sketch, Mr. Burrows (MP) visits Dr. E. Henry Thripshaw (JC) about his problems with word order; the Doctor decides to name the condition Thripshaw's Disease. The Broadway version and film version (a Hollywood costume drama by David O. Seltzer) includes a film clip from *E. Henry Thripshaw's Disease.* The Doctor is interviewed about the film, and tells of working on a new disease that he hopes to turn into a musical.

Silly noises follow.

A Man (GC) visits a Vicar (MP) who is only interested in drinking his sherry. Mr. Husband of the British Sherry Corp. (EI) calls on him to deliver more, and a group of Spanish dancers and singers (led by TJ and CC) sing about Amontillado and request dirty books.

Closing credits all contain suggestive phrases: Michael "Bulky" Palin; Terry Jones, "King of the Lash"; John Cleese, "A Smile, a Song, and a Refill"; Terry Gilliam, "An American in Plaster"; Graham "A Dozen Wholesale" Chapman; and Eric Idle, "Actual Size—Batteries Extra."

ALSO APPEARING: Carol "Four Revealing Poses" Cleveland
The Fred Tomlinson Singers
Rosalind Bailey

An announcer says that E. Henry Thripshaw T-shirts are now available.

☞ The title page of the script reads "*MPFC* with Very Few Naughty Words. 'At last, a real work of art,' Don Revie; 'I laughed till I dried,' I. MacKellen; 'Much better than a poke in the eye,' Connie Francis."

☞ The Rev. Arthur Belling was intended for Show 4, and was not included in this script. E. Henry Thripshaw was not intended for this show, either, but for Show 12.

☞ This script contains several lengthy sketches that never ended up in any of the TV shows. These include a big-nosed sculptor bit, an early, extended part of "Eric the Half a Bee" (the end of which was used on *Monty Python's Previous Record*), "Cocktails" (which was performed in part during the early stage shows), and a "Wine-Tasting/Wee Wee" sketch that was filmed, but got into trouble with the BBC censors.

☞ WEE-WEE

Although the "Wee-Wee" sketch was shot, it was never broadcast as part of the Python TV show, according to Graham Chapman. The scene involved a man showing a sophisticated guest through his wine cellar, allowing him to taste vintages that he confesses are actually wee-wee.

The sketch apparently fell victim to censorship from both without and within the group. "I had always imagined that the 'Wee-Wee' sketch had been broadcast, but I know it was controversial at the time," says Chapman.

"Lamentably, John was on the side of the authorities on that one, and in fact, almost alerted them to this 'Wee-Wee' sketch, which had, I think—partly subconsciously—been written with the idea of annoying John!" Chapman laughs. "Mike and Terry knew there was a raw nerve there in John Cleese, who just *couldn't* stand *anything at all* about early toilet training. Anything that had a reference in it to a childish word relating to that area would bring John out in a cold sweat or a rage, or both at the same time—had something to do with his mother, I imagine . . ."

Show 11—Dennis Moore

RECORDED AS SERIES 3, SHOW 8—PROD. #78413

"Boxing Tonight" sees British heavyweight champion Jack Bodell take on the tweed-suited Sir Kenneth Clarke in the boxing ring; Clarke (GC) discusses the height of the English Renaissance before he is knocked out, and Bodell becomes the new Oxford Professor of Fine Arts.

In the corner, the Man in the Dinner Jacket (JC), without his desk, announces "And now" through a ring mike, a fanfare is played by the Nude Organist (TJ) in another corner, while the "It's" Man stands in a third corner and says "It's"

Titles

Highwayman Dennis Moore (JC), with an impressive introduction and theme song (to the tune of "Robin Hood"), stops a carriage with a Vicar (EI), a couple (TJ and CC), and the driver (MP), and brags about his sharpshooting. They all discuss the trees he claims he can hit, then he robs them all of their lupines, as it is the Lupine Express. He rides off as his theme plays, gives the lupines to a peasant couple, Mr. and Mrs. Jenkins (MP and TJ), and "The End" is shown.

Mrs. Once Off (GC) and Irene Trepidations (EI) discuss astrology, and predicting the future; Mrs. Once Off's horoscope (her star sign is Basil) describes her as a huge lizard. Irene goes through a list of synonyms for precognition, and a sign listing several is lowered from the ceiling, as the audience is invited to read along with "foretoken, presage, portend . . ." A Doctor (TJ) is lowered on a rope; he smashes furniture in his struggle to open his bag. Once opened, the bag is full of money. He takes Mrs. Once Off's money at gunpoint, as well as money from a hand in her wall, and says "See you next week."

A Doctor (MP) making his hospital rounds takes money from the heavily bandaged Mr. Han-

Cleese as Dennis Moore makes another visit to rob from the formerly rich, including Palin and Jones. **Photo copyright BBC and Python Productions**

Mrs. Once Off (Chapman) studies her horoscope, as she and Mrs. Trepidacius prepare to embark on a Palin/Jones sketch that parodies the Cleese/Chapman writing style. **Photo copyright BBC and Python Productions**

son (TG), and other equally afflicted patients (including Mr. Millichope).

An animated Securicor Ambulance/Armored Car burgles a house, then hits a pedestrian and robs him; the loot is eaten by a frog with a man's head.

The "Great Debate" Number 31: TV4 or Not TV4? Ludovic Ludovic (EI) introduces the group (JC, GC, MP, TJ), they all respond with a yes or a no, and the credits roll.

Coming Attractions show "Victoria Regina," "George I, Episode Three—the Gathering Storm." A party is attended by several fops in elaborate dress and powdered wigs, including the Lord of Buckingham (TJ) and Grantley (MP). Dennis Moore swings into the ballroom on a rope, as they are all discussing history. He steals all of their lupines and takes them to the peasant Jenkins and his dying wife (TJ), his theme playing as he rides. Jenkins asks him to steal them medicine, food, blankets, clothes, and wood. He rides back, theme playing, to the ballroom and steals everything, taking a large bag of swag to the peasants. "The End."

The Fifteenth Annual Ideal Loon Exhibition includes: Kevin Bruce of Australia, ranked fourteenth in the World Silly Positions League; Norman Kirby of New Zealand, who stands behind a

screen with a naked lady; the Friends of the Free French Osteopaths performing rather silly behavior; Brian Brumas (GC), who for two weeks has been suspended over a tin of condemned veal; Italian priests in custard; and the Royal Canadian Mounted Geese. The highlight is the judging, and Justice Burke (EI) is pronounced the winner.

Animated plan 38A is put into effect by the police, and a huge hole is set up to trap victims.

In an off license, Mr. McGough (EI) is a solicitor who has caught poetry, and asks for a bottle of sherry from the sales clerk, Mr. Bones (JC). Bones then lapses into the story of Dennis Moore.

Though the rich have become poor, Moore robs them again and rides back (with his theme) to the former peasants' house. They are now living in luxury, and he realizes that redistribution of wealth is trickier than he'd thought, and there is stock film of Women's Institute applause.

The applause continues into "Prejudice," hosted by Russell Bradon (MP), in which they insult all races, creeds, and colors. He helps a viewer find something wrong with the Syrians, and the winning entries of a contest to find derogatory terms for Belgians are read (the winner is "miserable fat Belgian bastards"), and they end with a "Shoot the Poof" segment.

Dennis Moore robs a coach and tries to distribute the wealth evenly among all the occupants as the credits roll.

ALSO APPEARING: Carol Cleveland
Nosher Powell

Losing judges comfort each other on a bus after the contest.

☞ The judges on the bus originally followed the animation after the Ideal Loon, before the man in the off license.

☞ **PROGNOSTICATIONS OF PARODY**

"We kept on parodying each others' sketches and styles," says Terry Jones, explaining how he and Palin took off on the Chapman/Cleese use of *Roget's Thesaurus.* "We wrote a sketch that we didn't really mean seriously—it was a parody of one of John and Graham's sketches."

It involved two old ladies discussing astrology, just before a doctor is lowered to rob them. "They're going on about star signs and prognostications, and we go to all these other names for prognostication, pulling down a sheet, and getting the audience to do them.

"When we actually wrote it, we didn't intend it as a serious sketch—we were just ribbing John and Graham." Jones laughs. "We were surprised when it got into the show!"

👉 LEARNING LINES

Partially due to their training in university revues, the group generally didn't have much trouble learning their lines in the shows.

"I was always good at that," recalls John Cleese. "When I was studying law, I learned to start memorizing something early, and just repeat it a lot, and not try to do it two nights before. When I do the learning at the beginning of the week, by the time I get to the show, it's almost automatic. But I have to start early. If I leave it until late, panic sets in. The great thing about remembering lines is confidence—if I feel confident, I'll remember them."

Cleese says there is a great advantage in writing the material to be memorized (although not on such nonsense things as Johann Gambolputty). "If I've written it, I have a very clear memory of exactly why I wrote each line, from a writers' point of view. Therefore, I have the underlying logic in my head, which makes it easier to learn dialogue."

The man in the off license catches poetry (Idle), while the sales clerk (Cleese) begins the tale of Dennis Moore. **Photo copyright BBC and Python Productions**

Show 12 — A Book at Bedtime

RECORDED AS SERIES 3, SHOW 3—PROD. #75554

A caption reads that the show will start immediately with the opening titles. We then see the Nude Organist (TJ), the Man in the Dinner Jacket (JC), and the "It's" Man (MP), then the

Titles

"A Book at Bedtime" features Sir Jeremy Toogood (MP), a dyslexic, trying to read *The Red Gauntlet* by Sir Walter Scott. He has difficulty with most of the words, and is joined by stage managers, the director, and others (JC, EI, GC) trying to help.

The Lone Piper on the Battlements of Edinburgh Castle is hurled off, and the Queen's Own McKamikaze Highlanders are trained to leap from the castle. Their Sergeant Major (TJ) and Commander (JC) train them, until only one man, Mac-Donald (GC) is left. In an office, a Man (MP) visits a Kami-Kaze Advice Centre, and steps out the wrong door.

At the castle, the Commander wants to send the regiment on a mission, but MacDonald, the last surviving member, keeps trying to kill himself. The Commander says "No time to lose," a phrase the Sergeant Major has never heard before.

At a No Time to Lose Advice Centre, a Man (MP) tries to learn how to use the phrase correctly, and the Consultant (EI) tries to sell him the phrase.

The animation of "No Time Toulouse, the Story of the Wild and Lawless Days of the Post-Impressionists," is told as he fights a showdown.

Back at the castle, the last survivor continues to attempt suicide, and is sent on a mission with the Sgt. Major. MacDonald tries to jump from a truck, strangle himself, and is repeatedly run over. "A Book at Bedtime" continues briefly, and more people are trying to read.

An animated parody of *2001* sees a bone become a space station, and fall down onto a caveman.

"Frontiers of Medicine," Part II, presents The Gathering Storm, over films of penguins. The Host (JC) discusses accidental discoveries, and introduces Prof. Ken Rosewall (GC). He explains their theories, aided by charts, which claim the penguin is smarter than humans: if penguins were as big as men, their brains would still be smaller, but would be much larger than they were before. Dr. Peaches Bartkowicz (MP) stands under a sixty-six-foot-tall penguin and penguins are shown to be smarter than BBC program planners. Dr. Lewis Hoad (EI) explains that they are actually equal in intelligence to non-English-speaking people. Penguins are then seen taking over such important jobs as working the checkpoint on the Russo-Polish border, along with other animated jobs.

At the Kremlin, Russian officers (EI and JC) are attacked by MacDonald, the Scottish Kamikaze. They call the Unexploded Scotsman Disposal Squad (MP and TJ). A phone in a tree is seen ringing, the camera pans over and shows the Squad in a field, taking MacDonald's head off and putting it in a bucket of vodka.

"Spot the Looney," which includes a whole panel of loonies, features the Presenter (EI) displaying a variety of loonies in films and photos. The Spot the Looney Historical Adaptation presents a looney version of *Ivanhoe*, and buzzers go off whenever a looney is spotted.

An Introducer of Documentaries (JC) walks through the woods and begins a talk on Sir Walter Scott, and another Documentary Man (MP) grabs his microphone and begins to discuss replanting forests. The first Introducer grabs it back, and a fight breaks out over the mike. Angus Tinker (GC) begins his segment on Scott, but a Forestry Reporter (TJ) then grabs his microphone, and a car chase follows.

A slide reads "The End."

The closing credits show film of politicians, with the looney buzzer going off.

A BBC slide announces next week's "A Book at Bedtime," but the announcer can't pronounce *Black Beauty*.

The BBC also announces new comedy programs, including "Dad's Doctor" (with TJ and a nude woman), "Dad's Pooves," "On the Dad's Liver Bachelors at Large," "The Ratings Game," "Up the Palace," and "Limestone, Dear Limestone."

The set is then shut off.

☛ The sketch with Mrs. Zambesi 1 and Mrs. Zambesi 2, in which they order a new brain, was to follow the battle over the microphone. It wound up in Show 13.

☛ The show was to begin with a party political broadcast on behalf of the Conservative and Unionist Party, in which a Politician (JC) tries to dance while delivering his speech, and a Choreographer (EI) interrupts to help him. He is joined by six male dancers in a kick line, and gives a wave and cheesecake smile at the end. Two Labor MPs in leotards and leg warmers are rehearsing their upcoming speech, and an animated Wilson and Heath dance, as well.

☛ STILL MORE PENGUINS

There is no real reason for the Python obsession with penguins, admits Michael Palin, except that he considers them to be wonderful birds. "We all love penguins. There's something slightly silly about them, the fact that they can't fly very well, yet they've got these rather stubby little wings.

"The way they move is wonderful, very like Python characters. A group of penguins looks like a group of old ladies in supermarkets," Palin says, screeching "Wellll!" in a Pepperpot voice, "waggling their little flippers and looking self-important. We all rather like penguins, the same way we like haddock, or halibut—fish used to come in a lot as well . . ."

☛ MCKAMIKAZE PYTHON

Graham Chapman says his alcoholism had become quite a problem by the third series of Python, and had started interfering with his work. While playing the McKamikaze Scotsman he was required to lie in a road, while a truck ran over him several times.

"That was a very simple, straightforward thing to do," Chapman says. "In that particular show, I remember the difficult thing for me—because my romance with alcohol was very much in its heyday—was keeping my limbs stiff while pretending to be dead, lying flat on my back with my knees in the air. I had incredible difficulty, because of tremor. It's absolutely easy now, I just couldn't then. Big problem! Any sharp medical practitioner watching the show would say 'Ah!' Anyway, it's nice to feel better watching it now than I did back then."

Show 13—The British Royal Awards Programme

RECORDED AS SERIES 3, SHOW 12—PROD. #78817

A Thames TV announcer (David Hamilton*) introduces the evening's lineup on that channel, but first, "a rotten old BBC program!"

A fanfare by the Nude Organist (TJ), the Man in the Dinner Jacket (JC), and the "It's" Man (MP) precede

Titles for the British Show Biz Awards, presented by Her Royal Highness, the Dummy Princess Margaret.

*Another genuine article.

Nearly all of the Pythons played newsreaders at one point or another (including Eric Idle), in addition to the real British newsreaders. Photo copyright BBC and Python Productions

Dickie (EI), the Attenborough-like presenter of the British Show Biz Awards, gives an elaborate introduction for the remains of the late Sir Alan Waddle (TG brings in an urn, which is in black tie), who reads the first nominations. They include Edward Heath for the "Edward Heath" sketch, Richard Baker for "Lemon Curry," and the winner, the "Oscar Wilde" sketch.

"London 1895, at Wilde's residence." Wilde (GC) exchanges epigrams with James Mac-Neil Whistler (JC), George Bernard Shaw (MP), and the Prince of Wales, the future Edward VII (TJ), who is compared to a jelly donut and a stream of bat's piss.

Animation of a society party has a woman go to the bathroom and loudly "powder her nose." Charwoman sweeps away the last remnants of male chauvinism, she pounds on her chest and her breasts explode.

Back at the show, Dickie puts glycerine drops in his eyes and has the next nomination read by David Niven's refrigerator: the refrigerator, in black tie, is delivered (by TG). Pasolini's *The Third Test Match* (complete with credits), has come in sixth; it is a Bergmanesque cricket film dripping with sexual imagery. Pier Paolo Pasolini talks with a cricket team, and is seen on television by Mrs. Zambesi 1 and Mrs. Zambesi 2 (GC and TJ). They discuss giving blood. They decide to order a new brain—Curry's Own Brains, for thirteen shillings and sixpence. They call to place the order and answer "Yes . . . yes . . . yes . . ." and give their shoe size, then a Man (JC) arrives with a receipt. A dummy salesman, Mr. Rutherford, is thrown into the room, and a Second Salesman (MP) arrives and straps on the new brain, which malfunctions when they go to give blood. On their way there, they pass a Kamikaze Scotsman.

At the blood bank, Mr. Grimshaw (EI) asks the Doctor (JC) if he can give urine instead of blood. After the Doctor refuses, he steals some of the Doctor's blood so that he'll be allowed to donate urine.

"Wife-Swapping" stars Rickman (MP), the host of International Wife-Swapping from Redcar. Wives race from house to house, and Jack Casey (TJ), whose wife wins, is interviewed. Next is the team event: Northwest vs. the Southeast, swapping to the mambo. On "Grandstand," the Host (MP) spotlights a rugby match with a wife as the center of play. "Grandstand" features titles with various wife-swapping scenes, as the credits roll. The credits are shown over "Grandstand," with all the names matched up with various spouses.

ALSO APPEARING: Carol Cleveland
Caron Gardner

At the awards ceremony, Dickie cries with the aid of a stirrup pump that sprays tears, as he awards the Mountbatten Trophy to the cast of the "Dirty Vicar" sketch. The sketch is shown, in which the butler, Chivers (GC), introduces the new Vicar, Rev. Ronald Simms (TJ), who starts assaulting the women in the drawing room. Dickie interrupts the sketch to end it.

☞ E. H. Thripshaw was to follow the Wilde scene and its animation according to the original script; buying a brain was also in the previous show.

☞ The title page of the script credits "Thomas and William Palin; additional material by Cynthia Cleese" (their real-life children).

☞ THE NEWSREADERS' BALL

The Pythons managed to get several real TV newsreaders to appear on some of their shows in various roles; strangely enough, some of them were fans who were happy to join in. "That was a major sign that we were doing all right, when people like that would do it. We were very fond of newsreaders," explains Michael Palin.

"BBC newsreaders weren't too keen on joining in the fun, though on ITV*, the Thames newsreaders were very happy. In fact, we had a launch party for the first Python book, so we made it a Newsreaders Ball. The newsreaders were invited along, and we had a band. Suddenly people who had only seen these newsreaders from the waist up, saw all these full-length newsreaders there. There had never been a gathering all together of newsreaders, so it was rather nice."

*The privately owned TV stations.

MONTY PYTHON'S LOST EPISODES

THE GERMAN SHOWS

Many Python fanatics have virtually memorized the classic forty-five half-hour shows, but almost none of them have seen two original fifty-minute shows shot in the early '70s for German TV. The second show was broadcast in England on BBC 2, but the first program was seen only in West Germany, largely because it was shot entirely in German.

Throughout the years, the group has cannibalized a few of the sketches for use primarily in the stage shows, including the *Little Red Riding Hood* film, the "Silly Olympics," and the "Philosophers' Football Match." In addition, some of the other original bits have turned up on Python albums, such as "Stake Your Claim" and a somewhat different version of the "Fairy Tale" sketch.

All of the material was created especially for the show,

however, except for a Bavarian version of the "Lumberjack Song," sung in German, and the sketch in which Colin "Bomber" Harris wrestles himself. Graham Chapman has performed the latter in virtually all of the stage shows, and originated it long before.*

The shows actually came about through German initiative in 1972.

"There was great enthusiasm from a producer at Bavarian TV," Chapman recalls. "He had seen some of our work somewhere, and decided that we were amazing, and we ought to do a show for him. The idea of doing fifty minutes totally on film—at that point we were only doing studio stuff with a little bit of film—was something we wanted to have done.

"We went over there to have a look around, to see what might spark off ideas, and spent a couple of months writing each one. The first one was in German, the second one in English, which was later dubbed."

Language problems slowed them down a bit, although John Cleese says he speaks some German. "I spoke a little, and Michael can understand a little, but the others didn't at first. We worked with Germans who translated it. We would say 'What does this actually mean?' and they explained the translation to us.

"Occasionally, we were able to say 'Well, that's not really quite the sense we wanted. Do you have a word that's softer, a word that a schoolmaster would use to a schoolboy?' Cleese explains. "We managed to get the flavor as a result of that, though none of us speak German well enough to know whether we got it exactly. But we got it pretty much right, and parroted it off. I can still remember great chunks of it," he says, and demonstrates. "I know what it means, but I can't speak the language, as such."

Though the shows were filmed totally in Germany, and written specifically for German viewers, the Pythons didn't hold back. It was quite the opposite, as Graham Chapman recalls.

"They were kind of way-out; we didn't pull any punches. It was probably a stage farther on than any of the TV shows we'd done in England up to that point, in terms of absurdity and peculiar starts, and they lacked any sort of thread to keep the audience sane. Indeed, it was deliberately annoying for the audience, as we often were. It was quite a stupidly courageous thing to have done, I suppose." Chapman smiles.

"The first program was actually screened opposite an England-German football match that night, so I don't think anyone in Germany watched the TV show—except the critics. But they liked it. I suppose that's why we got asked back to do another one the next year."

Monty Python in Deutschland

A German lady announcer describes the background of the show and the performers. A flat behind her falls down, and she is revealed to be sitting in the open air, near a castle and lake. As she talks, two frogmen emerge and try to drag her in the water. She keeps talking, until they finally drag her underwater.

Animation leads into the opening titles.

"Live From Athens." An Olympic torch runner is run over.

An inaccurate documentary begins on Albrecht Dürer, when a program-planner type interrupts and apologizes for the inaccuracies in the show. They speak to an Australian in the outback drinking Fosters, but his appraisal of Dürer is heavily censored. An Anita Ekberg cutout sings "Al-

*"It's been with me off and on for most of my life," he recalls. The scene requires Chapman to put his body through rigorous physical contortions; backstage on the last night of the Hollywood Bowl show, he happily noted that "This is the last time I'll ever have to do this scene" (as it turned out later, he performed it for some of his lecture tours in the '80s).

162

brecht Dürer" to the tune of "Dennis Moore/Robin Hood." An appreciation of Dürer is abandoned for Part 4 of *The Merchant of Venice,* performed by the Bad Toltz Dairy Herd, with the aid of subtitles. Stock film of Women's Institute applause follows.

The Olympic torch runner becomes a cigarette commercial.

Next is a word from a Frenchman who has only been to the toilet once in the last five years. People who know him confirm this, including Willy Brandt, Nixon, the Pope, and a famous Berlin Specialist who describes their idyllic years together, while lush romantic music plays. A Farmer breeding Doctors interrupts their romp in the country.

"The Life and Times of Albrecht Dürer" resumes with animation; the Planner runs in, out of breath, and there is much cutting between the Farmer and Dürer.

Act I of *The Merchant of Venice* ends with the cows leaving the hospital. A Critic analyzes Shakespearean productions by animals, and the Doctors' version of *The Merchant of Venice* is shown, complete with a commercial for the "Victor" Surgical Truss.

The "Little Red Riding Hood" story is shown, with a less-than-demure Hood (JC) and a less-than-intimidating wolf.

L.R.R. Hood becomes manageress of a Holiday Inn in the United Arab Republic. On an Egyptian side street, an Arab tries to proffer dirty photos, dirty socks, dirty woodcuts, and a picture of Dürer, with animated woodcuts and engravings.

A Camper on the Olympic torch runner's shoulders fries an egg on the torch, and a tent is set up at the Pagodemburg, in the Nymphenberg Gardens, followed by ten seconds of sex.

Five Pepperpots arrive in Munich to get shopping accepted as an Olympic Sport, and the team is profiled. They practice counter approach, packing speed, complaining, and bargain spotting, but they specialize in arguing and gossiping. The "International Shopping Contest—Germany v. England" is held at the Marianplatz, with replays and slow motion effects. The winner, Mrs. Elsie Schweiz of Germany, acquires the lease and buys an entire shop.

Scenes are shown from the three-thousand-meter steeplechase for people who think they're chickens, as well as a marathon for incontinents, as they hop, step, and write a novel. A hammer throw leads into

A Wild West town, where Dürer enters a saloon. The program planner stops it, and calls for a panel game.

"Stake Your Claim" features Norman Vowles of Gravesend, who claims he wrote all of the works attributed to William Shakespeare. Mrs. M of Dundee is thrown off Salzburg Castle and buried, as part of her claim. Vowles returns, claiming he wanted to be a holzfeller (lumberjack), and the "Lumberjack Song" is performed in German, with a chorus made up of Austrian border police.

A letter of complaint leads into animation.

A wrestling match sees Colin "Bomber" Harris (GC) grappling with himself.

Film of the Free World's fight against fresh fruit and International Socialism follows.

Two flunkies carry a sedan chair. A nobleman enters, a flushing noise is heard, and they all leave.

Animated titles begin the "Bavarian Restaurant" sketch, in which the food, drink, and service is traditional beyond the point of being sensible, with more traditions than anywhere else in Germany. Coats are taken with musical accompaniment, as are sitting down, bringing menus, etc. The Maître d' recommends appallingly violent food, in the name of tradition.

Historical footage is shown to discover the history of the joke, including cavemen, Egyptians, Greeks (the trip and fall), Romans (the chair pulled out), and medieval times (the plank). Also included are Columbus and the banana peel, the Renaissance, leading up to Baroque comedy and modern-day jokes, with footage of Lenin telling a joke, and robots tripping each other.

The End

Animation features the castle.

The lady announcer emerges from the lake, still talking.

Show Zwei

The second German show was shot the next year, in October 1973. Also entirely on film, this one was later run as a special on BBC 2. It was performed in English, and dubbed for its original German broadcast. By this time, the writing partnerships were as loose as they had ever been, and John Cleese found himself writing with his then-wife, Connie Booth.

". . . In the second German show, we did a prolonged sendup of a medieval fairy tale, which Connie and I wrote. It was actually well-liked at the time, and we used it in the stage show at Drury Lane, though I don't think it was frightfully well directed," Cleese recalls.

"But it was a script that everybody liked, and Terry Jones actually wanted to base a feature on it. That was the first thing that Connie and I ever wrote together."

An abridged version of the "Fairy Tale" sketch appears on *Monty Python's Previous Album,* and the Cleese/Booth team went on to create *Fawlty Towers.*

Monty Python Blödeln für Deutschland

A William Tell blackout begins, followed by

Arthur Schmidt, stockbroker and international financier, who becomes Superbutcher! He is followed by Norbert Schultze, an economic theoretician who becomes Wilf, the Furry Tiger; and finally Gustav Pedersen, who changes into Mrs. Edith Griffiths. The Presenter becomes Linkman! He flies in animation to the

Titles

Mr. Zurk hosts a show on sycophancy, with Mr. Norman Thrombie and Mr. Twall, who just tries to be polite.

There is a profile of Frank Tutankhamun, who has dedicated his life to preserving mice (and has also opened a National Fish Park). Cowboys ride the four-thousand-acre Big Squeak Ranch, where eight white mice roam freely, and they rope and brand the mice. The Pied Piper of Hamelin is interviewed; he has had to diversify. Outside the "Little Furry Creature Saloon," mice are tethered, but there is a stampede. Elsewhere, a Prospector pans for chickens, and there is footage of the Great Chicken Rush of '49, with animation. Forged chickens are discovered (a cleverly reconstructed rabbit).

An animated opening for "International Philosophy" features German vs. Greek philosophers playing football.

"Learning to Swim," with Arthur Lustgarten, features Part 27, Entering the Pool; the Cowardly Announcer is afraid of the water.

Back in "International Philosophy," no one has moved, and Nietzsche is thrown out of the game for arguing with the referee, Confucius.

More animation leads to a Customer trying to buy a hearing aid from Rogers, a shop assistant. They get Dr. Waring to fit him for contact lenses. Another Customer enters who wants to complain about his contact lenses, and a fight breaks out.

In Happy Valley, King Otto and his daughter, Princess Mitzi Gaynor (CB) live in happiness, for sadness is punishable by death. Mitzi finds the Queen in a clinch with a black man, Mr. Erasmus, whom she claims is her new algebra teacher. Mitzi herself is engaged to Prince Walther; King Otto entertains himself by playing his organ and singing "Ya de buckety rum ting ptoo."

Prince Charming arrives and promises to slay a dragon for Mitzi. At the stadium the next day, he shoots a tiny dragon with his revolver, then starts jumping up and down on it. Walther vows revenge. A witch interrupts Mitzi and Charming's wedding, and changes Charming into a toad, a lampstand, a turkey, and several other objects. She finally changes the entire congregation into chickens, and the prospectors head toward the church as the credits roll.

The Linkman says "The moral is, if you don't have a good way of ending a fairy story, have a moral."

☞ In the spring of 1978, the filming of *Life of Brian* was anything but certain, especially after EMI pulled their money out. Whether *Brian* was filmed or not, the group still planned to do a movie that year.

"Our 'Plan B' is to use the two tapes that we made in Munich in '72 and '73," Michael Palin said in April '78. "They contain a lot of very funny material, like the Silly Olympics, the philosophers playing football, and John as Little Red Riding Hood . . .

"We could probably get together fifty or sixty minutes of material which would form the basis of a sketch show. We would then write and re-record other sketches to go around it in September and October. For a really modest outlay and total control, we'd have ourselves a little Python film to push around as a stopgap.

"It's not as attractive as *Brian,* which would stretch Python far more than doing old material again. On the other hand, the German stuff is good material, and we wouldn't have to bother with any sort of backers and people getting cold feet at the last minute. We'd be doing all that stuff ourselves."

Of course, the money came through for *Brian* from George Harrison, and the need for using the German shows once again ended. The two German shows were eventually screened in February, 1989, as part of the Python retrospective at New York's Museum of Broadcasting (during afternoon screenings on February 17 and 24). But the last remaining unseen Python TV shows still remain unseen by all but a handful, awaiting release at some future date.

THE FOURTH SERIES

AIRED OCTOBER 31–DECEMBER 5, 1974

*I*t came as no great shock to any of the others when John Cleese decided against doing another series of Python. He had been restless to move on to something different, which turned out to be *Fawlty Towers.* Reaction from the rest of the group ranged from regret to anger, but they decided to carry on with six more shows, though they felt mixed emotions at doing so. Cleese had left behind some unused material developed during writing sessions for *Monty Pyton and the Holy Grail,* and he allowed them to use it in the new series of shows. Much of what he wrote turned up in the "Michael Ellis" show, and can be seen in the script reproduced in the *Grail* book.

"*Holy Grail* meandered about in early writing stages, and it wasn't until Mike and Terry came up with the coconuts scene that we all began to fall for the idea of it being set in medieval times," Cleese explains. "But there was a lot of material in the first draft, which probably wasn't even called *Holy Grail* at that point, and something like ninety percent of the first draft was thrown out. It's in the book, and a lot of it is very funny.

"That was the stuff which I said I was very happy for them

to use in the six shows. But apart from the 'Toupee' sketch in the 'Michael Ellis' piece, I can't remember what the other material was. I've only ever seen three of those shows, one of which was excellent, one was pretty good, and one wasn't so good. Everybody said they weren't quite as good as the ones done with me, and the three I saw seemed to be playing with the same kind of average."

For the remaining five, the decision to move ahead on their own was a difficult one, and the final six shows were almost never made. "For a long time, the rest of us were caught between two schools—whether to just give up, or to try and do Python without John," says Michael Palin.

"Every time we thought 'Oh, we can't do Python without John, Python's got to have six people,' we would then get together and say 'Well, all of us want to do some more—we've got some great ideas.' Some of us felt that Python was just beginning to work, while others thought it had passed its peak. But just seeing all that material around and the will to do it together, it would be a shame not to. So we eventually did it. John was happy enough for us to use the 'Michael Ellis' stuff, but the other shows were written without John, which was a pity, in retrospect. It shouldn't have happened like that. Although I did enjoy making most of those shows, they weren't really Python."

The last six shows did away with most of the conventions and recurring characters from the previous three seasons, and a new set of animated titles was created. The name of the show was also shortened to *Monty Python* in Cleese's absence. Terry Gilliam took a stronger hand in the acting, while Neil Innes and others became more involved with the group.

Most important, the programs show a heavier Palin/Jones influence, with half of them involving a more linear storyline from beginning to end, a movement in the direction that would eventually bring forth *Ripping Years*. "The Golden Age of Ballooning" featured the Montgolfier Brothers as a continuing thread throughout the first show; "Michael Ellis" is the rather straightforward story of the title character and his attempts to buy a pet ant; and "Mr. Neutron" tells the story of the search for the most deadly and dangerous man in the world. Interestingly, "Ellis" is the only show-length Chapman/Cleese sketch, which can be attributed to its origins as a first draft of *Holy Grail*.

Nevertheless, if the fourth series didn't quite measure up to its predecessors, it can in part be blamed on the fact that the earlier shows set such a high standard for laughter and innovation. In any case, there are still plenty of gems left in the final TV shows.

Incidentally, it was the fourth series of shows that caused the Pythons' biggest legal battle in America. ABC bought the rights to the six programs to air as part of their "Wide World of Entertainment" late-night specials. Unbeknownst to the group, ABC cut, edited, and censored three half-hour shows down to sixty-six minutes and broadcast the results on October 3, 1975.

The Pythons then filed suit to prevent the network from cutting up the second three shows. Although they were unable to prevent the second special from airing on December 26, there was a brief disclaimer at the beginning of the show. The group continued their court battle with ABC, finally winning six months later, establishing a precedent regarding copyright laws, and eventually obtaining ownership of the Python shows.

Show 1—The Golden Age of Ballooning

RECORDED AS SERIES 4, SHOW 1—PROD. #95141

Animation opens "The Golden Age of Ballooning," introduced by a Plumber (MP) as he fixes a toilet.

Jacques and Joseph Montgolfier (EI and TJ) discuss bathing on the eve of their first flight, while the Butler (GC) tries to introduce Mr. Bartlett. The two animated brothers wash each other, before The End.

An advertisement appears for next week's "Golden Age of Ballooning"; other GAOB books and items are plugged. Part Two Follows, which features "The Montgolfier Brothers in Love." The GAOB titles are run on a home-movie screen in their workshop, where Joseph (TJ) works as his fiancée, Antoinette (CC), is floating like the bottom half of an airship; she complains that he is obsessed with balloons.

The Butler introduces Louis XIV (MP), complete with Glaswegian accent, and two

Joseph Montgolfier and his fiancée Antoinette (Jones and Cleveland) continue their experiments with lighter-than-air craft. **Photo copyright BBC and Python Productions**

advisors, who want to see plans of their proposed airship. Jacques and the King can't think of anything to say to each other, and he instructs the Butler to search for the claret, and shows their balloon plans to the King. Joseph bursts in with a shower cap and towels to prevent them from taking the plans to the Royal Archives, and points out that Louis XIV died in 1717, and it's 1783.

Part Three of "The Golden Age of Ballooning." The Great Day for France finds Sir Charles Dividends (GC) on a chat show, *Decision*, with Lord Interest (EI) and a Linkman (MP), who changes the current affairs show into the court of George III, 1781, and tips viewers off on the Montgolfier Brothers' plans.

King George III (GC) is read to (by EI), when they are interrupted by Louis XVI (MP) (after trying Louis XVIII), who sells them the plans and promises

169

to disengage their troops in America. They want their money immediately, but Joseph rushes in wearing a towel, and exposes the phony Louis the XVI. Another Butler (TG) announces the Ronettes, a trio of black women who come in singing "King George the Third."

Back in France, Antoinette paces as Jacques wonders about Joseph, and the Butler still can't find the claret. He announces that Mr. Bartlett is gone, to audience laughter, applause, pandemonium, and shouts of "More!" while being congratulated by the entire cast, as the credits roll.

ALSO APPEARING: Carol Cleveland
Peter Brett
Frank Lester
Bob E. Raymond
Stenson Falke

A voiceover credits Neil Innes for writing "King George the Third."

A BBC slide announces more "Golden Age of Ballooning" items, and introduces a party political broadcast for the Norwegian Party (EI), involving Norwegian gibberish with subtitles explaining the advantages of the Norwegian economy and Norwegian women.

"The Golden Age of Ballooning," Episode Six—Ferdinand Von Zeppelin: Pioneer of the Airship has one of the Zeppelin brothers, Benny (TJ), inflate himself.

Ferdinand Von Zeppelin (GC) hosts a party in his airship, but when his guests refer to it as a balloon, he throws them out. They all land in a small house and disturb a German couple, Helmut (MP) and Hollweg (TJ), as he reads to her. She finds the chancellor and Prince Von Bülow, along with the bodies of ten other military and political leaders in their drawing room. More film and slides of zeppelins are shown, and the director of GAOB, Mike Henderson, is revealed to be a descendant of one of the balloonists.

"The Golden Years of Colonic Irrigation" is next, followed by more ballooning as two *Mill on the Floss* characters float away.

☛ Cut from the final show was an animated sequence showing America becoming New Scotland, with a bagpipe version of the Stars and Stripes.

Also cut was a montage of Benny Zeppelin's life, including a scene at the "Royal Institute For Less-Talented Younger Brothers" with Harpo Nietzsche.

☛ **TIMELESS COMEDY**

One of the reasons the Python shows hold up as well as they do, decades later, is that they avoided using topical humor. This was a deliberate decision on their part, made for several reasons.

"Since we came along fairly closely after *Beyond the Fringe,* and the social consciousness and satirical label that they'd gotten—somewhat unfairly—we wanted to avoid being bracketed as being another offshoot of their methods," explains Graham Chapman.

"More importantly, however, a very practical reason was repeats. We'd written in TV for a few years, so we'd obviously realized at this stage that if we wrote something in a show that got repeated, then we would get another fee for it without having to do any extra work! Now, that looked like a good idea, and as the BBC didn't pay us very much in the first place, it was almost essential to have the thing repeated. Obviously, topical things were not favored, because they wouldn't work in a couple of years' time, so we did tend to avoid them."

Show 2—Michael Ellis

RECORDED AS SERIES 4, SHOW 2—PROG. #91562

The Titles roll, immediately followed by the closing credits (with a writing credit for JC).
ALSO APPEARING: Carol Cleveland
John Hughman

A Doorman lets in customers at a Harrod's-type store; he is kneed in the groin by an Old Lady, and parks the bicycle of Chris Quinn (EI), another customer. Chris walks in, and studies the directory.

At one of the counters, a Woman (CC) complains to an Assistant (TG) about a flamethrower, and one customer is burned. Chris walks by them, and approaches Another Assistant (GC), who mistakes him for a Michael Ellis. Chris demands a Third Assistant (MP), and then calls for the Real Manager (TJ). He tries to explain everything, and is told it's the store's Rag Week.* He is finally waited on (by MP), and explains that he wants to buy an ant. He picks one out that he names Marcus, buys him a cage, ant toys, and a book, but as he leaves, he is called Mr. Ellis.

Chris takes the ant home, where his Mother (TJ) complains about all of his other pets that he's lost interest in, including a tiger and sperm whale. She says Michael Ellis has been looking for him all day. He and Marcus watch University of the Air (hosted by MP) on animal communications; it features "Let's Talk Ant," a restaurant scene with an ant-speaking Waiter and Customer (GC and TJ). They begin discussing Michael Ellis when his mother turns the set off. When Chris turns the TV on again, an animated ant is being dissected. He learns that Marcus has two legs missing, and decides to take him back. An elevator lady gives him directions for ant com-

*When high school and university students indulge in harmless pranks, ostensibly for charity.

plaints, and he is directed to the Toupee Hall.

Chris enters to find an Old Lady (GC) at a Victorian poetry reading, where Wordsworth reads *I wandered lonely as an ant,* and Shelley reads an ant version of *Ozymandias.* Keats (EI) begins reading his *Ode to an Anteater,* but is pulled out of the hall. Queen Victoria (MP) enters, accompanied by her late husband Albert in his coffin. As she denounces ant poetry and begins to lapse into a German accent, Chris slips away.

Chris is pulled into the Toupee Hall (by TJ) and finds two other Men (MP and GC), all wearing shoddy toupees. He escapes from them and rushes into the complaint room. A Customer (CC) complains to the Clerk (MP) about the lack of a safety on her flamethrower, and sets his desk on fire. Another Man (GC) goes to complain, and they all become surrounded by flames. An announcement over the intercom says it's the end of Michael Ellis Week, and that it is now Chris Quinn Week.

Chris is at the End of the Show Department, and a Salesman (TJ) demonstrates their offerings, including the pullout, the chase, walking into the sunset, the happy ending, a summing up from the panel, a slow fade, and the sudden ending.

☞ Much of the "Michael Ellis" show is made up of material discarded from *Monty Python and the Holy Grail,* particularly the parts taking place in the Harrod's-like department store, which is why John Cleese received a writing credit here. Originally, portions of *Grail* were to take place in modern-day Britain, with the knights finding the object of their quest in the Grail Hall. Much of the original version of the script is reprinted in the *Monty Python and the Holy Grail Book* (see the comments

171

Queen Victoria (Palin) with husband Albert (in the coffin) at a poetry reading devoted to ants (Gilliam is seen over Palin's shoulder). **Photo copyright BBC and Python Productions**

landic Honey Week Man was to be in the line at the Complaint Department.

☛ **FIRE AND TIGERS**

Although the Pythons seldom took unnecessary chances while filming, the number of potentially dangerous elements somehow seemed to peak in the "Michael Ellis" show. Carol Cleveland played a woman who tries to return a defective flame-thrower, while another bit involved a live tiger in a cage. As Graham Chapman recalls, having such props around was fun, and invigorating.

"They obviously took a great deal of care, so there was very little actual danger, but I think we were all quite excited about the smoke and the flames. The guy [was supposed] to catch fire while having a conversation about being up north—some piece of madness—and [really] got set on fire, as well. But he didn't mind.

"I looked forward to the day when we had the tiger on the set, in front of the live studio audience. Terry was complaining about the tiger being on Mandies, how it shouldn't be getting more drugs because they only made it more stroppy. But unfortunately, the thing went to sleep." Chapman laughs. "It needed to be poked with a stick in order to move at all! They'd given it too much sedative before the show in order to keep it quiet, but played far too safe. It was nice having a tiger around, even if it was in a cage. Animals, in general, were always fun."

at the beginning of the Fourth Series by Cleese and Palin).
☛ A scene between Chris Quinn and an Icelandic Honey Salesman was cut, as well as a scene at the Paisley Counter. Also, the Ice-

Show 3—Anything Goes—The Light Entertainment War

RECORDED AS SERIES 4, SHOW 3—PROD. #95279

Two Tramps (MP and TJ) walk jauntily along, rooting through a garbage can and pulling out champagne and two glasses, while *Steptoe and Son* banjo music plays. They are run over by Alex Diamond (GC), as James Bond-like music plays. Diamond suffers from lumbago, which leads into Dr. Emile

Koning, who battles lumbago (and Dr. Kildare-like music plays). Koning's doorbell is near Rear Admiral Humphrey De Vere (EI) as naval music plays. It all becomes the story of his daughter, a nurse, but evolves into Len Hanky, henteaser (TJ). Following him are the Chairman of Fiat (EI), and several more men, rapidly named, ending with a chaplain, Charlie Cooper (TJ), in a fighter plane, and the story of the men who flew with him.

In 1944 England, a Squadron Leader (EI) reports to his superiors, Squiffy Bovril (TJ) and Wingco (GC), speaking in banter which they don't understand. A Pilot (MP) enters, and no one can understand him; he reports that London is being bombed by cabbage crates.

A Private (EI) reports to Gen. Shirley (GC) that they are being attacked by troops with halos and wands, and the enemy is accused of not taking the war seriously. They are accused of trivializing the war by dropping cabbages and such.

A 1940s courtmartial sees Sapper Walters (EI) accused of taking out an enemy outpost with wet towels. He is charged with carrying on the war by other-than-warlike means. Col. Fawcett (MP), the prosecutor, says the incident happened at Basingstoke in Westphalia, and the Head of the Review Board (TJ) tries to find the location on a map written by Cole Porter. Col. Fawcett insists it was compiled by a different Cole Porter, and sings a new version of "Anything Goes."

Walters is accused of having a pair of gaiters worth sixty-eight pounds, ten shillings, a present from the Regiment for the ways he used to oblige them. Walters then attacks the entire military system. The Head of the Review Board orders everyone to put on pixie hats, and they all sing "Anything Goes."

War film showing troops in halos and tutus serves as a trailer for a film about a soldier's love for another man in drag, *Coming Soon,* followed by

Titles

Mrs. Elizabeth III (TJ) and Mrs. Mock Tudor (GC) watch the beginning of "Up Your Pavement,"

Survivors of the Light Entertainment War—and the survivors of the Python TV show, in their last season. (Left to right: Jones, Palin, Gilliam, Idle, and Chapman). **Photo copyright BBC and Python Productions**

and administer a shock to an Arab Boy (TG) near the TV, and he turns the set off. Mrs. Elizabeth III says the programming is for idiots, and goes about proving to her friend that she's an idiot.

Programmers for TV decide viewers are such idiots that viewers would watch a film of the M4 Motorway, which they broadcast successfully. Programmers discuss televising more motorways, and try to decide on new titles for their repeats. A Man from Security (TG) enters and reports that no one is taking the World War series seriously.

Animation of the Television Centre follows as bombs are dropped, and new weather is constructed for a man.

"England 1942." At the manor of Mansfield Vermin-Jones (GC), he, his wife (EI), and his daughter Rebecca (CC) all discuss pleasant, woody-sounding words; his daughter is frightened by tinny-sounding words. Mansfield begins pronouncing sexual words, and is joined by the Pilot from the beginning of the show.

Elizabeth III and Mock Tudor shock their remote controller to change channels to the M2 Show, then to themselves watching TV, then to show jumping.

A woman on a horse jumps over the cast of *The Sound of Music,* followed by jumps over a minstrel show and the cast of *Ben-Hur.* They are interrupted by an announcement that World War II has reached the sentimental stage; the Germans started spooning at dawn and the British Army responded by gazing into their eyes, so the Germans have gone all coy. There is film of a soldier singing "Where Does a Dream Begin" (written by Neil Innes), while the credits roll.

ALSO APPEARING: Carol Cleveland
Bob E. Raymond
Marion Mould

John Cleese and Neil Innes both have writing credits for the show.

☞ SHOW JUMPING

The casts of *Ben-Hur, The Sound of Music,* and the minstrel show, which were jumped by horses, provided some of the strangest visuals in all of Python, but strangely, none of them can remember much about the shooting. Graham Chapman believes there were one or two real people mixed in, but Terry Jones says in the end, they were all dummies.

"Originally, we intended them to be people," says Jones, "but the horses were a bit nervous going over actual people . . ."

☞ TERRY GILLIAM'S CHEAP THRILLS

It was the fourth series that saw Terry Gilliam really come into his own as an actor, and he appeared in nearly every show toward the end. Although his animations took up much of his time, he enjoyed performing, though he admits it was for less than noble reasons. "It's nice to see one's face up there, and to be recognized, but it's also the cheapest of possible thrills. It's not for the actual joy of performing, it's for the fact that I'm identified and recognized. If I sit and work up in a little room pushing pieces of paper, it's very nice *occasionally* for people to say 'Oh, that's the guy that did it!' That's why I don't think I'm an actor—I don't think I'm doing it for the right reasons.

"Sometimes I enjoyed performing very much," Gilliam says. "I enjoyed *Holy Grail,* being the bridgekeeper, and being Patsy. There are a lot of things along the way that I was genuinely doing for the right reasons. What I don't like about doing them is that I don't like being second rate. I'm afraid that within the group, I am very second rate as a performer. They're very brilliant, so I desperately try to protect my ego, but it's tough going! Whatever I did, I always felt it was small potatoes compared to what they were doing. I would really go for cheap shots, because that's about all *I* could do—they're great performers!"

Show 4—Hamlet

RECORDED AS SERIES 4, SHOW 4—PROD. #95474

Titles roll for "Hamlet," Act I, opening with a car, driven by Hamlet (TJ), speeding down the street. He goes in to his Psychiatrist (GC), and tells him he really wants to be a private dick. The Psychiatrist repeats his "To be or not to be," traces his problem to sex. Another Psychiatrist (EI) claims the first was a bogus doctor, and he is chased out by a third (MP), who has papers to attempt to prove he is a psychiatrist. He then changes into a police costume and a Fourth Psychiatrist (TG) enters. All of them ask about his sexual problems ("So you've got the girl down on the bed and her legs up on the mantelpiece"). The Second Psychiatrist comes in again, claiming that it has all been part of a disorientation test, but he is soon chased out.

Dr. Bruce Genuine (TJ) of the Psychiatric Association gives assurances against bogus psychiatrists and discusses computer psychiatry.

"Nationwide" and its Host (EI) ignore World War III, and study sitting in a comfortable chair. A Reporter (GC) in a chair on a London bridge is then approached by a Policeman (MP) who tells him that his chair has been stolen from a Mrs. Edgeworth, who is standing across the street. He proves he is a policeman and then steals a chair from Mrs. Edgeworth so he can sit and talk to the reporter. As he discusses helmets, he steals lunch and beer from the passersby.

A couple necking on the other side of the bridge (TJ and CC) are to be married, but she tells him that her Father (GC) will have to live with and sleep in the same bed as them. The Father reads in bed with them, and when they turn out the lights, he tries to build a model in the dark.

Titles are followed by a Man (TG) pounding on the wall to stop the noise. He then climbs into a crowded bed and they watch *Hamlet.*

Animation exposes parachutists trying to enter a castle.

On "Boxing Tonight," a Fighter is carried into a locker room following a match in which his head and arms were knocked off. His manager, Mario Gabriello (MP), and Boy (EI) talk about what a great fight they have witnessed while they try to reattach his head. The press enters to question him; his head has come off in his last six fights.

The next week, doctors and patients in a hospital are listening to the fight on the radio, and heads and arms come off again. It is followed by a soap opera, "The Robinsons," which is also heard by Mrs. Gorilla (MP) and Mrs. Non-Gorilla (GC) as they sit in a park discussing piston engines. Mrs. Smoker (GC) throws cans and bottles at ducks, and is joined by Mrs. Non-Smoker (TJ), who has just purchased a piston engine, and they begin quoting Shakespeare.

Act Two: A Room in Polonius's House (introduced by MP) features live reports from a Dentist (TJ), a Housewife (GC), and a Real Estate Agent (MP), all of whom discuss Epsom and development. At the Epsom race track where the Queen Victoria Handicap is to be run, Brian McNult (EI) interviews several jockeys, of which only their caps can be seen. The race features eight Queen Victorias, and all of the announcers are dressed like Queen Victoria, as are Brian and Hamlet.

An animated Queen Victoria flies, as does a boy holding a bunch of grapes like balloons.

Act Five: A Ham in the Castle sees all of the Queen Victorias take their curtain calls, and bow to the audience as the credits (by William Shakespeare) roll.

ALSO APPEARING: Carol Cleveland
Jimmy Hill
Bob E. Raymond

Connie Booth
K. Joseph

"Additional blank verse" is credited to John Cleese.
"And then . . ." (MP)

👉 WHAT'S IN A NAME?

In almost every show, there may be characters called either Arthur or Ken, names that seemed to pop up with no particular reason. "That was because of Arthur Lowe, the comedian in *Dad's Army* and all that. I would frequently just say 'Arthur Lowe' for no reason at all. I suppose that's why it crops up a bit, but I was never really conscious of it at the time," says Graham Chapman.

"Jones and Palin were very fond of the name 'Ken' at one stage, I remember . . . It was 'Ken' everything at one point—'Ken, could you pass Ken that piece of Ken paper?' Which got a bit annoying after a time, but Ken was quite popular with them . . ."

Show 5 — Mr. Neutron

RECORDED AS SERIES 4, SHOW 5—PROG. #95563

Titles

Housewives deposit missiles and bazookas on a cart driven by a scrap-man (TJ). A Royal Mail van drives past and unloads a dais, microphones, bunting, chairs, guests, and officials for a ceremony to open a new post box, accompanied by a GPO Official (MP) speaking in several languages.

Mr. Neutron (GC), the most dangerous and deadly man in the world, steps off a train in a quiet English suburb, with an impressive animated introduction. He has tea with Mr. and Mrs. Entrail (TJ and MP), and she entertains him with stories about her children and their spouses. Her sour-looking husband Gordon hates everything and everybody.

At the headquarters of F.E.A.R. in Washington, D.C. (the Federal Egg Answering Room, a front name for the Free World Extra-Earthly Bodies Location and Extermination Center), Captain Carpenter (EI) contacts the Supreme Commander of Land, Sea, and Air Forces (MP) to report that Mr. Neutron is missing; all their forces in the world are alerted.

Mr. Neutron is meanwhile helping with gardening and chatting with a housewife (EI), Mrs. Smailes. Though there is no sign of Neutron in Washington, the Supreme Commander (who sniffs and examines himself) is assured that everybody is afraid of the armed forces. He orders Carpenter to search the Yukon for Teddy Salad, the most brilliant man in the world, to save them from Neutron. Salad is retired and breeding rabbits in the Yukon.

In the Yukon, Carpenter tells a Lumberjack (GC) in a cabin that he's from the U.S. Government Ballet, and asks how to find Salad. Meanwhile, Neutron is putting up wallpaper for Frank Smailes (MP) and cooking for him.

In a Yukon restaurant, the Italian Chef (MP), thinks Carpenter is ordering salad, and complains that all that the (British) Eskimos ever eat is fish, so he was happy to fix the salad. The Eskimos give Carpenter directions to find Salad; he spots a Trapper (TJ) with a dogsled, and the Trapper says one of the dogs in his team is actually Salad in disguise. Carpenter gives him a bone and takes him for walkies.

At 10 Downing Street, the Prime Minister (EI) hears a request from the American Secretary of State for a full-scale red alert, but Giuseppe (TJ), a gypsy violinist, plays so loudly that he thinks the

Americans are bombing them.

Meanwhile, Carpenter has taken Salad out chasing reindeer, and then has to take him for walkies again.

The Supreme Commander, now nude, orders bombings as the only way to stop Neutron, with animation of the bombs landing in all the wrong places, including Cairo, Bangkok, Cape Town, Buenos Aires, Harrow, Hammersmith, etc.

In a suburban sitting room, Mr. Neutron has fallen in love with a housewife, Mrs. S.C.U.M. (TJ). He has won five thousand pounds in a Kelloggs Corn Flakes competition, and wants her to be his helpmate in his plan to dominate the world.

Around a campfire, Salad talks about his other experiences, but is blown up before he can tell Carpenter where to find Neutron. The Supreme Commander is told that everything in the world has been bombed except for Ruislip, the Gobi Desert, and his office.

Meanwhile, Neutron makes Mrs. S.C.U.M. the most beautiful woman in the world, but as they are running away together, a bomb is dropped.

A Man from the Radio Times (EI) reveals that Mr. Neutron has escaped and what will happen next, and describes "the most lavish and expensive scenes ever filmed by the BBC," but the credits roll before they can be shown.

ALSO APPEARING: Carol Cleveland

Bob E. Raymond
Sloopy

"Conjuring Today" features a Magician (MP) about to saw a lady into three bits, but he is chased off by the police.

World Domination T-shirts are advertised.

☞ Neil Innes' "Protest Song" (performed at the stage shows) was to be performed at the very end of the show.

☞ MR. NEUTRON

As usual, Terry Jones and Michael Palin tended to write the longest sketches—something the other Pythons didn't discourage. "I liked the idea of bringing some creature from outer space into a mundane English suburban setting, and then being almost ignored, and absorbed into everyday English life," says Palin.

"Bits and pieces were snipped and added by the rest, but that was predominantly Mike and Terry," says Graham Chapman. "There was a great relief when they read off this enormously long sketch. We thought, 'Well, that's next week done! Jolly good—we can get off early this afternoon.'"

Show 6—Party Political Broadcast

RECORDED AS SERIES 4, SHOW 6—PROD. #95623

A party political broadcast on behalf of the Liberal Party features the finals of the "Worst Family in Britain" contest and the Garibaldi family. Mr. Garibaldi (TJ) is at the table eating Ano-Weets, saying they unclog him much better than Recto-Puffs. Mrs. Garibaldi (EI) irons clothing and a transistor radio. Kevin Garibaldi (TJ) is at the table eating, son Ralph (TG) lies on the couch stuffing himself with

beans, and Valeria (GC), with huge beehive hairdo, applies makeup. They discuss Rhodesia, and are visited by the Liberal Party candidate at the door.

The Compère (MP) explains that the Garibaldis in Droitwich in Worcestershire are the third-place winners in the "Worst Family in Britain" contest, while the Fanshawe-Cholmleighs of Berkshire, upper-class twits, won second place. The winners are the Joddrell family of Durham, but they cannot be shown due to obscenity laws.

Another awful family (EI and TJ) watching the show complains about favoritism, and is interrupted by an Icelandic Honey Seller (GC). He explains that there is actually no such thing as honey in Iceland and they have to import every drop—there is only fish to eat. He is there because it gives him an excuse to get out of Iceland.

Titles

A Doctor (GC) about to perform surgery blackmails a patient, Mr. Cotton (TG) with a naughty complaint. Another patient, Mr. Williams (TJ) enters. He has just been stabbed by a nurse and is bleeding profusely, but he has to fill in a form before he can be treated. Although he fails the questions on the form, the Doctor agrees to give him morphine if he can improve his answers on the history section.

Brigadier N. F. Marwood-Git, Ret. (EI), wearing a tutu, dictates a letter to a bishop, Brian (MP), pondering about the permissible.

An animated opera singer is shot by a very slow cannon.

This is followed by an appeal on behalf of Extremely Rich People who have absolutely nothing wrong with them (delivered by GC).

Mrs. Long-Name (TJ) gets instructions on how to finish her sentences (from EI), and then walks to Stonehenge to find a Linkman (MP) to introduce a Richard Attenborough program.

There is a quest to find the legendary Walking Trees of Dahomey, but they walk too fast for the camera crew. They discover a Turkish Little Rude Plant, an African Puking Tree, and the legendary Batsmen of the Kalahoni, who sit in front of a pavilion, and at intervals bring their hands together for no apparent reason. The young men of the tribe offer themselves as human sacrifices when the sun goes down by pouring harmful liquids into their stomachs. They are shown to be fierce warriors, however, and there is footage of them against Warwickshire at Edgbaston. Warwickshire's first man is killed outright and the last is seriously hurt. Everyone else tries to run away as the results are given, and the compère ends the show.

Closing credits roll, and the music is Neil's version of the Python theme, as played by one learning guitar.

ALSO APPEARING: Carol Cleveland
Bob E. Raymond
Peter Brett

Additional material is credited to Douglas Adams and Neil Innes.

As an office party proceeds in the background, the Nine o'Clock News is read (by EI), and leads into a series of silly cuts.

☞ Several references to Michael Ellis were in the original script, but were taken out; the Icelandic Honey Sketch was intended for Show 2. Also intended was a series on Ursula Hitler, a Surrey housewife who revolutionized British beekeeping in the 1930s. Though born with one of the most famous British Liberal names (Lloyd George), she had to keep changing it to avoid publicity. She was very puzzled in 1939 when a Mr. Chamberlain sent her an ultimatum on Poland.

👉 MORE WRITERS

In all of Python, only two other persons besides the six group members received writing credits on the show. Neil Innes received a writing credit, in addition to two musical credits in the fourth season; and Douglas *(Hitchhikers' Guide to the Galaxy)* Adams was credited with coauthoring a sketch with Graham (though there were other contributions by non-Pythons: Connie Booth cowrote some material with John Cleese for the German shows).

"I didn't work very much on the television side of things at all, but I wrote some things with Graham during that time," Innes recalls. "I don't know how it came about, really—it just happened that way. It was 'All right, you write something with Graham,' and I said 'Okay.'

"I cowrote the 'Awful Family' and their baked beans, and I seem to remember having something to do with the 'Appeal on Behalf of the Very Rich.' I didn't plan to write—I just got dragged into it, gradually, screaming . . . I've always maintained I could have had a decent individual career if it hadn't been for Python." He laughs.

Adams cowrote (with Chapman) a scene in which Graham played a doctor, and Terry Jones was a patient bleeding to death in his waiting room.

"Terry literally had a lot of additional plumbing put around his person, with plastic tubes—for some reason, they often use condoms in devices like that—but there was lots of plastic tubing wrapped around his person, so that he would gush blood," Chapman says.

"That is the one contribution of Douglas Adams to the whole of Python, writing that one with me. John had left, and I had been working with Douglas anyway, so we wrote something for the show."

👉 MORE BEANS

Though the fourth season is generally considered uneven by many of the Pythons, some of the material there ranks with the best of any Python sketches. A highlight is certainly the "Most Awful Family in Britain" competition, according to Michael Palin, with Terry Gilliam's acting particularly delighting him.

"One of my favorite Python characters is Terry G eating the beans." Palin smiles. "*Most* of the characters Terry G played I do enjoy greatly—he's just wonderful. He really threw himself into these awful roles—talk about grossness—he really had an absolute market to himself!

"But that sketch where he was eating beans, just sitting there with a primitive, primeval grunt coming out of him—'More beans, I gotta have beans!'—I like that. John Cleese was never totally comfortable letting himself go like that. That's why I quite enjoy seeing someone like Terry G, or Terry J, *really* throw themselves into things. They didn't mind looking like idiots."

Palin says that Gilliam actually had to be coaxed into acting at first. "He was a bit shy about it. He'd done a little bit of acting school. We'd found out that he was really a bit better than the parts he got. He was given awful parts to do. He was always encased in something like a suit of armor.

"Even during *The Meaning of Life,* many years later, when he was a major film director with a major career behind him, he was still putting on that rubber African outfit—which got stuck and wouldn't open at the right moment in the film. He got his cue, and couldn't open it. All we heard was "Uhh, uhh, can't get out. . . ." Palin laughs.

👉 CREDITS WHERE CREDITS ARE DUE

A great many talented people worked behind the scenes in a variety of roles. Most but not all of them received their recognition in the shows' credits. So here are the valiant crew members whose efforts helped bring us *Monty Python's Flying Circus* (the series each worked on is listed in parentheses). Note: every series was produced by John Howard Davies, while all the shows were directed by Ian MacNaughton (excepting the first four shows, which were directed by Davies); the only non-Python writing credits went to Neil Innes (4–3) and Douglas Adams (4–6).

RESEARCH: Sarah Hart Dyke (1); Patricia Houlihan (3); Suzan Davis (3)

MAKEUP: Joan Barrett (1, 2); Penny Norton (2); Madeline Gaffney (2, 3); Maggie Weston (4)

MAKEUP AND HAIRDRESSING: Jo Grimmond (4)

COSTUMES: Hazel Pethig (1, 2, 3); Andrew Rose (4)

FILM CAMERAMAN: James Balfour (1, 2, 3); Max Semmett (1); Alan Featherstone (1, 3); Terry Hunt (2); Stan Speel (4)

FILM EDITOR: Ray Millichope (1, 2, 3); Bob Dearberg (4)

SOUND: John Delany (1, 3); Jack Sudic (1); Peter Rose (2); Richard Chubb (3); Mike Jones (4)

LIGHTING: Otis Eddy (1, 2); Ken Sharp (2); James Perdie (2, 3, 4); E. C. Bailey (3); Bill Bailey (3)

DESIGN: Roger Limington (1); Geoffrey Patterson (1); Christopher Thompson (1, 3); Jeremy Davies (1); Robert Berk (2, 3, 4); Ken Sharp (2); Richard Hunt (2); Ian Watson (3); Valerie Warrender (4)

VIDEOTAPE EDITOR: Howard Dell (1, 2, 3)

PRODUCTION ASSISTANT: Brian Jones (4)

GRAPHICS: Bob Blagden (2, 3)

VISUAL EFFECTS: Bernard Wilkie (3)

PHOTOGRAPHY: Joan Williams (2)

SOUND RECORDIST: Ron Blight (4)

DUBBING MIXER: Ron Guest (4)

CHOREOGRAPHY: Jean Clarke (4)

ROSTRUM CAMERA MOUNTED BY: Peter Willis (3, 4)

SILLY EXTRA MUSIC BY: John Gould (3)

DOG TRAINED BY: John and Mary Holmes (4)

THE END OF THE BEGINNING

By the end of the fourth series, enthusiasm for continuing with Python had diminished considerably. Although some of the group would have happily continued, others were anxious to spread their wings in other directions. The success of *Monty Python and the Holy Grail* had whetted the appetite of some to expand into film (Terry Gilliam's *Jabberwocky* in 1977 was followed by Graham Chapman's *The Odd Job* the following year), while others had their eyes on new television projects after John Cleese's success with *Fawlty Towers* (Eric Idle's *Rutland Weekend Television* and Michael Palin and Terry Jones's *Ripping Yarns* followed not long after).

At any rate, the fourth series made it abundantly clear to some that continuing the Python TV series would be a mistake. According to Michael Palin, the departure of John Cleese threw off the balance of the show; he says the group now concedes that all six members are necessary for a Monty Python project.

"Everybody contributed something, although I don't think it was obvious until it was taken away," Palin says. "What John took away was a really good authority figure. That was John's great strength—he could play authority figures extremely convincingly, which was absolutely marvelous. One could never say

'Oh, it's a lot of little, resentful people having a go at some of the decent types of this country,' because John looked absolutely the personification of the decent, tall, stiff-upper-lip Englishman. He sent up that sort of character, and it was much, much stronger than if any of the rest of us would have done it.

"And, it also gave Terry and myself, the smaller Pythons, someone to play against. Irritating John's character onscreen was wonderful. Of course, he went on to do *Fawlty Towers,* which is all about being irritated by everything. Really, we lacked John's presence, although I think we were writing some quite good stuff in the fourth series. I thought the last of the six shows, which included the 'Most Awful Families of Britain,' had some very nice stuff," says Palin.

Just as Cleese had left after the third season, others were ready to call it quits after series four, even though the BBC wanted the show to go on. "They wanted us to continue, and I said 'No'—I was the one who said no at that stage," says Eric Idle.

"The BBC said 'Come and do six more.' I remember having a long walk around the common with Michael, and he said 'Come on, let's do it.' I felt that, whereas before we had this balance between Terry and John, and the others fell down the middle, without John we didn't have that balance to Terry's enthusiasm, which tended to carry things into an area just slightly more loaded. John's input had always countered that. If we'd gone on, we would have gotten worse and worse as a TV show, and we wouldn't have done anything else."

Fortunately, the end of the TV series only marked the passing of one aspect of the Pythons' careers. The group would continue with record albums, books, stage shows, and of course, films. In addition, the six individual careers that have emerged during recent years have given us an embarrassment of riches, comedic or otherwise, in virtually all media.

With their own projects flourishing, another Monty Python film appears unlikely in the near future. Their successes have made them so busy

Late-period generic group shot, actually shot on the sands of Tunisia while the Pythons were beginning to shoot Life of Brian **(left to right: Cleese, Gilliam, Jones, Chapman, Palin, Idle). Photo copyright Python Productions, Ltd.**

that coordinating schedules can be difficult. Although the subject has come up, John Cleese continues to discourage the thought.

"The idea of another Python film doesn't set the adrenaline running," Cleese explains. "It might in another five years, but it has nothing to do with what I want to do at the moment, nothing at all."

Graham Chapman has said there will be another film when one of them comes up with an idea so good that it would virtually write itself, and Cleese says there is some truth in that.

"I always used to say that in the time it took us to write *Meaning of Life,* any pair of us could have written at least two movies, probably two and a half. So, I would have reckoned that if we'd split into three groups, we could probably have written five or six movies during the time we took to write that one! That's what puts me off another Python film," Cleese says.

Whatever the future of Python, the classic forty-five shows still stand as a benchmark of TV comedy, to be watched, studied, and enjoyed by generations to come. But frighteningly enough, the world nearly never saw *Monty Python's Flying Circus* after its initial run. *Python* started around the beginning of the video age, and was one of the first entertainment-oriented shows kept by the BBC. Many of the best BBC shows created just before Python were erased or thrown out, including BBC shows with Peter Cook and Dudley Moore, and Spike Milligan—including *Q5.* Only a few *Do Not Adjust Your Set* shows still exist, while only the filmed segments remain from *The Complete and Utter History of Britain.*

The influence of Python has not always been easy to determine, although wherever anarchic, innovative comedy springs up, an admiration for—or at least an awareness of—Python is seldom far behind. Lorne Michaels was a great fan of the show when he started *Saturday Night Live,* and in fact the creators of *Cheers* had *Fawlty Towers* in the front of their minds when they were developing that program.

Still, it would seem the Python attitudes in humor skip a generation, or at least a decade, according to John Cleese. He says that although he enjoyed some of the British sitcoms in the years that followed Python, there was nothing particularly startling or innovative about them.

"In retrospect, the most remarkable thing is that I remember constantly looking around for whatever good, young comedy group was coming up behind us, and never seeing anyone within miles," Cleese says. "There have been a huge number of first-rate young comics with completely different styles since *Not the Nine O'Clock News,* but there was an incredibly barren period in the ten years following the beginning of Python where there was nothing that interesting going on, in my arrogant opinion . . ."

According to Terry Jones, *Monty Python's Flying Circus* was a product of its times, and would probably never have come about under different societal attitudes.

"I think Python started something in the late '60s and early '70s, and it came out of a period that was very optimistic," says Jones. "There was a great feel of optimism at that time, a feeling that anything was possible and the world was on the verge of improving. Perhaps that optimism is there in Python as well; Python's got a joie de vivre about it which is very difficult to encapture in the '80s, where everything seems to have turned sour . . ."

Graham Chapman looks back on Python as anarchic, surreal humor that followed in the footsteps of *The Goon Show* and *Beyond the Fringe,* but notes that one of its most important contributions involved its use of television.

"In some ways, I suppose we became a television equivalent to the Goons," says Chapman. "We were one of the few television comedy programs to actually use the medium of television, and use some of the tricks of the trade for comedic effect. Obviously, there are certain things we could do that we couldn't do with film. We made progress in that direction, and also in pushing back the barriers of what is considered 'good taste.'

"There were things the BBC thought one couldn't do before we started doing them; we were often able to do them purely because the BBC didn't really like us very much, and didn't pay much attention to us to begin with. We were able to get away with quite a lot before they even thought us serious enough to read the scripts at an executive level.

"When executives did begin to read the scripts, a few little disputes did break out, but by then, we usually had a precedent to point at. For instance, we could say that we said 'shit' in program two, and they would then have to go back and check and find out that we had in fact said 'shit' in program two, and that no one had written in to complain. Therefore, they would allow us to say it *once* in this program, but not the three times that we wanted." He laughs. "That's the sort of petty bargaining that went on . . .

"We felt it rather strange that comedy should be dealt with differently than drama, that because one was ostensibly serious, it could therefore have rude words in it, whereas something comedic couldn't. It was just bizarre, really. Perhaps the higher the status, the more rude words one can say. I suppose we did push back the barriers a bit more in terms of sex and violence, but in a very minor way . . ."

One Brief, Shining Moment

After a recent session looking through his diaries and old notebooks, Michael Palin balks at trying to summarize the Python years.

"One tries to pigeonhole Python and make neat little epigrams about what it was like and what it did," says Palin. In fact, he remembers the show as a phenomenon that could not be repeated, and says they were all in the right place at the right time.

"I realize now that I was in some tremendous, uncontrolled mass of outpourings of material by six people who were ripe at just that particular time. Everybody wanted to write and play these extraordinary characters; each show gave us tremendous pleasure, with a huge amount of energy coming out . . . A lot of it was wasted, a lot was crossed out and never got on, a lot was completely unplanned, but somehow, we held it all together.

"Right from the start, I always felt Python was a centrifugal thing; it wasn't six people who wanted to work together for the rest of their lives. It was six people getting together as a stroke of genius on somebody's part. Yet, from the day we did that discussion about the first show, the seeds of the breakup were there, because people were going off in their various different directions.

"But for a while, for maybe thirty-nine shows—some people say only twenty shows—we actually held it together so well that we got the combined fire of six people working on all cylinders. That's what was so good about Python, but we just couldn't keep that up.

"I think the shows still stand up today because they're so *rich.* Not because they're so good—there's a lot of tedious stuff in there sometimes. Some things go on too long, some don't really work, and they certainly can be improved technically. But they're so rich! I always found that twenty minutes into a Python show, I'd think 'This must be the end,' yet there's more and more! So it's like a thick, well-filled comic book. People are always finding new things in Python. It was layer after layer, because one person would write the basics, someone else would have an idea, someone else would say 'While you're doing that sketch, let's have something on the wall that looks good.' So, we'd have a sketch where people have bits of raw meat on the wall, which one doesn't really see because the sketch is going on. But if one sees it forty-five times, like some people in America have, they get around to noticing the things on the wall. So there's always something new.

"It's that feeling of vivacity which really made Python work, and still makes it work. It wasn't such controlled, polite, carefully programmed, well-worked-out television; the BBC barely kept control over it—that's what was so good. Most television now, they're prepared for everything. When they do something surreal and strange, one can bet they'll have good advertisers to back it, and it's all been worked out. The risk and the danger are not there. They were in those Python shows."

The Python phenomenon is one that can't

be re-created, Palin says. "When people ask 'Are there going to be any more Python television shows?' I tell them there really couldn't be. There are certain things right for certain times, like Elvis. All of Elvis's best stuff was really before he went into the Army. He did some nice stuff after that, but the really good *Blue Suede Shoes* Elvis that I remember did it all in a period of two or three years.

"That sort of burst of creativity is like a sunspot. It flares up, very intensely and brilliantly, for a very short period. If it lasted any longer, it would never have been as brilliant in the first place."

BEYOND THE BEEB

CAPTURED LIVE

*C*apturing the spirit of the TV shows onstage before a nightly audience would seem to be difficult, if not impossible. Yet somehow, the Pythons managed to transfer much of their television work to the stage most effectively.

The surreal animations that were so vital to the stream-of-consciousness flow of the shows were presented on huge screens, either lowered onto or placed adjacent to the stage, where the occasional film segments were shown as well. Other real-life cartoon gags were actually reproduced with life-sized props, including a giant hammer wielded against Carol Cleveland and Neil Innes, and the Hand of God, a gigantic cardboard cutout used to finger the guilty suspect in the "Salvation Fuzz/Church Police" sketch. If there was some loss in the expansiveness or mobility of the scenes, it was more than made up for by the excitement and energy of the performances before the delighted crowds.

The Pythons were not averse to taking the scenes directly to their fans. The "Bruces" sketch performed live always involved Eric Idle leading the audience in the "Philosophers' Song," while the words are projected on the screens; in addition, the first few rows are sprayed with Fosters' Lager, while additional cans are pitched into the usually appreciative audience.

The "Albatross" sketch generally involved Cleese, in ludicrous drag, walking through the rows trying to sell his bird, when he is approached by Terry Jones. The "Travel Agent" sketch usually ended with Eric Idle being pursued through the audience, still spouting complaints about package tours as he is pursued by Cleese.

Now used to working in TV, the group had to adjust to performing the same show regularly, recalls costumer Hazel Pethig, who accompanied them on the Canadian tour. "For the first few shows, they found it very difficult doing the same thing every night. They weren't used to stage work. But they kept up, and eventually it got better and better. The 'Parrot' sketch got so good that it was exciting. They'd walk onstage to do a certain sketch, and there would be great roars of recognition, like a football crowd—and *nobody* got bored! They adapted very quickly to the stage."

The Pythons generally managed to fit in all of their

Jones takes a trip on a banana peel as Chapman (behind podium) lectures on the history of humor. Although Palin and Gilliam are there to help demonstrate, Jones always gets it when the pies start flying. **Photo copyright KHJ**

most popular sketches that could be transferred to the stage, and Neil Innes, performing solo versions of several of his songs, became a staple of the live shows.

Of course, the "Dead Parrot" is included, with a stuffed bird standing in to suffer the prolonged, choreographed beating delivered by Cleese to prove the bird is definitely deceased. To his inevitable irritation, Silly Walks is always included, and always well received, even though he has long since tired of it. Even more rigorous is the "Colin 'Bomber' Harris" sketch, in which Graham Chapman plays a wrestler who grapples with himself, throwing himself around the ring rigorously.

Of course, the shows always conclude with the "Lumberjack Song," performed by either Idle or Palin, with fans joining the Mounties in the chorus. This is where a few ringers have been slipped in. On separate occasions at the City Cen-

ter, a rather inebriated Harry Nilsson and a virtually unrecognized George Harrison both took their turns singing.

Despite the reliance on "Greatest Hits" sketches, there is usually some new material mixed in with the old favorites. Film from the German shows has included the "Philosophers' Football Match," the Cleese/Booth "Little Red Riding Hood," and the "Silly Olympics." The "Secret Service/Cocktail" sketch was performed in some of the earlier stage shows, and can be found on the *Monty Python Live at Drury Lane* album.

Terry Gilliam's film *The History of Flight* has been included, along with some other animation, while Neil Innes's songs have never been done in the Python TV shows. Some of the original sketches have been expanded as well, including the aforementioned "Bruces' Philosophers' Song" and a longer "Travel Agent" sketch.

The most notable "new" scenes, however, are the "Custard Pies" and "Four Yorkshiremen," both actually predating Python and never performed on the Python TV show. The former sees Graham Chapman as a college professor lecturing on the history of humor, with Palin, Jones, and Gilliam demonstrating his examples of slapstick (and Jones always getting the worst of it). It was generally so messy that it was performed just before intermission, to allow the three assistants time to clean off the pie and take off their padding. The latter involves four men sitting around playing "Can You Top This?" with stories of their deprived youth. It has also been seen and performed in film and the Amnesty International benefits.

The Python stage show has been rather effectively captured on film in *Monty Python Live at the Hollywood Bowl*. Although some sketches have been removed and the running order completely changed, the performances are typical of the feel of the show, and capture the playfulness as the group performs onstage together for the first time in four years.

The shows are also captured on two different record albums, *Monty Python Live at Drury Lane* and *Monty Python Live at The City Center*. The former is available in America only as an import, and contains some sketches, like "Secret Service" and "Cocktail Bar," that have seldom been seen or heard in any form in the U.S. The contents of *City Center* differ somewhat, and the sound quality is far inferior—Arista Records insisted that the soundtrack album be released before the group finished their three-week run in New York. This was accomplished by recording the first shows, when such sound problems as microphone placement had not been resolved.

Monty Python's First Farewell Tour was actually a three-week series of one-nighters throughout Britain, beginning in Southampton. By

After receiving his lumps, Jones takes off his padding and cleans off the excess pies, during intermission. **Photo copyright KHJ**

Idle plays Michaelangelo to Cleese's Pope as he describes his first draft of the Sistine Chapel ceiling. **Photo copyright KHJ**

the time they ended, on May 24, 1973, they had played a peculiar variety of venues before tiny audiences and groups of thousands. One night proved particularly memorable for Neil Innes, however.

"We were in Birmingham on Michael's birthday, and so we got Eric's mother, who looks *exactly* like Mary Whitehouse, the self-appointed guardian of television standards. At the end of the 'Parrot' sketch, instead of saying 'Do you want to come back to my place?' and Cleese saying 'Yeah, all right,' and then going offstage, Cleese suddenly said 'No,' and grabbed Mike in a viselike grip.

"On came Eric in his horrible emcee's gold jacket, saying how it was a very special evening, and it was Michael's birthday, and they'd gotten Mary Whitehouse to present him with a cake. And brought on Eric's mother. We had the whole audience *totally* convinced it was Mary Whitehouse!" says Innes.

"Michael, with great presence of mind, realized who it was. He took some flowers and said 'Well, I'd just like to say this to the old shit,' and adopted his Gumby voice, and said 'We take the flowers, and put them in the cake.' The audience was convinced that we'd perpetrated this massive insult on Mary Whitehouse! That's one of my favorite Python memories . . ."

Later that year, they embarked on an extensive, sometimes grueling tour of Canada. Upon finishing, John Cleese—who had informed the others at the beginning of the tour that he wanted out of the TV series—went back to England, while the others headed for Hollywood. In a notorious episode, the Pythons made their first—and only—

191

group appearance on the *Tonight Show.*

Joey Bishop, guest-hosting for Johnny Carson that evening, introduced the group by saying "Now here are five lads from England. *I'm told* they're very funny."

"Can you imagine being introduced like that?" Terry Gilliam laughs. "Anyway, we all came on, and they showed a couple of tapes of us. It was a disaster! The audience just sat there with these wonderful blank looks on their faces—they didn't know what to make of us. They just sat there staring with their mouths hanging open. It was great! A total disaster—complete silence.

"We shouldn't have expected much, though. The first sketch they showed was something with Eric in drag, and the audience had no conception at all of what was going on." He chuckles. "We all had a good laugh about it later."

Python humor may never appeal to a mainstream American audience, particularly *Tonight Show* viewers. That evening, any Python dreams of succeeding in America were completely and utterly crushed. They returned to England, and the following February did a stint at the Theatre Royal, Drury Lane.

It was just over two years later that the Pythons returned to America in triumph, following the success of the TV shows and *Monty Python and the Holy Grail* (actually, they had all spent

The Pythons' farewell message to their audience is flashed on the screen at the Hollywood Bowl. Photo copyright KHJ

quite a bit of time in the States in 1975 to promote *Holy Grail*). Warming up by performing at the *Pleasure at Her Majesty's* Amnesty International benefit in London on April 1, 2, and 3, the group then did a three-week run at New York's City Center from April 14 through May 2, 1976, which was a major success, and endeared themselves to their American fans even more. Reviews were good as well, with *Time* magazine noting that "No matter how high the brow or how low, *Monty Python Live!* creases it with jet-propelled mirth," even though a picture of Michael Palin as a camp judge was incorrectly identified as Neil Innes. The group itself enjoyed working before the live audi-

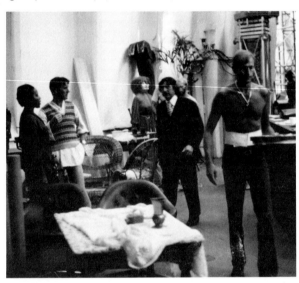

Backstage at the Bowl: Palin waits in Gumby sweater, Jones is in formal attire prior to exploding during "Never Be Rude to an Arab," and Chapman carries off a box of Whizzo Chocolates. A wireless radio mike is visibly strapped onto Chapman. Photo copyright KHJ

ence, though they began to tire of doing the same material night after night. In fact, the three weeks at the City Center was the last time they would perform the show for such an extended period.

"City Center was a lot of fun," recalls Neil Innes. "I took my family to New York that time, and we had an apartment over at West 74th Street. It was quite a phenomenon, because everybody knew the material. . . . There was a great feeling of everybody sharing something, no matter how silly it was."

By the time they finally returned to the stage in 1980, the Pythons only performed for four nights. They took the stage at the Hollywood Bowl

September 26–29, with an open dress rehearsal prior to opening night. This was the most elaborate presentation of the live show yet. A large screen for the backstage projection of films and animation was hung over the stage, while two larger screens were hung on either side. These two were also used to project closeups of the Pythons, so that even the last rows could see the smallest details onstage. As the Hollywood Bowl was not designed for the type of show presented by the Pythons, each had to be wired for sound. Individual wireless microphones were painfully taped to each of them, which caused sound-quality problems up until opening night.

The show was also recorded for possible presentation on a premium cable system, or as a theatrical film, with Terry Hughes (who directed *Ripping Yarns*) at the helm. The end result, *Monty Python Live at the Hollywood Bowl,* saw a limited theatrical release and eventually came out on videocassette and cable. *Hollywood Bowl* is representative of the Pythons live onstage, though the show contains new material taken from *Monty Python's Contractual Obligation Album,* which had been released earlier in the year. Terry Jones makes several attempts to sing "Never Be Rude to an Arab," while a barbershop quartet moons the audience after performing "Sit on My Face."

The group actually decided to do the *Hollywood Bowl* shows out of frustration, when they were getting nowhere attempting to write what would eventually become *The Meaning of Life.*

"After about thirteen weeks, I said 'Let's just leave it for a few months,' " says John Cleese. "At the time, we thought 'Well, we spent thirteen weeks not doing anything, and we need a bit of cash. What about the Hollywood Bowl?' We'd been invited to California, and we'd said no because we thought we'd be writing the final draft of the movie. There's very little money to be made out of the show itself—there's only four nights, and one can imagine what it costs. But, out we came!"

Cleese says that, although the show is not that difficult to prepare for, the Hollywood Bowl posed some special problems. "When we're in the Hollywood Bowl, we can very easily lose control of the whole thing, because if the mike dies on us, we are dead," he commented backstage midway through the run. "There's nothing we can do about it. We didn't get enough rehearsal, because it was a very complicated thing to put up,

and it was distinctly rough for the first couple of nights."

He is interrupted by Palin, who notes that "The real dress rehearsal was on opening night. I wonder if the Beatles had these problems . . ."

Some of the funniest parts of the stage show were the result of unplanned moments or

A constant stream of celebrities was swarming around the backstage area at the Bowl; Cleese poses with Saturday Night Live's *Laraine Newman.* **Photo copyright KHJ**

near-disasters. Palin and Cleese broke each other up fairly regularly during "Silly Walks" and "Dead Parrot," with Palin claiming that he found it so easy to break up Cleese, that he felt almost guilty about it. The "Church Police" always contained shaky moments; the "Hand of God" fingered the wrong suspect; and Terry Jones's Pepperpot kept losing his wig on one memorable night, resulting in the rest of the group cracking up considerably.

Reflecting on the success of Python, Cleese says they had no idea when they were first writing that they would be performing more than a decade later before thousands of people in America.

"The funny thing about all this is that it was just written in two or three peoples' little houses," says Cleese. "Then we suddenly find it's successful with the BBC, we hear they like it in Australia, and then they're selling it in Germany and Denmark. The next thing we hear, it's beginning to catch on in America. If it all happened at once, it might drive us crazy, but when it happens very gradually, we sort of accept it.

"These little things were all so private when we wrote them—just two people in a room in London. When we finish up doing them to eight thousand people in California, there's something slightly strange about it."

The Program

The running order for the various stage shows varied, but the major sketches generally remained in all the incarnations. The *City Center* shows contained most of the elements of the early shows, as well as some that were only included in the later shows. The running order is as follows:

The "Llama"
Animation—Nini Nana
"Gumby Flower Arranging" (with Michael Palin)
Animation—Conrad Poohs and his Dancing Teeth
"Link to Secret Service" (with John Cleese as a
    recruiter)
"Wrestling" (Graham Chapman wrestles himself)
"Silly Olympics" (from the German TV shows)
Neil Innes—"Short Blues"
Animation—*2001*
    leads to
    "World
    Forum/Com-
    munist
    Quiz"
Neil Innes—"I'm
    the Urban
    Spaceman"
"Silly Walks" leads
    to *Silly
    Walks* film
"Mary, Queen of
    Scots on the
    Radio"
"Salvation Fuzz/
    Church
    Police"

"Bruces' Philoso-
    pher's Song" plus the Song Sheet
"Crunchy Frog"
Neil Innes—"Protest Song"

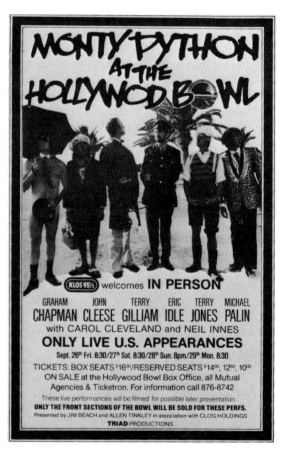

Handbills promoting the City Center and Hollywood Bowl shows. Photo copyright Python Productions, Ltd.

194

Animation—Charles Fatless
"Travel Agent"
"Custard Pies"
"Dead Parrot" (with John Cleese)
"Two Camp Judges"
Animation—Flasher Love Story
"Blackmail"
Neil Innes—"Stoop Solo"
The History of Flight film
"Albatross and the Colonel Stopping It"
"Nudge, Nudge"
"Idiotting" (demonstrations of idiocy

under strobe lights)
Neil Innes—"How Sweet to Be an Idiot"
Philosophers' Football film–Part 1
"Four Yorkshiremen"
Philosophers' Football film–Part 2
"Argument"
Terry Gilliam's Song on a Wire
Little Red Riding Hood film
"Courtroom"
The "Lumberjack Song"
Opening Titles film
"Pet Shop" (with the Parrot)

The Amnesty International Benefits

The members of Monty Python have taken part in several of the annual Amnesty International benefit shows held in London, performing with members of *Beyond the Fringe,* the Goodies, *Not the Nine O'Clock News,* and numerous other British comedy stars. Contents ranged from old Python sketches to completely new material, with various groups mixing up personnel. John Cleese, in particular, became a powerful force behind the shows, serving as director for several of them.

With *The Secret Policeman's Ball,* the focus of the shows began to swing away from comedy and move toward rock music, with performances by Pete Townshend, Donovan, Eric Clapton, and Jeff Beck. Eventually, the rock stars seemed to take over the Amnesty benefits. The various Pythons all continue to be involved with various charities and benefits, although not as a group.

Pleasure at Her Majesty's, presented April 1–3, 1976, involved all the Pythons (except Eric Idle), along with Carol Cleveland, the Goodies, and most of *Beyond the Fringe.* The show has been preserved as a TV documentary, *Pleasure at Her Majesty's* (shown in America on PBS), a record album, *A Poke in the Eye With a Sharp Stick,* and even an unauthorized film called *Monty Python Meets Beyond the Fringe,* which consists of noth-

ing more than the TV documentary with the backstage scenes edited out (an unscrupulous impresario in Washington tried to pass it off as a new Monty Python film).

The Pythons' contributions include the "Dead Parrot," a courtroom sketch with Peter Cook filling in for Idle as the defendant, and Graham Chapman lecturing on the history of practical jokes, while Jones, Palin, and Gilliam assist him. Cleese and Jonathan Lynn portray the Pope and Michelangelo in a scene recorded for *Monty Python Live at the Hollywood Bowl.* And Terry Jones appears with the *Fringe* in their Shakespearean sketch "So That's the Way You Like It." The show ends with Palin and the entire cast singing the "Lumberjack Song"; in the documentary, he forgets some of the words and is assaulted by the cast members.

An Evening Without Sir Bernard Miles, presented on May 8, 1977, featured John Cleese and Connie Booth, as well as Terry Jones. The rest of the cast included Peter Cook and Dudley Moore, Jonathan Miller, and Peter Ustinov. Directed by Jones and Miller, a record album of the show was released entitled *The Mermaid Frolics.*

The Secret Policeman's Ball, presented in June 1979, and its followup, *The Secret Police-*

man's Other Ball, were the largest and most successful Amnesty shows, with resulting books and record albums. The two shows were combined and released in America as *The Secret Policeman's Other Ball,* and again contain contributions from all the Pythons except Idle. A subsequent Amnesty benefit, *The Secret Policeman's Third Ball,* contained only a brief appearance by John Cleese in which he appeared in a sketch to accept an award, which spoofed his refusal to participate in that show.

PYTHON ON FILM

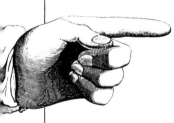

And Now For Something Completely Different

The success of the TV series caught the attention of numerous entrepreneurs, including Victor Lownes of the London Playboy Club. A great fan of the group, Lownes apparently felt that Python would go over well in the States, and the best way to introduce Monty Python to America would be with a feature film.

Lownes approached the group with the idea of refilming some of the best television material for the big screen. He convinced them that the project would make them a great deal of money, and break them into the American market. In fact, with a budget of only eighty thousand pounds, the movie quickly regained its costs, though the Pythons themselves earned very little from it.

So, for five weeks in October and November 1970, the Pythons shot at a former dairy in north London, repairing to the country for some location footage. The group had assembled sketches from the first and second series, and, except for some new linking material, the scenes were nearly the same as their TV originals.

Directed by Ian MacNaughton (who was also at the helm of their TV shows) the group found themselves under the close scrutiny of Lownes. He made suggestions about the design and contents of the film, and probably tried to exert more control over the group than the BBC had at that point. He strongly objected to a sketch featuring Michael Palin as Ken Shabby, and subsequently, Shabby did not appear in the film. Palin has characterized the film as consisting of a lot of men behind desks, and removing Shabby for no logical reason left more sketches behind desks.

Lownes was not content with the removal of Shabby, however. Terry Gilliam designed many of the titles in the typical grandiose *Ben Hur* blocks of stone, and Lownes wanted him to redesign the titles to include his name in such a fashion. Gilliam refused, and yet another battle broke out.

Not surprisingly, the Pythons are not particularly fond of their first screen effort. Although the material is good and the performances tend to be up to par, the feature isn't appreciably better than the TV shows. In fact, *And Now For Something Completely Different* looks much like the TV sketches blown up for the big screen, despite their refilming.

The feature opened in Britain in December 1971, and received mostly good reviews, but due in part to poor publicity and distribution, it failed when it was released in the States in late spring 1972, confirming the opinion of some of the group members that the show would never work in America. It was only when the TV series began to catch on in America in 1974–75 that *ANFSCD* surfaced again, and is now a perennial favorite on campuses and cable, and in revival houses.

☞ AND NOW FOR SOMETHING COMPLETELY DIFFERENT
KETTLEDRUM/PYTHON PRODUCTIONS FILM, DISTRIBUTED BY COLUMBIA (UK), 1971 88 MIN.

AND NOW . . . CONTAINS THE FOLLOWING SKETCHES FROM THE FIRST AND SECOND SERIES OF *MONTY PYTHON'S FLYING CIRCUS:*

"How to Avoid Being Seen," followed by the Man in the Dinner Jacket (JC) and the animated Titles. A Theater Compère (TJ) introduces a man with a tape recorder up his nose. A Hungarian (JC) visits a tobacconist but uses a faulty phrase book, and the author is taken to court.

An animated sequence features a garden of hands, and a careless shaver cuts off his head.

Arthur Putey (MP) and his Wife (CC) visit a marriage counselor (EI), who takes a special interest in Mrs. Putey.

Animation involves a hungry baby carriage, and Michelangelo's *David.*

A City Gent (TJ) is annoyed by Another Man (EI) and his innuendoes in a pub in "Nudge, Nudge," followed by a Drill Instructor (JC) trying to teach his men self-defense against fresh fruit. The

Colonel (GC) warns the show about getting too silly, after which a group of old ladies, Hell's Grannies, goes around attacking young people. This is followed by a group of military fairies swishing and drilling.

An animated fairy tale features a Prince who notices a black spot on his face. It soon kills the Prince and goes off on its own.

A Young Man (EI) tries to join a mountain-climbing expedition led by Sir George Head (JC), whose double vision has inspired him to build a bridge across the twin peaks of Mt. Kilimanjaro. A link follows with several women in bikinis and the Man Without his Dinner Jacket (JC), leading into "Police Fairy Story" (MP and JC); and a Flasher (TJ) who walks along the street frightening women.

Animated Communist Chinese attack, but are stopped by Uncle Sam, followed by commercials for Crelm Toothpaste and Shrill Oil, 20th Century Frog, and Conrad Poohs and his Dancing Teeth.

"Ken Ewing (TJ) and his Musical Mice" involves a nightclub performer who tries to play "The Bells of St. Mary's" with a mallet and a group of specially tuned white mice, but is chased off by disgruntled patrons.

"It's the Arts" features an interview with director Sir Edward Ross (GC, by JC), followed by a Milkman (MP) who is led into a trap.

"Joke Warfare" follows, in which the funniest joke in the world is written, and anyone who hears it dies laughing; it is quickly put into use by the military.

Animation sees "The Killer Cars," and a dancing Venus, which leads into the "Dead Parrot": Mr. Praline (JC) tries to return a dead parrot to the pet shop from which he has just bought it. The Proprietor (MP) of the shop reveals his desire to be a lumberjack, and launches into the "Lumberjack Song," accompanied by a chorus of Mounties.

A link by the Man in the Dinner Jacket (JC) as he is roasting on a spit, leads into the "Restaurant" sketch, which sees a Couple (GC and CC) in an elegant restaurant given a dirty fork, and the place is eventually turned into a shambles with subsequent apologies.

Animation sees Rodin's "The Lovers" become a musical instrument.

A Masked Bandit (JC) tries to hold up a lingerie shop, under the mistaken impression that it's a bank. Two coworkers (EI and JC) in an office high-rise watch falling stockbrokers and accountants fall past their window, followed by a letter of complaint. An animated sequence sees a caterpillar undergo a metamorphosis.

The "Vocational Guidance Counselor" sketch features the dull, boring, timid Arthur Putey (MP) visiting the Counselor (JC) in hopes of becoming a lion tamer. "Blackmail," hosted by Wally Wiggins (MP), is a quiz show that attempts to extort money from viewers. In a link, the Colonel (GC) is caught in an embarrassing position before introducing the Batley Townswomen's Guild, which reenacts the Battle of Pearl Harbor in a field of mud. After this, a Couple (TJ and CC) in bed watch suggestive films.

Finally, the "Upper-Class Twit of the Year Contest" sees the Pythons compete in such events as the "matchbox jump" and "waking up the neighbors" before the winners are announced, and the credits roll.

Monty Python and the Holy Grail

The true turning point for Python was the success of *Holy Grail* in 1975. By that time, the TV series had ended for good, and the members of the group were preparing to go their separate ways. Had *Holy Grail* been a failure, they would have likely drifted apart permanently, despite the return of John Cleese for the filming and the success of the TV shows in America.

But for the first time, the Pythons were about to make some significant profits for their work, and discover just how widespread their popularity had become.

The group had toyed with the idea of writing a full-length feature since the beginning of the third series of shows, and they had all begun writing with an eye in that direction.

"I was very keen to do a movie," recalls Terry Jones, "and John really wasn't at that time. John had been very keen on *And Now For Something Completely Different,* and Victor Lownes had been very close to John about that. I think John thought we were going to make a lot of money out of that movie, and we didn't. So, he wasn't that interested when we were setting up *Holy Grail,* but everybody else seemed to be keen on the idea.

"With the first script, *Holy Grail* was just going to be another Python mish-mash again, half in modern-day, half medieval. We had some time off, and during that time I thought to myself 'I'd much rather do it all medieval'—I was in my Chaucer period at that time. When we all met again, I said 'Let's make it all medieval.' I thought everybody was going to object. I was surprised when everybody went along with that."

The Palin/Jones team in particular was turning out material dealing with the Middle Ages, although many of the sketches were set in modern-day Britain, as well. The original idea had been for the knights to buy a grail in the Grail Hall at Harrod's in London, because Harrod's had everything. The Pythons had to watch their budget carefully, which also restricted their possibilities.

The lack of money, however, didn't restrain their creativity during the writing process. "We've never really restricted ourselves in writing, even in *Holy Grail,"* Michael Palin observed years later. "We never said 'We can't do this.' We wrote it, then pared it down if someone said we couldn't do it. We'd been very heavily financially controlled in the TV series, and after that, Python has always been spreading our wings to come out into films. Rather than make economics that ruin sketches or scenes, we write the scenes first, then find a way of doing them."

In fact, it was the idea for the coconuts (knights accompanied by squires clapping coconut shells together, making a sound like horses' hooves) that marked a turning point. They were able to perform without real horses, and decided to set the entire film in the Middle Ages, which Terry Jones had been studying extensively anyway (in preparation for his *Chaucer's Knight* book).

As the creative aspects were being assembled, the business side was hammered out as well. Theatrical producer Michael *(Rocky Horror Show)* White put together a group of investors for the low-budget project that included members of Led Zeppelin, Pink Floyd, and three record companies. The result was a movie made for the astonishingly low cost of 229,000 pounds. The Pythons performed virtually for free in return for the (hoped-for) profits.

While on the set of *Meaning of Life,* Michael Palin reflected on the changes in less than ten years of Python films. "With *Grail,* we had to do everything ourselves. We only had a budget of 500,000 dollars, and here, we have about eight million, so it makes things a bit easier. I get driven to the studio in the morning, instead of having to drive myself and three other Knights of the Round Table in a pickup truck."

The writing proved first rate and very funny, with all of the group turning out some of their best material. Although the Cleese/Chapman team usually wrote most of the verbal material, one of the funniest visual jokes was written by them as well, involving the killer bunny rabbit attacking the knights.

"John and Graham wrote that very early on," says Terry Jones. "They got more visual while Mike and I got less visual, and that's one of the best examples, actually. . . . It was one of those things that we were dying to do—it sounded like such a funny idea, and it looked so good."

The team wanted to retain as much control as possible, and opted to direct their first original feature themselves; Terry Jones and Terry Gilliam shared the duties. "From the beginning, I was very involved in the shape of the shows when we

The group, in good spirits, during the Grail *filming. Left to right: Chapman is King Arthur, Idle is Sir Robin the Brave, Palin is Galahad the Chaste, Jones is Bedevere the Wise, and Cleese is Lancelot the Brave; in the front is Gilliam as the brave and loyal Patsy.* **Photo copyright Python Productions, Ltd.**

did the TV series, and I was always involved in the editing of them. I felt a very strong commitment to the finished product, and actually seeing the thing right through to the final edit," explains Terry Jones, who says they really were only concerned with protecting what they had written.

"I don't think there was any desire to direct in the first place. It was just a result of seeing things get screwed up that we knew should be done a better way."

Still, it proved difficult for the group to have the two Terries calling the shots. In fact, it actually created divisions within the group.

"We really weren't working as happily as we normally did, and there was more friction," Gilliam explained a few years later. "Where Ian MacNaughton got all the shit before, suddenly there was Terry and me to be picked on, because we were the ones who'd been doing it wrong, even though we knew we were doing it better than they could have.

"The group actually started splitting internally. I mean, we'd always argued, but suddenly there were almost two groups. There was the group of four that were just acting, and the other two who were running around doing ten million jobs. Working on a film is a reasonably boring job if we're just acting, because we sit around all day waiting for the directors and the cameraman and everyone else to get their jobs together. Then we go out and do our bit, which only seems to take about a minute, whereas it seems to take about forty-five minutes to set up the shot.

"Everybody gets bored waiting, and I thought tempers went off a lot. And, I think Terry and I were trying to prove that we could direct. Actually, it was the first thing we had ever done, so we were very tense," says Gilliam.

"There were great moments, it was a great hoot a lot of times, but I still thought directing *Holy Grail* was very rough. I think directing is a really shitty job, unless it's my own project. Doing a group film, and having to shout at people to get something done that they wrote, gets a bit irritating. I was actually shouting, and got fed up with the whole thing."

The greatest portion of *Holy Grail* was shot at a castle in the Scottish countryside, and conditions were far from good. The weather wouldn't cooperate—it seemed to rain nearly every day, the crew was dissatisfied, and morale plummeted.

In addition, Graham Chapman's drinking was worse than ever. As he tells it, he made the decision to stop drinking on the morning of the first day of filming. As King Arthur, he was preparing to cross the Bridge of Death, over the Gorge of Eternal Peril. Early in the morning, out in the countryside, Chapman was disturbed to find that neither he nor any of the crew had brought any alcohol along, and he began shaking. It was then that he admitted to himself that his work was suffering because of his drinking, and decided he was going to quit (which he did, successfully, in December 1977).

Costumer Hazel Pethig also recalls that his drinking had, by this point, started to cause prob-

Dressed as King Arthur, Chapman contemplates his greatest real-life battle, as he resolves to quit drinking. **Photo copyright Python Productions, Ltd.**

Crossing the Bridge of Death over the Gorge of Eternal Peril proved to be dangerous for the cast, and Cleese confesses that a professional mountaineer actually performed the stunt dressed as Sir Lancelot. **Copyright Python Productions, Ltd.**

lems. "We were all loving Graham, he wasn't short of love, but when he was forgetting his line—well, we all cared about him so much, but it meant that getting his gloves off was a job, because his hand was shaking so bad."

Ironically, it was Chapman who came through when tensions were at their peak. According to David Sherlock, a Chapman collaborator, morale was dragging during the first two weeks. "The cast and crew were really being worked very hard, and they had lost a lot of feeling about what they were doing a week and a half into the filming. They still hadn't seen any rushes, so they really didn't get an idea of what they were doing. Terry J and Terry G were pushing them awfully hard. I don't think they realized at the time just how the crew felt."

Sherlock says that the crew had almost reached the point where they were ready to mutiny—actually walk out.

"Somehow, Graham seemed to sense it. That night, he had the whole cast and crew meet in the bar, and started buying drinks for everyone. Graham had started up a singalong, and I don't think he let anyone else buy a drink all night. Graham is really quite shy, so the whole evening was hard for him at first. But that night, the whole

unit seemed to develop the unity that had been lacking; they developed the strong bond that made them keep going.

"The next night, the rushes finally came in, so everybody got a chance to see what they were working on. They saw they had a winner, so they went all out for the film from that point on," Sherlock says.

Neil Innes, who composed and performed the music, also acted in a variety of roles, notably as the minstrel singing "The Ballad of Sir Robin" ("To call it acting is a bit generous." Innes laughs. "Just say I appeared onscreen."). He recalls that they had to keep each other's spirits up.

"It was pretty miserable, up on the Scottish mountainside in string chain mail, with wet feet, but we did have a bit of fun once in the car, dressed as these silly k-nigets. Filming is a very lengthy process, and when one runs out of crosswords halfway up a Scottish mountain, one tended to think of other silly games to play," Innes says.

"I said it would be fun to decline the verb 'to sheep-worry.' John came up with the future pluperfect 'I am about to have been sheep-worried.' It was the sort of thing we did to pass the time."

Even though morale improved, the filming still ranged from unpleasant and uncomfortable to grueling. The tiny budget forced them to cut corners and take chances that they would rather have avoided. John Cleese recalls that many of his most uncomfortable, dangerous moments in all of Python occurred during the *Holy Grail* filming.

"The toughest shot for me was swinging backwards and forwards on a rope, because I was getting tired after five or six takes," Cleese explains, describing the scene where Sir Lancelot disrupts a wedding party by slaughtering several of the bridal party and their guests.

"The other dangerous one was playing Tim the Enchanter, up on a very high mountain peak. Every time I stood up to do a take, the wind would catch my clothes, and I'd get blown backwards slightly. There was actually a drop behind me that would have killed me if I'd fallen, and I was only operating in an area of about three by six feet. That was a bit hairy, particularly as the explosives kept going wrong, and I was up there over an hour."

The only Python stunt Cleese ever backed out of was in *Holy Grail,* as well, and involved running across the Bridge of Death. "I had tried crossing it the previous day," Cleese says. "I walked across, to try to work myself up to running across it. I came back and said 'There's no way I can run across there!' It was slippery, and we were in those strange, knitted-string chain-mail outfits. On the soles of our feet was just a plain bit of leather, nothing on them at all—no rubber, no indentations—so, they got a mountaineer to do it. He ran across it as though it were a road. Quite extraordinary! That's the only bit I ever chickened out of."

Pethig confirms the problem. *"Holy Grail* was very difficult for them, wearing all that string-net armor, with wet ground underfoot, and helmets. They weren't very pleasant costumes at all. And the things they had to do—Michael had to look as though he was eating mud. It was very uncomfortable for him, lying around in the mud, cold and wet . . .

"Because it was their first feature, there was very little money. I worked as a wardrobe mistress, the wardrobe van driver, the costume designer, and a dresser; we didn't have any facilities. I remember dragging bags of costumes up mountainsides with no one to help us. It was never the Pythons' fault," says Pethig, noting that they suffered more than anybody. "It was their first feature, and they hadn't been backed properly . . . It was challenging to manage with so little money, and it was terribly hard work. I was happy to just get through and finish it without having a nervous breakdown."

Despite all the trials and tribulations of the filming, however, the final result was most impressive. Audiences and critics alike praised it,

Although all the group met in New York City to promote the American opening of **Holy Grail,** *they split up after the initial publicity push to concentrate on regional screenings. Eric Idle and Terry Gilliam traveled to the West Coast, while Graham Chapman and Terry Jones flew in to Chicago, appearing at the theater for its Midwestern premiere, answering questions from the audience, and handing out free coconuts to the first 500 people.* **Photos copyright KHJ**

but it meant even more than that to the Pythons. It was the group's first major success away from the BBC, so it built their confidence, and proved to them that they could contend with longer forms of comedy.

And it proved as much of a joy to watch as it was an ordeal to film. It was an immediate hit, and they all seemed to realize that the real future of Monty Python would be in movies.

☞ MONTY PYTHON AND THE HOLY GRAIL
RELEASED APRIL 1975 BY CINEMA 5/ COLUMBIA (US) AND EMI (UK) 90 MIN.

The film begins with King Arthur (GC) and his servant Patsy (TG) approaching a castle, Patsy banging coconut halves together to simulate hooves of a nonexistent horse. Arthur is unsuccessful attempting to recruit knights for his court at Camelot, as the residents of the castle are more interested in where he obtained the coconuts.

A Man (EI), collecting dead bodies of plague victims, has trouble with an Overeager Customer (JC), and they identify the King as he passes.

King Arthur encounters a pair of Peasants (TJ and MP) who refuse to acknowledge his authority, citing constitutional theory.

The King encounters a fearsome Black Knight, who tries to prevent him from passing. A fierce and bloody battle leaves the Knight the worse for wear, but still belligerent.

During their quest for the Holy Grail, Arthur and Bedevere encounter the fearsome Knights Who Say Ni.
Copyright Python Productions, Ltd.

An angry mob captures a Witch (CB), but Sir Bedevere (TJ) questions their judgment, and helps them apply logic and scientific method.

Arthur and Bedevere are joined in their quest by Lancelot (JC), Galahad (MP), and Robin (EI), and they approach Camelot, where an elaborate song and dance fest is in full swing. They see an animated vision telling them to seek the Holy Grail, and they begin their quest at a French castle, where they are taunted by a Frenchman (JC). A plan by Bedevere to attack the fortress with a giant Trojan rabbit fails. A modern-day historian lectures until he is slaughtered by a medieval knight, and the adventure of Sir Robin begins.

Accompanied by a band of minstrels (led by NI) who sing of his courage, Robin encounters a giant three-headed knight, and bravely runs away.

Sir Galahad the Chaste tries to track down the Grail at the Castle Anthrax, where 160 young, beautiful girls are living by themselves. They try to tend to his every need, but he is rescued by

Lancelot, who tries to launch an attack on the girls.

Arthur and Bedevere encounter an Old Man (TG), who gives them a vital clue to the Grail, and the two of them meet the Knights Who Say Ni, and are sent on a mission to find them shrubbery.

An animated sequence finds a monk disturbed by the "bloody weather," and at Swamp Castle, an Angry Father (MP) holds his son, Prince Herbert (TJ), captive before his wedding. His two dim-witted guards (EI and GC) are instructed to keep him in the room, but Lancelot arrives to rescue the Prince, slaughtering several guests and the bride's father.

Meanwhile, Arthur and Bedevere encounter Roger the Shrubber (EI), and complete their mission. They rejoin Robin and the others, and time passes during an animated sequence.

The knights meet Tim the Enchanter (JC), and he leads them to the Cave of Caerbannog, where they have a fierce, bloody battle with the creature guarding the cave. They defeat the small, white rabbit, but do battle inside the cave with the animated Black Beast of Aarrgghhh.

The group finally makes it to the Bridge of Death over the Gorge of Eternal Peril, and have to correctly answer three questions or they will be hurled to their deaths. Some of them make it across during an intermission, and once again encounter the French Taunters, before the final climactic battle.

The film was promoted rather extensively in America; the entire group flew in to New York for the U.S. premiere, which proved extremely successful. A subsequent *Variety* ad showed fans lining up outside the theater beginning at 5:30 a.m. Following the New York premiere, Eric Idle and Terry Gilliam flew out to the West Coast for the L.A. premiere, while Terry Jones and Graham Chapman attended the Midwest opening in Chicago, in which coconuts were given out to the first five hundred patrons. In addition, several cities featured men hired as knights, who walked around in armor passing out handbills, and carrying huge *Monty Python and the Holy Grail* banners.

It was subsequently sold to CBS in the States by accident, and turned up as the Late Night Movie on two occasions in early 1977, cutting it to remove suggestive words and situations, and excess blood. The group subsequently regained the rights to the film, and it was later shown uncut on PBS in America. It is now available on videocassette.

The Life of Brian

RELEASED AUGUST 1979 BY HANDMADE FILMS FOR ORION PICTURES AND WARNER BROTHERS, 90 MIN.

The Pythons had been talking about a followup to *Holy Grail* even before they had finished filming it. Toward the end of the shoot, Eric Idle came up with the joke title *Jesus Christ: Lust for Glory*. The title went no further, but the idea of a Python Bible story remained. A rough draft was ready as early as Christmas 1976, and work progressed slowly but surely. The Pythons had pretty well drifted off on their own, but as the writing continued they regrouped for such projects as the City Center stage shows.

The concept of a Python life of Christ evolved into the story of Brian, the thirteenth apostle. The group found that there was nothing about the life of Christ that invited ridicule, and so diverted the film into an attack on religions that pervert the teachings of Christ, and those that blindly follow—all years before the televangelist scandals.

"The Gospel According to St. Brian" was to be the story of the least-known disciple, the one who looked after the business side of things while none of the others were making any money. Cleese explains that Brian always missed the most significant events, such as arriving late for the Last Supper because his wife had friends over that evening.

The group discovered yet another problem in hammering out the storyline: every time Christ would make an appearance, the laughter stopped. More rewrites were called for, and the film turned into the story of a man whose life paralleled Christ's, now titled "Brian of Nazareth." The group decided to go off together on a working holiday in Barbados for two weeks in January of 1978 to finalize the script and the concepts. It paid off, giving them a much clearer idea of the final story. As Cleese wrote shortly after the session, "It is now called *The Life of Brian*. Brian is no longer a disciple, just a bloke in Judea in 33 A.D. . . . ."

"That was the first time, really, that all the Pythons had been together for such a prolonged period of time in years, and it was very productive," explained Michael Palin a few months later. "Ideas got thrashed out and worked through very fully, and the script is very much tighter as a result. So we're all very pleased with the script, very committed to the movie, and every single member of Python is raring to go on it."

Arranging the finances proved to be more difficult than they had anticipated, and they suffered a major financial setback. Originally planning to shoot in Tunisia in April 1978, the project was delayed for six months, during which time the script was revised and polished. The result was a very different film than would have originally been shot.

A representative of EMI had encountered the Pythons in Barbados during their writing session, and the company had agreed to give the group two million pounds to make the film. A month later, however, the head of EMI read a copy of the script, and backed out of the deal, leaving the Pythons high and dry. So in April, instead of shooting *Brian,* Michael Palin found himself in New York hosting *Saturday Night Live,* where he discussed the situation.

"Lord Bernard Delfont and EMI, the British company that had given us the money, got cold feet for some reason—partly money and partly taste. I think mostly taste," explained Palin. "He was worried that he might get involved in a film that had imaginative content, and that he might possibly be called upon to justify his support for in the next life. He was unwilling to take this risk with immortality.

"The offer of money was so firm that we

A rather bored-looking Chapman and Palin relax in Pilate's audience chamber; this is the costume Palin had contemplated wearing on his **Saturday Night Live** *appearance.* **Photo copyright KHJ**

had actually started on the film, and we're attempting to recover the money by legal methods. At the moment, we've put the film off until September. Our producer, John Goldstone, is in America at the moment talking to various people, and we hope to get the money together soon. So we have the script, we have done quite a bit of preliminary work on locations, we have costumes being made. I was trying on Pontius Pilate's costume the other day—I thought I might wear it on *Saturday Night Live,* but no . . ."

Palin explains that if the money hadn't come through, they would still have turned out a Python movie that year. If necessary, they would have combined the two German TV shows into a sketch film.

Of course, *Brian* was by far the most attractive option, and the financing finally came through from a rather unexpected source. George Harrison had long been a fan of the group, and met Eric Idle during the Los Angeles opening of *Holy Grail.* When Idle explained their money problems, Harrison told him that he would give the group the two million pounds. Proving as good as his word, Harrison and business manager Denis O'Brien formed Handmade Films, and became the executive producers of the film, simply because Harrison, a Python fan, wanted to see the movie.

Construction crews were sent to Tunisia during the summer to prepare sets and locations under the watchful eyes of Terry Gilliam. After a week's worth of rehearsals, shooting began on Saturday, September 16, in the city of Monastir. The first scene shot was the stoning, in which Cleese plays an official in charge of a prisoner to

Chapman and Cleese consult with director Jones inside the Tunisian ribat. **Photos copyright KHJ**

be stoned to death for saying the word "Jehovah." Since, in biblical days, women were not allowed at stonings, the Pythons portrayed women who were disguised as men by wearing false beards.

"We've got a very complicated convention going there," Cleese noted shortly after shooting the scene. "It starts out simple, in that women aren't allowed to go to stonings, so they have to put on beards to go there as men to be allowed to go at all. The complicated thing was, two of the women were being played by Eric and Michael. Also, Charles McKeown and Terry Baylor were playing two of the other women, so we had a picture in which four out of the nine faces were men pretending to be women pretending to be men. I suspect that's too difficult for an audience, and I hope we're able to reshoot it with at least three more obvious girls between Mike and Eric, just to help the clarity of it.

"There was an odd atmosphere about that first day, and I couldn't work out what it was. Then I suddenly realized that there was absolutely *no* sense of occasion. If anybody had walked on the set, they could have thought it was the fifth week. It was a lovely feeling, everybody knew just what they were doing, and went about their tasks in a very efficient, unhurried way," Cleese observed.

In fact, the filming was as easy and comfortable as *Holy Grail* had been difficult and unpleasant. As Michael Palin noted on the set, "Compared to *Grail,* working on *Brian* has almost been a holiday. The weather has been beautiful, whereas it was almost constantly raining at the locations in Scotland, and everything is going as smoothly as can be. If this keeps up, I'll almost feel guilty about taking the money."

The group views *Brian* as a comedy epic, given the large scale on which the comedy could be played out. In fact, the "Latin Lesson," which was shot on the second day, took on a different tone than most comedies. Upon joining a revolutionary group, Brian is sent to write "Romans, Go Home" on the palace walls, where he is caught by a sentry.

"When I saw the rushes, I was very struck that here we were, shooting the scene in the Roman Forum at midnight, in very real colors, just as though it were a proper adventure story, and the audience would be on the edge of their seat," notes John Cleese. "I'd never seen a comedy scene played in this slightly forbidding, cool blue light. It's much more like something out of a drama film. Although we may lose a laugh or two because it is shot at night, I think the overall effect is to enhance its quality. It's rather interesting."

Most of the shooting took place at the Ribat (Arabic for "castle") in Monastir, an ancient Moslem landmark, and a building next to it that was built a few years earlier for Franco Zeffirelli's *Jesus*

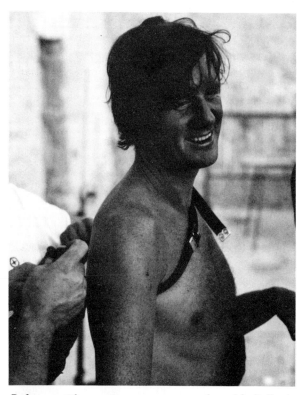

Before setting out on a commando raid, Palin is fitted with a battery pack for his electric lantern. "All of this electricity forces one to be rather careful when having a pee," he noted . . . **Photos copyright KHJ**

Inside a dungeon, Palin confers with a cheerful crucifee (Idle), as the stammering jailor (Gilliam) looks on. **Photos copyright KHJ**

the film is devoid of animation, so Gilliam was able to devote all his time to design. "The closer we come to doing real stories in Python, like this one is, the less room there is for animation. The animation was really a linking device, and now that the thing has such a solid story flow to it, there's no need to link."

Two of the most challenging scenes in the film were tackled early in the production; both involved large crowds that had to react in specific ways to the actors. As Pilate, complete with speech impediment, addresses the crowd, the mob below must react with gales of uproarious laughter. And when Brian, totally nude, throws open his windows after spending the night with Judith, the huge group of followers must react to him and his mother.

With the forum jammed with Tunisian extras, a professional Tunisian comedian was hired to entertain the crowd, in order to get the people laughing properly for the reaction shots to Pilate's speech. However, the mob proved adept at taking Terry Jones's direction, through an interpreter, and the comedian wasn't really needed.

"The 450 Tunisian extras were sensational," enthuses John Cleese. "When they first fell to the ground laughing . . . it was one of the funniest sights I had ever seen. They fell in waves, like something out of a land-based Esther Williams movie."

Although a group of English tourists were

of Nazareth. Filming in that area lasted about five weeks, including four days' filming in Sousse, a few miles north of Monastir (where the unit utilized the ancient city wall on the same spot "where Robert Powell was crucified for Lew Grade," Eric Idle joked). Zeffirelli had shot in many of the same locations as the Pythons did later, and the two stoning sequences were filmed on the same spot.

Terry Jones served as lone director on *Life of Brian,* with Terry Gilliam stepping back and designing the production instead. Still, as he commented halfway through the hoot, he was kept busy enough with his chores. "This is bigger than any of the films we've done before, so there's plenty of pressure to get the stuff ready in time," Gilliam says. "The scale of the amount of things we've built here— it's huge, it's a real epic! I haven't been able to stop the whole time down here."

Except for the spaceship sequence and the opening credits,

A little rain delays the shooting of the crucifixion party, as Jones, Gilliam (out of his jailor makeup), and Palin confer. The rain bonnet on Palin is to protect the curly-haired wig. **Photo copyright KHJ**

recruited for the scene outside Brian's bedroom, most of that group (nearly 750) were also Tunisians, and devout Moslems. As a nude Graham Chapman throws the shutters open to face the crowd— many of whom were forbidden by their religion to view a naked man—he says he heard shrieks and screams from the local women, which somewhat undermined his confidence.

"Those two big crowd scenes could have been real buggers," notes Cleese, "but we got them under our belts, and they all worked."

The interiors of the bedroom scene, shot the next week, saw Brian's mother (played by Terry Jones) discover Judith in her son's bedroom. While Jones was in front of the camera acting, Cleese stood by to help with the performances. "I know how, as an actor, I need two things from a director. Helpful suggestions and criticisms are fine, but what I really need is faster or slower, and bigger or smaller. If I get that, I basically get it right. Graham was a little bit too big at the start, so I brought his performance down, and he really performed beautifully after that. It took Terry a long time to loosen up in the first half, as we need that loose expansiveness to make a comedy scene work at its best. It was not helped this morning by the fact that Terry's entrance was through an extremely small door; in his second entrance, he caught his foot and skinned his instep. All of this builds up pressure, and makes it difficult to build up the really good flowing timing that makes it funny. But we got a really good take just at the end, and

The crucifixion party sets out, with Idle and Chapman (as Brian) in the lead. **Photo copyright KHJ**

we're there now."

The original bedroom scene was written by Cleese and Chapman, and was considerably different from the finished version. "When Brian woke up, he had two girls in bed with him called Cheryl and Karen, and when his mother Mandy knocked on the door, he hid them behind a curtain," Cleese says. "Eventually they giggled, because they didn't think this was quite the behavior of a man who was likely to lead them out of captivity. Mandy found them and asked Brian who they were, and he said 'They're two of my disciples, Mum.' And she said 'Disciples? They haven't got a thing on! What are they doing here?' And Brian said 'We were discussing eternal life, and it got a bit late, so they stayed.'

"We decided to take that out

Camping it up for the camera, with Cleese (center), Kim "Howard" Johnson (right), and Bernard McKenna (far right) with Tunisian extras. **Photo copyright KHJ**

Looking uncharacteristically less than stylish, Palin, in costume as Ben (who has been hanging in manacles for years), sips his tea as makeup girl Elaine Carew prepares another assault on him. **Photo copyright KHJ**

After falling from a balcony, Brian (Chapman) lands on a very boring prophet (Palin), with the help of some of the crew. Palin's boring prophet entertained the crew by improvising long stretches of extremely boring, mundane matters while shots were prepared. **Photo copyright KHJ**

Chapman poses with a dummy double, who will fall from a tower and land on a flying saucer in his place. **Photo copyright KHJ**

in the next draft in Barbados. Judith disappears from the story from about the time Brian goes on the raid. We wanted to get her right back in there just as soon as we could, and this was the first time we could put her back in the story. The scene went through about three different stages."

While shooting in Sousse, where most of the commando scenes in tunnels were filmed, *Goon Show* chief Spike Milligan stopped by while on holiday to visit with the Pythons. The comedic hero and inspiration of the group while they were growing up, Milligan agreed to appear in a scene the next day outside the city wall in Sousse, when the mob following Brian divides itself into shoe, sandal, and gourd factions (which the Pythons refer to as the "entire history of religion" in two minutes).

A couple of weeks later, their financial angel, George Harrison, took a break from mixing his next album to fly down for an overnight visit. He agreed to make a cameo appearance as Mr. Papadopoulis, the man who rents Brian's group the mount for next weekend (his only line is "Hello").

Two weeks of shooting followed near the desert at Matmata near Gabes (where the *Star Wars* desert sequences were filmed). Most of the large outdoor sequences were done there, including the opening sermon and the Wise Men scene. A scene involving a group of shepherds singing the praises of their sheep was also shot there; although it was originally intended as the opening

The life-size model of the flying saucer after it crashes to earth was constructed in a courtyard of the Tunisian castle. It was actually carved from polystyrene of a large statue of Caesar used earlier in the shooting. **Photo copyright KHJ**

sequence of the movie, it was eventually cut to speed the flow of the story. A few final days were spent filming the coliseum scene in Carthage, with Neil Innes joining them as the Christian who battles the gladiator. The post-production was all done in London over the next few months.

One scene had to be completely filmed in the studio, however. When Brian falls off a tower, he is rescued by a spaceship, occupied by two strange-looking aliens. Pursued by an enemy craft, the ship zips off into outer space for a brief battle, which damages both ships. Brian's flying saucer crashes to earth at the exact same place he just left, and a band of Roman soldiers resume their pursuit.

"We were all saying 'We need some animation,' and Graham said 'Why isn't Brian rescued by a flying saucer at this point?' We all thought it was a good idea, though it turned into Terry Gilliam's creation when we did it," explains Terry Jones.

The sequence inside the spaceship was actually the last to be shot, and had to be done two months later in London. At the time, Chapman was living in America, and for tax purposes, he was only allowed twenty-four hours in England.

"I arrived in the morning from Los Angeles, and was driven straight to the studio," Chapman says. "I was put into the box made up to resemble a spaceship, with lights and wires. I was dressed as Brian, shaken around a lot, then taxied back home for a few hours sleep before being put on another plane to L.A. I wasn't in England for more than twenty-four hours, and eight of those were spent in a box. Rather the reverse of one of those relaxation booths—sort of a 'tenser booth.' And it worked, too! I didn't know where I was in the world, or the time, space, anything, for a week after that."

The filmed script ran about two and a quarter hours, and the group had to then edit that down to about ninety minutes. There was some talk of running the entire film, as written, with an intermission. At one point there was even talk of turning it into a two-part film. Finally, it was simply edited down. The shepherd scene was removed, as was an extended subplot to raid the castle and kidnap Pilate's wife (played by six-foot nine-inch John Case in drag), who demolishes her attackers. Perhaps the most controversial scene removed involved Eric Idle as King Otto, leader of a suicide squad. The fascistic, rather Teutonic King told Brian of his plans to "establish a Jewish state that will last a thousand years!" Only a brief appearance at the end, while Brian is on the cross, suggests the vanished scene.

Still, the film proved controversial enough without it. Fundamentalists, most of whom had never seen the film, picketed and protested to have it banned. Life followed art, as thousands wrote angry letters and made angry calls at the suggestion of their religious leaders, attempting to suppress a film whose chief message was "Think for yourselves." One of John Cleese's favorite moments in all of Python is during Brian's address from his bedroom window to his crowd of followers. He says "You've all got to work it out for yourselves," and the crowd of 750 shout "Yes, yes! We've got to work it out for ourselves." Brian says "Exactly," and there is a pause. Then, the entire group shouts in unison, "Tell us more!" Cleese notes that it seldom ever gets a laugh, but

A protest outside the Warner Communications building by another religious group made up largely of people who haven't seen the film—and have yet to learn how to work it out for themselves. **Photo copyright KHJ**

it says all that needs to be said about the protesters.

The film was banned in some southern states in America, and a number of countries as well, but it is still as funny and powerful as when it was first released. Several of the Pythons consider it their best work, and it remains the longest narrative produced by the group.

"It's more natural for six people to produce short spurts," says Terry Jones. "I was always interested in the progression from *Holy Grail* to *Life of Brian*, the fact that in *Life of Brian*, we were actually able to make a story. In retrospect, the failing of that film is that we didn't have enough confidence in the concept of story. We speeded it up so much, in the way that we've always done

Cut from the final print of the film, six-foot, nine-inch British actor John Case played Pilate's wife in the kidnapping attempt. His only remaining role in the film is as Eric Idle's helper in the haggling scene. **Photo copyright KHJ**

212

for sketches, that it actually is too fast now. I would love to recut *Brian* to make it slower. I think it would work better."

After *Life of Brian,* and with the nurturing of Handmade Films, Cleese, Palin, and Gilliam made, respectively, *Privates on Parade, The Mis*sionary, and *Time Bandits* for the company (plans for Handmade to handle *Yellowbeard* did not pan out). Python began drifting even farther apart, but would still reunite for a stage show and a big-budget studio film.

Monty Python Live at the Hollywood Bowl

RELEASED 1982, THE MONTY PYTHON BEGGING BOWL PARTNERSHIP, THORN EMI VIDEO, 78 MIN.

The four nights Monty Python performed at the Hollywood Bowl in 1980 were recorded at the time with an eye on packaging the show for HBO or Showtime. While the show was being presented live, cameras captured the action. It was shown on large screens so that even the back rows could see the closeup expressions on the performers' faces. The shows were edited and eventually released to theaters, though the final film received rather limited promotion and release; it was released on video not long afterward.

The film version differed from the stage show in running order and length. Sketches were rearranged in an effort to improve the flow. In addition, the film runs only seventy-eight minutes—considerably shorter than

***The group relaxes during their successful four nights at the Hollywood Bowl.*
Copyright 1982 Monty Python Begging Bowl Partnership**

the live performance. The film does include several shots of the crowd, and the rabid Python fanatics dressed in various silly costumes. Although most of the material is available elsewhere, the film does include special performances of songs from the *Contractual Obligation Album,* as well as contributions by Carol Cleveland and Neil Innes.

The Meaning of Life

UNIVERSAL, 1983, THE MONTY PYTHON PARTNERSHIP, 103 MIN.

After *Life of Brian,* the Pythons had hoped to turn out a followup film not long afterward. In fact, *The Meaning of Life* took much longer than any of them had anticipated, and almost didn't happen at all.

Although the group had come up with a great deal of material, they hadn't managed to agree on a storyline, and the project stalled. At one time, they were considering "Monty Python's World War III," which was little more than an umbrella title for a series of sketches. During the hiatus in which they were unable to decide on a theme, they ended up doing the stage show at the Hollywood Bowl.

An early version began with a warning that a picture of a huge male penis would be flashed upon the screen soon, and the implications of this were discussed at length. The "middle of the film" section was written to include unbilled cameos by such celebrities as Clint Eastwood and Barbra Streisand. The search for the missing leg also took up a much larger portion of the story than was eventually used.

The possibility of another Python film appeared more and more doubtful, but based on the success of the sojourn to Barbados to polish *Brian,* a writing trip to Jamaica was proposed, possibly out of desperation.

"We decided we'd actually force ourselves to finalize the script," explains Michael Palin. "We actually went to Jamaica with less confidence than we had with *Brian* at that stage. We seemed to be going downhill after three or four days, and nothing new happened."

"There was one point in the writing where we all thought 'This is it, we'll never do anything else again,'" says Terry Jones. "We had a format and sixty percent of the material, and couldn't get it into a shape. On the way there, we all read the script and thought it was disastrous. When we got there, instead of putting the finishing touches to a script that we already had, we were suddenly back to square one trying to decide on a format. After a couple of bad days, I remember waking up with a sinking feeling in the pit of my stomach, feeling this was just not working out.

"Then, I think it was Wednesday morning, I woke up and thought 'I've *got* to do *something,* this is terrible!' I realized that I had a script with the timings on it. I hadn't thought it would be any use, but I brought it along just in case. When I read it, I realized that we'd practically gotten a film. We had sixty or seventy minutes, so all we were talking about was another twenty minutes!

"I came down to breakfast feeling cheerier and more positive. Mike suggested that we all go home and turn it into a TV series, but I said that all we needed was the last twenty minutes. I'd always gone on about it being a life story, only nobody could agree about whose life story it was going to be. At this point, I thought everybody was going to go 'Ooohh, Terry's going on about it,' because that's what I'd been saying for the last two years. But suddenly Eric or John—I can't remember who—said 'It could be *anybody's* life story.' And Eric came up with 'It's the meaning of life!' Over that breakfast, it just returned from the brink of disaster."

The "meaning of life" idea seemed to spark everyone, and the Pythons began creating more material almost immediately. "We clicked onto a very rich vein, and started writing again," says Michael Palin. "In particular, John and Graham went off and wrote a very good opening sketch about a hospital, the birth sequence, which was right up to the very best Python standards. That gave us all confidence, and we came back from Jamaica with the film virtually a definite starter."

The result was a movie that resembled a sketch film, but had a strong connecting thread running through it with the Python version of the Seven Ages of Man.

"Actually, it doesn't feel like a sketch film," says Jones. "It has this weird feeling, this momentum that keeps one hoping it's all about the same thing. It's not like *And Now For Something Completely Different* or *Hollywood Bowl,* which *are* sketch films. It has a continuity of progress in it. While it's not a conventional type of story, it *is* a story.

"Although the structure is much looser than *Brian,* there is a theme, a certain unity to it," says Palin. "I think 'sketch film' sounds dangerously as though we'd put together bits of our old material. I've been saying to people that it's more of a sketch film, but that's wrong. It has a unity and theme."

The Meaning of Life takes aim at a greater variety of targets than *Life of Brian.* "Every Sperm is Sacred," a Palin/Jones song attacking the Vatican's stance on birth control, succeeds on virtually every level, from comedy sketch to social satire to song-and-dance number. Cleese is a headmaster who, with the aid of his wife, demonstrates sexual techniques to a terribly bored and distracted group of schoolboys. Terry Jones as Mr. Creosote forces regurgitation to new highs (or lows) in a gross-out scene so expertly staged and performed that it becomes a triumph of excess.

Other scenes range from a modern-day hospital birth which sees the mother as unqualified to assist the doctors, to the Zulu Wars; from a World War I trench, to a Bergmanesque sequence with the Grim Reaper interrupting a dinner party. The film actually begins with the "Crimson Permanent Assurance," a short subject conceived and directed by Terry Gilliam, which sees elderly accountants sailing their building off for corporate raids.

There is music here, as well, including the title song, the Noël Coward-like "Penis Song," the show number "Christmas in Heaven," and Eric Idle's wonderful "Galaxy Song." *The Meaning of Life* is rich in its variety, and while some sketches misfire and others run long, the winners outnumber the losers, and a few, like "Every Sperm" and "Mr. Creosote," are worth the price of admission in themselves.

Once again, Jones served as sole director of the film, with Gilliam working on his own short subject parallel to the main body of the movie. The majority of the film was shot at EMI–Elstree studios outside of London, although there was a bit of location work.

"The problem really only occurred when we left the studio," says Palin. "There were one or two dangerous moments, where we had shellfire, rockets, and bombs going off, that we filmed just after the IRA had bombed Hyde Park. There were old ladies complaining that they were seeing mushroom clouds in the sky about Elstree, in the middle of the London suburbs . . ."

The "Zulu Charge," shot near Glasgow, Scotland, was the scene of a minor uprising. The black extras apparently claimed they were never told that they were going to be natives charging up a very cold Scottish hillside, and refused to wear loincloths. They claimed it was typecasting, and all went home.

"Actually, it was an absolute blessing in disguise," says Jones. "Because it was a gray day, and the one thing we wanted was a blue sky, because it was supposed to be Africa. Scotland with a gray sky looks like Scotland. I was biting my lip, hoping something would happen that we couldn't do it, and it was amazing—they had this revolt!"

"We had to shoot the next day, with white people blacked up," says Palin. "It was very sad. We deliberately tried very hard to get authentic black people in Glasgow, which is in itself quite difficult, so we ended up with three hundred unemployed shipyard workers. We could only black up the fronts of them, because we didn't have enough blacking to do their whole bodies—just their fronts were seen as they charged. If we'd filmed the retreat, we'd have had to spend a lot more money."

Python seldom improvised. As writers, they tended to have a great respect for the written word and generally followed their scripts with great care, although they occasionally improvised one-liners during the "Vox Pops" bits during filming sessions. One of the few true improvised lines in Python occurred in *The Meaning of Life.*

"One of my favorite lines in *Meaning of Life* was something Mike suddenly threw in when we were actually shooting it," says Terry Jones, laughing. "When Death visits the dinner party, the ghosts all get up to go. Mike was going, and they were all going on about the salmon that poisoned them all. Just as the ghosts were suddenly going out the door, Mike's character suddenly says 'Hey, I didn't even eat the salmon!' He just threw it in on that take."

Working with their biggest budget yet, the Pythons labored in comparative luxury. For Palin, his most difficult costume was as the American Nancy Reagan-like socialite (wife of Terry Gilliam) in the Grim Reaper scene. "I was very expensively dressed, with blonde, coiffured hair. By the time I got my makeup on—my eyelashes, punitively painful earrings, and a long red cocktail dress—I looked quite extraordinary, like a real old banger!*

"But it was fairly uncomfortable, and it was one of those sketches that just went on and on. It was fairly simple in terms of lines, but technically quite difficult. It involved location work on a very windy, rainy moorland in North Yorkshire, which I think is the single wettest spot in the British Isles," says Palin.

"One day we didn't film anything at all, but had to be dressed, up there, and waiting. While John went out and was filmed doing his bit, I was still dressed as this socialite on the top of this moorland in this hostel. It was really a hostel for walkers, people who go hiking, men with hairy hands who carry backpacks and all that. The look on their faces when they saw me coming down the stairs in the morning to get my cup of coffee had to be seen to be believed.

"That was quite humorous for a bit, but this went on. We must have spent almost a week on this scene, and having to get up and into this gear every day really put me off transvestism as a career!"

Terry Gilliam was busy with his own project, as well. The "Crimson Permanent Assurance" was originally intended as a three-minute segment in the middle of *Meaning of Life.* Eventually, however, it grew to occupy over fifteen minutes of screen time, and as much time to shoot as the rest of the film put together. The story of the elderly accountants who become pirates intrigued

*Jalopy. Or sausage.

Gilliam, who had finished *Time Bandits* not long before.

"I had always liked the idea of buildings that sail, so I thought I'd write something around that," Gilliam explains. "Piracy was in the air, Graham was working on *Yellowbeard,* and I always fancied doing piratical-type films. It all started tying together, and so the piratical accountants came to the fore."

Gilliam says it was an interesting attempt to do more and different special effects than he'd done before, but it proved much more complicated than he had first thought. "When I approached it, I thought it would be a piece of cake, but it was more complicated—there was a major panic from a production point of view, because nobody took it seriously until it was too late. Then they realized they had something as complicated as the entire rest of the film.

"This thing just grew. What I thought was going to be a five- or six-minute section done with animation, suddenly became seventeen minutes long, because with live action, everything spreads. That's the joke now, it's one-fifth of the film. It's one thing to draw it as a storyboard for animation, but real people take longer to do physically. I can't just go 'Zip!' across the screen—somebody actually has to walk . . . I really just designed it as a cartoon, and we're trying to do it for real," says Gilliam.

Despite the complications with his pirate short, the most difficult part of *Meaning of Life* for Gilliam may have been the bits of animation. "I don't actually 'think animation' very well anymore. I'm much more interested in live action," he says. "The shortcuts one does in cutout animation, all these quantum leaps every two seconds—my mind doesn't work that way now, and it's proven to be extremely difficult. I have to rethink what I was doing, because I don't do it anymore. I think I'm washed up."

Although he does do some acting in the main film, Gilliam says his main interest is actually doing his own movies. Although he still feels a strong bond to Python, he says working on *Meaning of Life* was rather frustrating for him.

"All of the group have such different styles of working now, it makes it harder and harder to keep together. The film was done very luxuriously, and the money that was spent doesn't seem to be on the film. It's spent on creature comforts and more relaxing working, which is all very pleasant.

It's more enjoyable, as a group, working on this film than anything we've ever done before—but I find it hard to work that way. It's too pleasant!''

The final result puzzled the group. As brilliant as it was, it was simply too long to fit in its place in the middle of *The Meaning of Life*. Though they contemplated releasing it as a separate short subject, it ended up as the first reel of the film, although the pirates do show up briefly in an attack on a boardroom.

The Meaning of Life was quite well received at the box office, easily earning back its eighty-million-dollar initial budget. Feelings within the group were mixed, however. Cleese was not delighted with the final result, while at the opposite end of the spectrum—as usual—was Jones, who felt it was the funniest thing they had ever done. While Cleese says he didn't enjoy shooting it, Jones calls directing *The Meaning of Life* "quite enjoyable.''

As much as he liked making *Brian,* Jones says that he enjoyed *Meaning of Life* even more. "When we were away in Tunisia, there was more of a group feeling, because we were all away at the same time, and saw each other every day,'' says Jones.

"I sometimes felt I was making *Meaning of Life* on my own, in that it was always me there. It would be either me and John for a week, or me and Graham for a week, or me and Mike for a week. There weren't many times when it was everybody together. It was great fun to do, but it was slightly more analytical, because we were working in the studio, and coming home to our families.''

Palin concurs that the "location feel" was missing from *Meaning of Life,* even though it wasn't a difficult film to make for him. "The schedule was reasonable, and we were based at home most of the time. But it lacked the 'location friendliness' that we had with *Brian* and *Holy Grail.* We were all away together, and there was a great feeling of the cast and crew being involved on a project, being friendly and mixing much more.''

The question of another Python film is raised less often than it used to be, largely due to the many successes of all of the group members. Still, even those members of the group less anxious to reunite will never rule it out.

Of all the Pythons, Palin remains one of the more firmly committed to new group films and other projects. Despite his many and varied solo successes, he says he hopes to include Python with his own future works.

"I regard Python as something I can only do with the five other Pythons. It brings something out in me as a writer/performer, a satisfaction I can't get in the same way from doing my own stuff. For me, it's terrific if Python keeps going. However successful anything I do, I would love to have the fact that I can go back to Python,'' says Palin.

"In a way, Python is funnier than anything any individual does. For example, *Fawlty Towers* is unquestionably brilliant, but it isn't as unique and special as Python. I have a suspicion that John knows that, too. I'm not belittling any individual projects, but Python is the one really unique feature of all our acting and writing lives.''

INDIVIDUAL PROFILES

Graham Chapman

The tall, blond Graham Chapman was born in Leicester on January 8, 1941. A policeman's son, one of his earliest memories was being taken around by his father to the site of a wartime air raid, and encountering parts of bodies scattered around the area. This may have influenced his decision to seek a career in medicine, as it had his older brother.

It was, however, his love of comedy and his admiration of the Cambridge Footlights Society that led him to study medicine at Emmanuel College, Cambridge. After mounting his own cabaret show, he was invited to join the Footlights at the same time as first-year law student John Cleese, with Eric Idle joining the following year (David Frost was serving as secretary at the time).

Keeping up his medical studies while appearing in the Footlights' production of *Double Take,* he qualified as a doctor at St. Bartholomew's Hospital in London. At approximately the same time, he was invited to tour New Zealand with the

Footlights. To obtain his parents' permission, he parlayed an off-the-cuff comment by the Queen Mother, whom he met at a school function, into a Royal Command to tour Australia, which sufficiently impressed his mother. Putting his medical career on hold, he joined John Cleese on tour with *A Clump of Plinths,* which was retitled *Cambridge Circus* when it ran on Broadway in October 1964, for twenty-three performances.

Returning to England, his medical career proved useful when he started writing for the "Doctor" series, with both Bernard McKenna and John Cleese, including *Doctor at Large, Doctor in Charge, Doctor at Sea,* and *Doctor on the Go,* serving as medical consultant for the series.

Writing for *The Frost Report* followed, where he met and became familiar with Michael Palin and Terry Jones. Chapman began doing more writing with Cleese, who was also performing on Frost's show during this time. With Cleese, Chapman wrote for Marty Feldman's *Marty, The Illus-*

Resting before another Python stage show, Chapman contemplates having to wrestle himself once again. **Photo copyright KHJ**

lock. He also helped to write, along with Eric Idle and Barry Cryer, two series for Ronnie Corbett,* *No, That's Me Over Here,* and *Look Here Now.* In fact, Chapman recalls one period while he was simultaneously writing Python, a Corbett series, and a "Doctor" series, doing one in the morning, another in the afternoon, and the third at night.

Of course, Chapman appeared in all of the Python TV shows and films, playing King Arthur in *Holy Grail* and the title role in *Life of Brian.* The Chapman/Cleese writing partnership began drifting apart, and so Chapman began doing some writing with Douglas *(Hitchhikers' Guide to the Galaxy)* Adams; in early 1976, they collaborated on a BBC special titled *Out of the Trees.*

It was during the period following *Holy Grail* that Chapman fought his most difficult personal battle, and stopped drinking. At his peak, he was consuming two quarts of gin a day. Unfortunately, one of his best friends, Who drummer Keith Moon, fell victim to alcohol and died just before he was to join the Pythons' rep company in *Life of Brian.*

The alcohol-free Chapman turned to his own project before filming *Brian.* He produced, cowrote, and starred in *The Odd Job,* released in England in October 1978. Costarring David Jason, Simon Williams, and Diana Quick, and directed by Peter Medak, the low-budget production was well received, though never distributed in America (the title role, played by Jason, had been written for Moon).

trated *Weekly Hudd,* and of course *At Last, the 1948 Show* just prior to beginning Python. The pair also wrote several screenplays during this pre-Python period, including part of *The Magic Christian,* in which they both appeared with Peter Sellers and Ringo Starr, Chapman playing the head of a rowing team. The two also collaborated on *The Rise and Rise of Michael Rimmer,* and another screenplay that was eventually released under the unfortunate title of *Rentadick* in 1972.

Chapman and Cleese also collaborated on a script for Peter Sellers that was never filmed. Chapman has since rewritten the script titled *Ditto* with David Sher-

Of course, his largest post-Python project was the pirate spoof *Yellowbeard,* on a scale so large that Chapman later felt that he simply lost control over it. With a cast consisting of Marty Feldman, John Cleese, Peter Cook, Cheech and Chong, Peter Boyle, Madeline Kahn, Eric Idle,

On the Life of Brian *set, Chapman, assisted by rep company member Andrew McLachlan, indulges in one of his regular passions, even in the wilds of Tunisia—The Times crossword puzzle.* **Photo copyright KHJ**

*Well-known British TV comic, and half of the Two Ronnies.

220

Kenneth Mars (and many others) its Mexican locales, and filming on MGM's *The Bounty,* all the elements were there. But reviews were mixed and audience response was lukewarm. Chapman himself was unhappy with the final version, even offering to edit the footage himself. The result, though entertaining, fell short of his expectations, and he resolved to maintain control of any future films. He has also developed a script based on his experiences with the real-life "Dangerous Sports Club," a group of Englishmen who hang-glide over active volcanos and launch themselves from catapults.

He is also the only member of Python to write his life story, titled *A Liar's Autobiography, Volume VI.* The highly entertaining, mostly truthful book is alternately witty and startlingly frank as he discusses his alcoholism, homosexuality (including

Speaking to a packed house at Drury College in Springfield, Missouri, on one of his U.S. lecture tours. **Photo copyright KHJ**

an hilarious account of his "Coming-out Party" and the reactions of his guests), and his various misadventures. He actually began writing a sequel on his word processor, but tragically, the nearly completed work was lost during a burglary at his home, when the computer discs were taken.

Following *Brian,* Chapman lived in Los Angeles for a period, where he made numerous TV appearances. Perhaps the most unusual was a week on the *Hollywood Squares,* Nov. 5–9, 1979, and two evening shows. While promoting *The Secret Policeman's Other Ball,* he made a cameo appearance on *Saturday Night Live* wearing a tutu, and was a regular on NBC's short-lived *The Big Show,* a weekly variety hour in which he performed both new and older material (including a version of the "Bookshop" sketch found on the *Contractual Obligation Album*).

It was during an American tour to promote his book that the seeds were planted for an entire-

ly new activity. Attending a screening at Facets Multimedia in Chicago on March 2, 1981, he discovered on his arrival that he was supposed to address the overflowing crowd. He turned the ordeal into a question-and-answer session, and after reviewing tapes of his performance, decided to hit the road with a series of lecture tours. He performed at scores of American colleges during the mid-'80s, delighting the students who had always wanted to see a Python in the flesh. "An Evening with Graham Chapman" evolved into a full-fledged lecture, with clips of Python and the Dangerous Sports Club. Chapman became quite polished and confident, in marked contrast to his shyer, more insecure persona.

In November 1988, a growth was discovered on one of Graham's tonsils and he entered hospital, where it was diagnosed as cancer. He battled valiantly for several months, though the cancer had spread to his spine. His morale was high throughout, however, and he kept making plans to return to work. He signed a deal with Imagine Entertainment and planned to make an appearance at the Chicago Museum of Broadcasting in the first week of October 1989 to observe the 20th anniversary of Monty Python. He joined the other five Pythons and Steve Martin to film a sketch for *Showtime,* playing his role from a wheelchair, but very much enjoying the reunion; the day resulted in talk of another Python project. He was released from hospital in mid-September, feeling fit and pronounced cured.

At the beginning of October he was rushed to hospital where he died two days later. It was October 4th, 1989, the day before the 20th anniversary of the first Python broadcast. A memorial service was held two months later.

John Cleese

Born October 27, 1939, at Weston-Super-Mare, John Marwood Cleese (he once went through a period of using "Otto" as his middle name; and his family name was originally "Cheese" until his grandfather changed it) was tall even as a child, and claims he developed his sense of humor to fend off any teasing by his classmates. He spent five years, from 1953–58, at Clifton College, getting A levels* in physics, math, and chemistry. He then taught at his old prep school for two years while waiting to go to Cambridge's Downing College.

Cleese began studying law, but was invited to join the Footlights his very first year there through three sketches he had written with Alan Hutchinson. In the Footlights he met future writing partner Graham Chapman. He appeared in the 1962 and 1963 Footlights Revues, the latter of which *(Cambridge Circus)* played for five months at the Lyric in the West End. He then took a job at BBC Radio, for fifteen hundred pounds a year, writing jokes for the *Dick Emery Show*. He wrote a Christmas show called *Yule Be Surprised,* with Brian Rix and Terry Scott, a program Cleese claims people still mention to him whenever they want to embarrass him.

Rejoining *Cambridge Circus* in 1964, he toured New Zealand in July, then played on Broadway for three weeks that October (as well as an appearance on *The Ed Sullivan Show*), and continued off-Broadway until the following February (in what is now the Bottom Line).

During this period, Cleese was recruited to appear in a fumetti feature for *Help!* magazine.

In barbership costume and apron, ready to perform "Sit on My Face." Photo copyright KHJ

The assistant editor was a young American named Terry Gilliam.

After *Cambridge Circus* folded that February, Cleese stayed on in New York to appear in the U.S. production of *Half a Sixpence* for six months, as the man who embezzles Tommy Steele's money. During his tenure with the show, he claims that his spectacular lack of musical ability caused the director to insist that he never sing, but stand in the back and mouth the words to the songs.

After an unsuccessful two-month stint writing on international politics for *Newsweek,* he then joined the *American Establishment Review* to perform in Chicago and Washington, before returning to London at Christmas time.

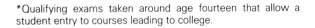

*Qualifying exams taken around age fourteen that allow a student entry to courses leading to college.

Cleese had written some sketches for David Frost's *That Was the Week That Was,* so when Frost asked him to join *The Frost Report,* he resumed his writing partnership with Graham Chapman. Eric Idle, Terry Jones, and Michael Palin were all writing for the show at the time as well, while Marty Feldman, the Goodies, and the Two Ronnies also did some writing or performing for Frost. Cleese performed as well; particularly notable are sketches done with Ronnie Corbett and Ronnie Barker which featured

A family shot on the set of Time Bandits, *with the six Bandits in the front row; in the back are Terry Gilliam and daughter Amy, film executive George Harrison and son Dhani, a costumer David Warner, and John Cleese with daughter Cynthia.* **Handmade Films/Time Bandits**

them as upper-, middle-, and lower-class characters. Cleese repeated his role as the upper-class gentleman years later on several of *The Two Ronnies* shows.

During the same time, Cleese was also writing and performing in *I'm Sorry, I'll Read That Again* for BBC Radio, with a cast that consisted largely of the *Cambridge Circus* crew, as well as performing on *I'm Sorry, I Haven't a Clue.* Most notably, he began *At Last, the 1948 Show* in January 1967, with Chapman, Feldman, and Tim Brooke-Taylor. Of course, the latter led into Python.

Cleese began 1968 by marrying American actress Connie Booth, and he and Chapman worked on screenplays and TV scripts during the period from February 1968 through August 1969. They collaborated on *The Magic Christian* screenplay, and Cleese appeared onscreen as a Sotheby's auctioneer; the pair also cowrote *The Rise and Rise of Michael Rimmer,* and *Rentadick.* Cleese performed in several films around that

time, including *The Bliss of Mrs. Blossom, Interlude, The Best House in London, The Love Ban,* and *The Statue.*

Becoming restless after the second series of Monty Python, Cleese did not leave the group until after the third series. During that time, his daughter Cynthia was born, and he had founded Video Arts, his industrial training film company, in December 1971, shooting their first film the following summer. Despite leaving the TV series, Cleese did appear in the subsequent stage shows, and shot *Holy Grail* in April and May of 1974. Later that year, he and Connie Booth cowrote and starred in *Romance With a Double Bass,* a forty-five-minute film adapted from a Chekhov short story.

The most celebrated Cleese/Booth collaboration soon followed. The couple shot the pilot for *Fawlty Towers* in December, while the first series was done in August and September of 1975. The pair cowrote and performed the six-part series in which Cleese plays Basil Fawlty, the henpecked

Cleese resting and relaxing on the Brian *set.* **Photos copyright KHJ**

award for best performance in a comedy for his appearance in *Cheers* on March 5, 1987. In "Simon Says" he portrays a celebrated marriage counselor who advises Sam and Diane. He says he did it because he was a fan of the show, and because he was curious about working on an American situation comedy. Although he enjoyed the people and the experience, he found the pace more frantic than he was used to, with script changes coming throughout the week. Nevertheless, he would still like to return. A *Cheers* scheduled for April 13, 1989 was to feature him reprising the Simon role (he was to return to collect the money owed him by Frazier Crane from his first appearance), but scheduling conflicts could not be worked out.

For the big screen, he wrote and performed in the award-winning short subject *To Norway: Home of Giants,* as well as smaller roles in *The Great Muppet Caper, Silverado,* and Terry Gilliam's *Time Bandits.* He took larger, more featured roles in *Privates on Parade* and *Clockwise,* but did not meet with his biggest onscreen success until 1988's *A Fish Called Wanda.* Cleese had long hoped to collaborate with director Charles Crichton, and had become friends with Kevin Kline during the shooting of *Silverado.* He had always wanted to work with Jamie Lee Curtis, and the addition of Michael Palin to the group seemed natural. In addition, his real-life daughter Cynthia plays the same role in the film. Well received by critics and audiences alike, it became his most successful solo project.

Not all of his interests involve performing, however. When his first marriage was breaking up, Cleese became involved in group therapy, and finally wrote a book, *Families and How to Survive*

owner of a small English hotel who is constantly frustrated in his attempts to deal with his wife, employees, and guests. The show proved extraordinarily popular everywhere it was shown, in some places surpassing the popularity of Monty Python. Even though Cleese and Booth were divorced in August 1978, they went on to create another series of six *Fawlty Towers* early the following year. He later married American actress Barbara Trentham, whom he met at the *Hollywood Bowl* shows, and with whom he had another daughter.

Cleese has done an extensive variety of film and TV work in his post-Python days, along with various commercials for products all over the world. In addition, he has done countless walk-ons and cameo appearances that include *Dr. Who, The Goodies,* the aforementioned *Two Ronnies, Not the Nine O'Clock News,* and *The Avengers.* More extended roles include a 1978 appearance hosting *The Muppet Show,* a 1977 film for London Weekend Television called *The Strange Case of the End of Civilisation (As We Know It)* in which he played Arthur Sherlock Holmes, as well as several roles in *Whoops Apocalypse.* One of his most unusual, and acclaimed, TV roles was that of Petruchio in the 1980 BBC production of *Taming of the Shrew,* in which he was directed by Jonathan Miller.

In addition, Cleese won an American Emmy

Them, with his therapist, with a followup centered on using psychological strategies in the business world. Provisionally titled *Life and How to Survive It,* the book occupied most of his time following *Wanda,* although he did do a small role (as Halfdan the Black) in *The Saga of Erik the Viking* for Terry Jones.

Cleese maintained his links with live theater by performing with the various Amnesty International shows, even directing *The Secret Policeman's Ball* onstage.

His most lucrative enterprise, however, still seems to be Video Arts, Ltd. and its comedy management training films. Cleese and other British comedy stars appear in a great number of them, and they have won awards for their use of comedy to put across simple principles of modern business by showing the wrong way of doing things. Titles include "It's All Right, It's Only a Customer," "How to Lie With Statistics," and "Decisions, Bloody Decisions" (the films are available in America by phoning 1-800-553-0091, or 312-291-1008 in Illinois).

In "Meetings, Bloody Meetings," Cleese plays a manager who has nightmares over his ineptitude in conducting meetings. **Photo copyright Video Arts**

☞ *FAWLTY TOWERS*

By far, Cleese's most successful non-Python TV project has been his portrayal of Basil Fawlty in *Fawlty Towers.* Written with and costarring Connie Booth, Cleese says the series actually came about because the two of them, married at the time, had wanted to work together when Cleese left Python. After the couple had written a sketch for one of the German Python shows, and scripted and per-

formed a short film, *Romance With a Double Bass,* they briefly considered doing some man-woman sketches. But when the BBC approached Cleese about doing something else, it took them only one hour to hit on the idea of a hotel.

"It was based on a hotel I'd stayed at back when I was filming Python—the manager was just wonderfully rude," Cleese recalls. "He was like Basil, but much smaller, a skinny little guy about five-foot four-inches, with a large wife who dominated him. We reversed the sizes.

"I had written some *Doctor in the House* TV shows, and had set one of the episodes at a hotel that had been based on this one. An old friend of mine said to me, 'There's a series in that hotel.' I thought 'Bloody television producer, can't see a program without thinking about a series.' The extraordinary thing was, he was absolutely right. When Connie and I sat down three years later, it was the second or third idea that came into our minds."

There are several advantages to setting a series in a hotel, according to Cleese. "We could have almost anyone we wanted walk in, without trying to find an explanation. Plus, we had our basic regulars. It's a situation which almost everyone understands. Everyone knows what it's like to walk up to a front desk, what it's like if someone's casual, rude, or inattentive. We didn't have to explain or set anything up. It's all very straightforward and conventional, so we could start right away with the jokes."

Michael Palin, who has kept a journal for many years, confirmed Cleese's account of that legendary hotel in Torquay with his notes:

Tuesday, 12th of May. Our hotel, the Glenea-

gles, was a little out of Torquay, overlooking a beautiful little cove, plenty of trees around. Eric and John were already there, sitting beside the pool. Decor was clean, rooms nice. However, Mr. Sinclair, the proprietor, seemed to view us from the start as a colossal inconvenience. When we arrived back at 12:30 a.m., having watched the night's filming, he just stood and

"Balance Sheet Barrier," which co-stars Ronnie Corbett, sees Cleese as a *"sophisticated"* manager who is taught the basics of business finance by a crude, but knowledgeable, small businessman (Corbett). **Photo copyright Video Arts**

looked at us with the same look of self-righteous resentment and tacit accusation that I've not seen since my father waited up for me fifteen years ago. Graham tentatively asked for a brandy; the idea was dismissed out-of-hand. And that night, our first in Torquay, we decided to move out of the Gleneagles.

Back at Gleneagles, avoided breakfast. Graham, Terry and I have been fixed for one night at the Osborne, from then on at the Imperial. Asked Mr. Sinclair for the bill. He didn't seem unduly ruffled, but Mrs. Sinclair made our stay even more memorable by threatening us with a bill for two weeks, even though we hadn't stayed. But off we went, with lighter hearts . . .

The acclaim that the shows received surprised Cleese; especially gratifying was their success around the world. "Connie and I did something we thought would get a smallish but friendly audience on BBC 2, and we finished out with about three times the audience we had originally guessed," says Cleese. "We thought it was almost a private little joke, and I'm still astounded to find that it plays in Hong Kong in Cantonese! I

don't understand it—Basil must be some kind of archetype."

Strangely enough, there were two separate attempts to adapt *Fawlty Towers* to American television. The first was a pilot starring Harvey Korman, while the second, titled *Amanda's* (which actually ran briefly on ABC), starred Bea Arthur. Both attempts were quickly, and rightfully, forgotten. "I asked the American company how the adaptation was looking, and they told me 'It's looking good. We've only made one change.' They wrote out Basil Fawlty! Incomprehensible."

☞ FAWLTY TOWERS INDEX

The first series was aired in Britain beginning September 19, 1975, while the second series began February 19, 1979. Both season featured the same cast of regulars:

Basil Fawlty . . . . John Cleese
Sybil Fawlty . . . . Prunella Scales
Manuel . . . . Andrew Sachs
Polly . . . . Connie Booth
Major Gowen . . . . Ballard Berkeley
Miss Tibbs . . . . Gilly Flower
Miss Gatsby . . . . Renee Roberts

FIRST SERIES

Show 1: "A Touch of Class" Basil tries to attract a higher class of clientele to Fawlty Towers by advertising in upper-class publications. Thus, when a "Lord Malbury" checks in, Basil gives him royal treatment.

Show 2: "The Builders" The Fawltys go away for the weekend, leaving Manuel and Polly in charge. Against Sybil's strict orders, Basil hires a cheap builder to do repairs at the hotel while they are gone.

Show 3: "The Wedding Party" Sybil rents a room to an unmarried couple. Basil is outraged, and tries to have them thrown out.

Show 4: "The Hotel Inspectors" Basil hears that three hotel inspectors are in the area, and rolls out the red carpet to a likely looking trio.

Show 5: "Gourmet Night" Basil attempts to host a gourmet night at the hotel, which goes awry when his chef gets drunk and Basil must take charge.

Show 6: "The Germans" While Sybil is in the hospital, Basil attempts to hang a moose head, run a fire drill, and host some German guests.

SECOND SERIES

Show 7: "Communication Problems/Mrs. Richards" A troublesome elderly guest accuses the staff of stealing her money.

Show 8: "The Psychiatrist" While trying to prove a young bachelor has smuggled a girl into his room, Basil finds himself in a variety of compromising positions.

Show 9: "Waldorf Salad/The Americans" Basil must contend with an overbearing, obnoxious American guest who challenges his limited abilities as a host.

Show 10: "The Kipper and the Corpse/Death" After a guest dies overnight, Basil and the staff try to remove the body without being detected by the other guests and a health inspector.

Show 11: "The Anniversary" When Sybil walks out after an argument with Basil just before an anniversary party, he recruits Polly to impersonate his wife.

Show 12: "Basil the Rat" Manuel's pet rat, named "Basil," escapes while a health inspector is expected, and the real Basil deals with a poisoning scare.

BOOKS AND RECORDS

Two books of scripts were released; *Fawlty Towers* in 1977, and *Fawlty Towers 2* two years later. Both trade paperbacks are fully illustrated with stills from the TV shows, and contain all the text of the first series of shows.

Finally, *The Complete Fawlty Towers* was released in 1988, containing the scripts from all twelve shows, but with a limited number of photos in the volume.

Three soundtrack albums were released by BBC Records: 1979's *Fawlty Towers* contains "The Hotel Inspectors" and "Mrs. Richards." *Second Sitting,* released in 1981, includes "The Builders" and "The Rat." Finally, *At Your Service,* recorded in 1982, features "Death" and "The Germans."

Terry Gilliam

Terry Vance Gilliam was born in Minneapolis, Minnesota, on November 22, 1940, and moved to Los Angeles eleven years later. In 1958, he enrolled in Occidental College, where he edited *Fang,* the university's humor magazine.

Graduating with a degree in political sci-

Terry Gilliam, deep in thought, with the weighty worries of a feature film as opposed to cutout animation. **Handmade Films/Time Bandits**

ence, he traveled to New York in 1962 in hopes of working for Harvey Kurtzman, one of the creators of *Mad* magazine, who was currently publishing his own *Help!* magazine. Good timing on Gilliam's part had him arrive just as Associate Editor Charles Alverson was resigning, and Gilliam found himself employed. He did a number of freelance cartoons and illustrations for *Help!* and other magazines around this time, but his most notable work was a fumetti strip which featured John Cleese as a man who falls in love with his daughter's Barbie doll.

After *Help!* folded in 1965, Gilliam traveled around Europe, and returned to Los Angeles the next year where he illustrated children's books, failed as a freelancer, and went to work as a copywriter and art director for an advertising agency. He soon discovered that this attempt at a respectable job was boring, and moved to London in 1967, where he found work doing freelance illustration for *The Sunday Times Magazine* and other publications. During this time, he also drew for some American comic magazines like *Car-Toons* and *Surf-Toons* as a freelancer. He became artistic director of *The Londoner* magazine, which also went under not long after he joined it.

Finding himself jobless once again, he turned to John Cleese, who introduced him to producer Humphrey Barclay. He sold two sketches to *Do Not Adjust Your Set,* and was befriended by Eric Idle, becoming the resident cartoonist for *We Have Ways of Making You Laugh,* which occurred between the two series of *Do Not Adjust Your Set.* It was for this show that Gilliam did his very first piece of animation, to help them deal with a tricky spot. Although given only two weeks and four hundred pounds, he impressed them enough to be asked to do more, and ended up doing three animated films for the second series of *Do Not Adjust Your Set.* He became more friendly with Michael Palin and Terry Jones, and the following year was asked to join a new project called *Monty Python's Flying Circus.*

Working chiefly as the animator, he would seldom appear onscreen, although as the series progressed, he began performing more often. But it was in his new-found career as an animator that he made his mark on Python, influencing the feel, shape, and flow of the shows, giving Python a look unlike any other program.

Even while working on Python, he pursued outside projects as an animator. In 1970, he cre-

In the set of **Time Bandits,** *Cleese as Robin Hood happily waits for the next shot, while director Gilliam consults with some of the Bandits.* **Handmade Films/Time Bandits**

ated the title sequence for the film *Cry of the Banshee,* and the following year animated twenty-five minutes worth of material for ABC's *The Marty Feldman Comedy Machine.* He shot his first commercial in 1972, part of a campaign for the British Gas Board, and also designed the title sequence for *William,* a CBS special on Shakespeare.

When *Monty Python and the Holy Grail* was conceived in 1974, the group wanted to maintain as much control over their material as possible, so Gilliam and Terry Jones codirected the film, whetting Gilliam's appetite for the big screen. He has, of course, maintained his Python relationship—although Terry Jones directed *Life of Brian* and *Meaning of Life* on his own, Gilliam designed *Brian,* conceived and directed "The Crimson Permanent Assurance" sequence for *Meaning of Life,* and acted in both.

Following *Holy Grail,* Gilliam

On the **Brian** *set, Gilliam, in full jailer's costume and makeup, talks with* **Jabberwocky** *cowriter Charles Alverson.* **Photo copyright KHJ**

was approached by producer Sandy Lieberson to direct a World War II documentary feature called *All This and World War II,* with a soundtrack made up entirely of Beatle songs. Gilliam had been keen to do a short film for the BBC based on Lewis Carroll's *Jabberwocky,* however, and turned him down. Lieberson then asked Gilliam to do *Jabberwocky* as a feature for him.

In 1977, Gilliam's *Jabberwocky* was released, starring Michael Palin, with brief appearances by Terry Jones, Gilliam, and Neil Innes. The script was cowritten by Charles Alverson and Gilliam. The dark medieval comedy/fantasy followed young Dennis (Palin), a cooper's son who goes to the city to make his fortune and ends up confront-

ing the feared Jabberwocky. Unfortunately, the film was promoted in some areas as "Monty Python's Jabberwocky" and even "Jabberwocky and the Holy Grail," which, understandably, made Gilliam furious. It would not be his last battle with the film establishment.

His first book was released in 1978 (although he did illustrate a volume called *Sporting Relations* two years before). *Animations of Mortality* was conceived as a "how-to" book on animation, using a great deal of Gilliam's old artwork. He created Brian the Badger to take the reader through the whole process. Throughout the book Gilliam tells the story mostly with pictures—at least until Brian is killed by the Black Spot . . .

Gilliam also made a few peculiar solo appearances following Python. During the City Center shows, he appeared on the game show *To Tell the Truth.* Two of the panelists had seen the show and disqualified themselves, while the other two voted correctly for Gilliam.

He also made a brief cameo appearance as an actor a few years later in the Chevy Chase/Dan Ackroyd film *Spies Like Us.* But Gilliam's future was clearly on the other side of the camera.

After the success of *Brian,* Handmade Films was eager to work with Gilliam on his next film. When they rejected what would eventually become *Brazil,* he came up with the basic story for *Time Bandits* over one weekend.

It was 1981's *Time Bandits* that made him an individual to be reckoned with inside the film industry. A bigger money-maker than any of the Python films, Gilliam cowrote and directed the story of a boy who encounters six dwarves who have stolen the map of the Holes in Time and Space from the Supreme Being. He accompanies them through history, where they meet real-life and fantasy legends, including King Agamemnon (Sean Connery), Napoleon (Ian Holm), and Robin Hood (John Cleese). Michael Palin, who cowrote the script with him, plays a dual role with Shelley Duvall, as star-crossed lovers in Sherwood Forest, and on the *Titanic*.

The success of *Time Bandits* allowed him to virtually write his own ticket. He was besieged by offers to direct such projects as *Enemy Mine* and *The Princess Bride*. Gilliam stuck to his guns, however, and insisted on directing an original film, his beloved *Brazil*. Written along with Charles McKeown and Tom Stoppard, Gilliam created his own world to tell the story of Sam Lowry, a lowly clerk in the Ministry of Information Retrieval.

In a story often compared to *1984*, Lowry challenges the repressive bureaucracy when he falls in love with a beautiful revolutionary (Kim Griest); his best friend (Michael Palin) becomes

Gilliam in a rare shot without unpleasant costumes and makeup. **Photo copyright KHJ**

his torturer, and an air-conditioner repairman (in a hilarious cameo by Robert DeNiro) becomes their greatest hope. The true star of *Brazil,* however, is the world designed by Gilliam, which incorporates elements of the past, present, and future existing simultaneously with Lowry's flights into fantasy.

Of course, the controversy with Universal over the release of Gilliam's version of the film often threatened to overshadow the movie itself. The details are presented in Jack Mathews's *The Battle of Brazil.* Essentially, Universal objected so strongly to the dark tone of the picture (even though the studio had previously read and approved the screenplay) that a fight broke out between the director and the studio. The latter demanded that he totally reedit the film and include a happy ending, and refused to release the film in America until Gilliam's version won the L.A. Film Critic's Best Picture Award. Although Gilliam won the battle, the movie suffered at the box office because, according to the director, they still refused to properly promote and distribute *Brazil*. The film continued to arouse controversy years after its initial release. Universal's savagely edited version of the film was finally shown when *Brazil* made its debut on commercial TV early in 1989. Gilliam's 131-minute movie had over half an hour cut from it, including most of the fantasy sequences, and the happy ending Gilliam had fought so hard against was reinstated by the studio. Gilliam wanted his name removed from the TV version and even contemplated a lawsuit to prevent its further showing, but instead decided to let the matter die.

Controversy seemed to dog Gilliam's efforts, but the problems on his next film nearly overshadowed all of his previous troubles. Shooting on *The Adventures of Baron Munchausen* was behind almost before he began, with the movie rushed into production long before Gilliam was prepared. The project ran over budget, and the studio threatened to take the picture away from Gilliam in the middle of the shoot. He found himself battling the studio to retain control of his film, and also fighting to complete the shooting. His efforts were not in vain, however, and *Munchausen,* with Eric Idle and John Neville in the title role, was completed as Gilliam had hoped.

Undaunted, however, Gilliam began planning his next project even before *Munchausen* was completed. He decided to direct the adaptation of the DC Comics series *The Watchmen* for producer Joel Silver. Created by Alan Moore and scripted by Sam *(Batman)* Hamm (with rewrites by Gilliam and Charles McKeown), Gilliam says he wanted to do the dark story of real-life superheroes in part because he was a bit tired of carrying entire projects through from beginning to end. *Watchmen* is expected to be released in late 1990.

Gilliam continues to look ahead, though, and his next project after *Watchmen* will probably be Gilliam from start to finish. He is currently interested in continuing in his historical fantasy vein by taking aim at the legend of *The Minotaur* with Michael Palin.

In Time Bandits, *scripted by Palin and Gilliam and directed by Gilliam,* Cleese appears as Robin Hood "played as the Duke of Kent"; here he appears with the gang of six time-traveling dwarves. **Photo copyright Handmade Films/Time Bandits**

☞ THE MINISTRY?

Although *Brazil* was not released until 1985, Terry Gilliam had been planning it for many years. He had hoped to film it shortly after *Life of Brian* in 1978, but that was not to be. Unable to raise the money for such an ambitious project, he was instead forced to come up with a more commercial movie. It was the enormous financial success of *Time Bandits* that gave him the power, influence, and reputation to write and direct 1985's *Brazil.*

It was seven years prior to that, however, that Gilliam first sat down to describe his plans for the film. In the top-floor studio of his home in Hampstead (on August 19, 1978), while preparing to leave in a month to shoot *Brian,* Gilliam talked about his dream project.

"At one point, I was going to call it *Brazil,* just because I like the song. We're going to use a lot of Latin American music, terrible 1940s Carmen Miranda stuff all through it, so it's all lush and romantic, even though it's very gray and grim. It was going to be called *Brazil,* but getting into the Ministry of Torture, we might just call it *The Ministry* and let it go at that," Gilliam explains.

At the time, he said, he was working on the story with Charles Alverson, his collaborator on

Jabberwocky. Interestingly, his basic concepts seem to have remained much the same in the years from conception to final edit.

"I've been working off and on for the past year. It's a thing that floats around," Gilliam explains. "After I wrote it, I decided to get someone who is better at dialogue than I am—I'm terrible at dialogue and Chuck's very good, and we work well together. After I got Chuck in, we went through it and fiddled around, and we're ready to hand the treatment over and see if someone will give us the money to get on with it.

"At one point, I was going to say it takes place everywhere in the twentieth century—I'm not sure what that means, but it sounds right. It's a very odd film about someone who works at the Ministry of Torture, and leads an incredibly elaborate fantasy life at night. He blindly goes through his job all day long, without thinking of the consequences of being a small cog in this great machine, what it's all about; he maintains a job for eight hours a day, then goes home and lives his real life, which is amazingly adventurous in his dreams.

"He suddenly changes from being a cog in the system to one of the victims. He has to make a choice between living in reality, in fantasy, or in madness, and I won't say which choice he makes, because it's very odd. In the fantasy sequences, I'm trying to do what I did in the animation, but with live action—real mind-blowing stuff, really amazing things.

"I'm not sure how I'm going to do it yet, but I'll probably combine models, animation, and live action to produce the fantasy images. The real world where these horrible things are happening is a very gray place, and most of the horrifying aspects of it all, like the torture, are never seen—we see or hear the results, but never any of the nastiness. People's attitudes in the film are like the attitudes now: if they don't see it, it's not happening; everyone's getting along with shopping."

The sound effects employed many of the same methods Gilliam had originally considered. In 1977, Gilliam, as a director, was more worried about maintaining the proper balance between fantasy and reality (in fact, early drafts contain longer, more elaborate flights into fantasy, but those were trimmed significantly for budgetary reasons).

"When we got done working one day, Chuck said 'I think we've got a horror film on our hands here.' On one hand, the fantasies are really a good adventure, but the other stuff is fairly strong. I don't know whether I can pull off this odd balance. People are going to come to see the fantasy sequences, and they're going to be surprised by all this other stuff, because it's probably more serious than they expected. It's going to be a fine line. I still haven't worked out where to draw the line between a film that's saying something, and a film that's entertaining."

The basic concept for the film arose when Gilliam watched an oil refinery spewing forth fire and smoke near the seaside, and the image clicked in his mind. "The city will look just like an oil refinery at night, all metal and hard and gray. We might just move into a steel refinery and turn it into a city! We're going to re-create the whole world—it's almost like a science fiction film, in a way.

"The public transportation is like a series of cages, and people are shuffled around like animals. Nobody minds it, because that's just how things are," Gilliam explains, and says his hero's home is automated. "His flat is ultra-efficient—he pushes buttons, and his breakfast comes up. It's all mechanized."

Although some concepts were changed—the public transport in cages didn't survive, for example—most of the images Gilliam developed made it into *Brazil* in one form or another, including the memorable sequences involving the repairmen played by Bob Hoskins and Robert DeNiro.

"The room is very barren-looking, but when things start going wrong, the repairmen come and start pulling wall panels off. It looks like guts behind the wall, except it's all mechanical. It's like taking a car apart, and the whole room gets taken over by all the tubes and stuff behind the walls. It would be amazing if we could do it, but I'm not sure if anyone's actually going to give me any money."

The battle for the money took almost seven years, and then Gilliam had to fight another battle with Universal to release the film his way. But the *Brazil* he ended up with was remarkably similar to the story he visualized long before.

Eric Idle

Born at Harton Hospital, South Shields, on March 29, 1943, Eric Idle lived in Oldham and Wallasey, before being sent to boarding school (Royal School Wolverhampton) in 1952. Deciding to major in English, he went to Pembroke College, Cambridge in 1962, and was voted into the Footlights the following March, where he met upper-classmen John Cleese and Graham Chapman. It was in September of that year, while performing in the Footlights Review at the Edinburgh Festival, that he met Terry Jones and Michael Palin, who were performing in the rival Oxford Review.

Elected president of the Footlights in 1964 (his first act was to initiate a bill allowing women to join), he appeared in their revue *My Girl Herbert,* touring with it

Receiving the last touches as King Otto, in a sequence all but removed from the final version of **Brian;** *Idle plays the leader of a crack suicide squad that pledges their support to an unwilling Brian.* **Photo copyright KHJ**

in 1965. After graduating that year, he performed some cabaret with John Cameron at the Blue Angel, was featured in the Richard Eyre production of *Oh, What a Lovely War* in Leicester, and

spent part of the Christmas season in the farce *One For the Pot,* also in Leicester.

His writing career began to blossom in 1966. He wrote for many of his old Footlights colleagues on BBC Radio's *I'm Sorry, I'll Read That Again*; he was recruited by David Frost to pen "clever ad libs" for *The Frost Report,* and wrote for Ronnie Corbett's series *No, That's Me Over Here.*

In 1967, Idle joined Palin and Jones for two seasons of *Do Not Adjust Your Set,* where he met and befriended Terry Gilliam. Between the two series, he and Gilliam both appeared on *We Have Ways of Making You Laugh,* notable for Gilliam's very first animation. When Idle went back for the second series of *DNAYS,* he brought Gilliam back to do cartoons for them.

The year 1969 brought two very big changes to Idle's life with the advent of *Monty Python's*

Flying Circus, and Idle's marriage to Lyn Ashley on July seventh (during the first week of Python filming). He appeared in all the Python TV shows, films, and stage shows, and was also principally responsible for putting together the Python books as well.

As the TV series drifted to a close, he was eager to begin his own projects. Idle wrote his first (and to date, only) novel, *Hello, Sailor,* in 1975, but he planned a return to television.

In 1975 and 1976, BBC 2 broadcast two six-show series of *Rutland Weekend Television,* purporting to be Britain's smallest, cheapest independent TV station. It was written by Idle and included Neil Innes, who did much of the music. A comedy album, *The Rutland Weekend Songbook,* and *The Rutland Dirty Weekend Book* both resulted.

Idle had met George Harrison, a long-time Python fan, in L.A. at the opening of *Holy Grail.* The two became friends, and Harrison appeared on one of the *RWT* shows to sing the "Pirate Song," which he cowrote with Idle. The Python also directed the films *Crackerbox Palace* and *True Love* for Harrison's *33⅓* album, performing a Pepperpot voice on "This Song."

It was a Beatle-related sketch on *RWT* that turned into one of his biggest successes. Idle and Innes had cleverly parodied the Beatles with a brief film and song featuring the Rutles. When Idle hosted *Saturday Night Live* on October 2, 1976, he showed the "Rutles" clip, and left to do a Canadian publicity tour for the book (he vowed at the time it would be his last publicity tour). He then spent Christmas in Barbados with *SNL* producer Lorne Michaels, who persuaded him to do a full-length Rutles TV film for NBC. Idle began writing in New York and, the following February, appeared on a *Saturday Night Live* prime-time special from the Mardi Gras in New Orleans. Idle hosted once again on April 23, with Innes as musical guest (performing the very Lennon-like "Cheese and Onions"). After great ratings, all was "go" for the Rutles.

Innes wrote nineteen "new" Rutles hits for the soundtrack album, Mick Jagger and Paul Simon were interviewed on the influence of the Rutles, and Idle had his appendix removed at Arab Hospital in St. John's Wood, London. The final script was completed in July, and filming began later that month in London, Liverpool, and New York. Innes recorded his songs in two weeks,

Idle is always up for a cricket game, even in Judea, 33 A.D. **Photo copyright KHJ**

while the editing took three months.

The result was an incredibly accurate parody of the Beatles, with Innes's uncanny music echoing all the phases of their careers. The cast included Dan Ackroyd, John Belushi, Bianca Jagger, Bill Murray, Michael Palin, Gilda Radner, and George Harrison as an interviewer. First broadcast on NBC on March 22, 1978, ratings for *All You Need Is Cash* were disappointing, but it was roundly praised as an artistic triumph. Two singles were released, and Idle followed them up with a single recorded with Riki Fataar as "Dirk and Stig" (their Rutles characters), "Ging Gang Goolie/Mr. Sheane."

He was also divorced in 1978 (he subsequently remarried in 1981; he met his wife Tania during his *SNL* days), and hosted yet another *SNL* in December, after returning from Tunisia and *Life of Brian.* He spent much of the following year putting together the *Brian* book, and attempting to produce his own version of *The Pirates of Penzance.*

His talents are spread among film, books, and records, but his strongest interest has been in writing. He has been quite prolific, but admits a reluctance to go through the politicking necessary to get his scripts produced. In addition to *Pirates of Penzance,* he has also turned out *National Lam-*

poon's *Australian Vacation* (he appeared in *European Vacation* as a hapless, ever-polite British tourist), a science fiction comedy called *The Road to Mars* that suggests a modern-day Hope-Crosby "Road" film, a Faustian farce called *Taxi to Hell,* and a musical called *The Back Page* about royalty and cricket. He has also planned a Rutles-like TV documentary on a fictitious Hollywood producer, to be called *The Legendary Sid Gottlieb.* Idle also wrote a play entitled *Pass the Butler,* which ran briefly in London's West End. His theater work has not been confined to scripts, however—he received good notices for his role in *The Mikado* in London, directed by Jonathan Miller in 1986. Unfortunately, when the production was taken to L.A., Dudley Moore was brought in to take over Idle's part in an attempt to cash in on the actor's film success.

One of his more interesting diversions—not unlike Palin's and Jones's children's books—was the result of his friendship with Shelley Duvall, the producer of Showtime's *Fairy Tale Theatre.* For her, Idle directed Robin Williams and Teri Garr in his version of "The Frog Prince" in 1983, and three years later starred in the title role of "The Pied Piper of Hamelin."

Although he has done some American television appearances (mostly for friends, as in *Laverne and Shirley* on Feb. 24, 1981, and a brief appearance on *Steve Martin's Greatest Show Ever*), he has been most active recently performing scripts written by others. In addition to several commercials, he appeared in Graham Chapman's *Yellowbeard* in 1983, and more recently, Idle was featured with Pierce Brosnan in NBC's 1989 remake of *Around the World in 80 Days.* Also in 1989, he starred in the short-lived NCB-TV comedy series *Nearly Departed* (originally titled *Ghost Story*); the spirited comedy ran from April 10 to May 1. Of course, his appearance in *Baron Munchausen* as Berthold, the world's fastest man,

reunited him with Terry Gilliam, a reunion welcomed by both. Nineteen eighty-nine proved to be an active year for Idle, as he also spent several weeks filming *Nuns on the Run* for Handmade Films.

☞ **THE RUTLES**

The greatest group never in the history of rock music, the Rutles' career actually began with a clip of them performing "I Must Be in Love" on *Rutland Weekend Television,* later shown on *Saturday Night Live.*

All You Need Is Cash, the ninety-minute "docudrama," was first aired on NBC on March 22, 1978, and chronicled the career of the Pre-Fab Four: Dirk McQuickly (Idle), Ron Nasty (Neil Innes), Stig O'Hara (Rikki Fataar), and Barry Wom (John Halsey). The rest of the cast included Mick Jagger, Paul Simon, Dan Ackroyd, Terrence Baylor, John Belushi, George Harrison, Bianca Jagger, Bill Murray, Michael Palin, Gilda Radner, Gwen Taylor, and Ron Wood. Scripted by Idle and codirected by Idle and Gary Weis, Lorne Michaels served as executive producer; in addition to America and Britain, the show was also sold to Canada, New Zealand, Japan, Belgium, Denmark, Iceland, the Netherlands, Sweden, Austria, Norway, and Finland.

Shot on location in London, Liverpool, New York, and New Orleans, the production values are superb, expertly re-creating the feel of the time period covered. For the few not familiar with the Beatles, it holds up on its own as simply a very funny documentary parody; for the rest of us, it is a near-perfect parody as timeless as its targets. It demolishes all of the old Beatle myths, and at the same time elevates them to even loftier heights.

As Neil Innes recalls, they had help in get-

Remnants of Rutlemania, the greatest group never in rock and roll. Photo copyright KHJ

ting it all started. "George Harrison showed Eric and me the film Neil Aspinall had made of the real Beatles. We watched this, and it got depressing, because it was real. When they broke up, it really was a downer. When Brian Epstein died, it just became a bit too real, and the fun definitely stopped. The general feeling was, we could probably tell the story as accurately with the Rutles, but in a more palatable way, because it wasn't really them—it was the Pre-Fab Four, not the Fab Four," says Innes.

"George Harrison was in it up to his neck. Michael Palin played Derek Taylor, and George played Mike!"

All You Need Is Cash effectively touches on all of the high points of the Rutles' careers: their beginnings at the Rat Keller in Hamburg, the fifth Rutle, Leppo, their trousers, Rutlemania, the concert in Che Stadium, *A Hard Day's Rut* and *Ouch!*, Sgt. Rutter, The Rutle Corp., their breakup, and the lawsuits.

At the same time the film was aired, Warner Brothers released the soundtrack, *The Rutles*, containing fourteen all-new Rutles classics written and performed by Neil Innes. It was packaged as a retrospective of the group's greatest hits, including "Hold My Hand," "Doubleback Alley," and "Love Life." Innes uncannily captured the Beatle sound while writing completely original songs, although one song heard in the film, "Get Up and Go," was reportedly not included on the album because of a too-close resemblance to "Get

Back." The album was packaged with a twenty-page booklet highlighting the Rutle years with excerpts and photos from the film. In England, the album received a silver disc for sales of over 150,000 pounds; in America, it was nominated for a Grammy Award as Best Comedy Recording of 1978.

"The songwriting wasn't easy, but it was a labor of love," says Innes. "I didn't listen to any Beatles stuff at all. The hardest songs to write were the early ones, when I had to remember what it was like to hold a girl's hand for the first time, and make it sound meaningful. Those early songs were the hardest to emulate—they're probably more exposed, and they had to be good in a simple way."

Innes assembled some musicians to record the songs, and decided to treat them as a real band. "The cleverest thing I did was to have everybody work together and live together at Hendon for two weeks, rehearsing just like a group, and we made the album in two weeks because of that. And the feel of it was just wonderful. We've got the quarter-inch tapes of the Rutles Live at Hendon someplace. We really sounded like a group, because there was no overdubbing or anything," Innes says.

Although further plans for the Rutles failed to materialize, Idle did release a subsequent single with Fataar, billed as "Dirk and Stig." When asked about a Rutles followup project, Innes turns to the show: "To quote Mick Jagger: 'I hope not!'"

Terry Jones

Born February 1, 1942 at Colwyn Bay, North Wales, Terry Jones attended Royal Grammar School, Guilford in 1953. Studying history, he went to St. Edmund Hall, Oxford, in 1961, and eventually became attracted to the theater scene. He appeared in the Oxford Revue * * * * at the Edinburgh Festival and at the Phoenix Theatre in London in 1964. Jones also played the condemned man in *Hang Down Your Head and Die*,

an anti-capital punishment revue presented at Oxford, Stratford, and London's Comedy Theatre. It was around this time that he met Michael Palin.

Graduating a year before Palin, he found himself working for the BBC Light Entertainment Script Department, as a script editor, producer's assistant, gag writer, and whatever else needed to be done. Joined by Palin, the two contributed to *Late Night Line-Up, The Ken Dodd Show, The*

Jones's first solo directing job was Brian, *though he would eventually make his way into lensing non-Python films, to critical acclaim.* **Photo copyright KHJ**

Billy Cotton Bandshow, and *The Illustrated Weekly Hudd,* and did various kinds of writing for Lance Percival, Kathy Kirby, Marty Feldman, and *The Two Ronnies.* The pair made short films for *The Late Show,* and in 1967, became script editors for *A Series of Birds* and *Twice a Fortnight.* More significantly, the two began writing for *The Frost Report,* which included other future Pythons among its writers. The pair also collaborated on two pantomimes for the Palace Theatre, Watford: *Aladdin* in 1968, and *Beauty and the Beast* in 1969.

It was 1967 that saw the first of two series of *Do Not Adjust Your Set,* a children's show written by Jones, Palin, and Eric Idle, with animations by Terry Gilliam, as well as appearances by Neil Innes and the Bonzo Dog Doo Dah Band, all of which led into *Monty Python's Flying Circus* in 1969. During the second season of *DNAYS,* the pair wrote and performed in an acclaimed six-part series called *The Complete and Utter History of Britain* for London Weekend Television.

"Mike and I were doing the last season of *DNAYS* at the *same time* we were doing the Complete and Utter Histories. It was absolutely manic!" says Jones. "The basis of the Complete and Utter Histories was that it was history as if

there had been television cameras there—things like William the Conqueror in the showers after the Battle of Hastings, all done with an ITN sports reporter asking what the battle had been like. It was like a football match, with a playback of the battle.

"They weren't very satisfactory in many ways, but they did have funny material in them. I think it was the Complete and Utter Histories that got John Cleese keen on doing something together . . ."

Jones and Palin wrote together for all the Python TV shows and films, both on their own as well as with the group. The pair had always tended to write longer pieces that would not fit into the half-hour Python format; one of those was a short play called *Secrets,* which aired on BBC 2 in August 1973. The story of a chocolate company that becomes successful overnight (after a body falls into the vat), was turned into the 1988 film *Consuming Passions* with Vanessa Redgrave, though Jones and Palin had little to do with the production. The Jones/Palin team also wrote two short plays for the Sheffield Crucible Theatre, under the single title *Their Finest Hours,* which were presented in 1976.

When the Python TV show came to an end, Jones and Palin set their sights on another series. The pair wrote the pilot for *Ripping Yarns,* aired in January 1976; "Tomkinson's Schooldays" was successful enough for the BBC to authorize a

Consulting with longtime friend and collaborator Palin in Pilate's audience chamber. **Photo copyright KHJ**

series of six, broadcast in the fall of 1977, and a second series of three, aired two years later. The writing was first rate, as were the production values, but as well received as the shows were, they were too expensive for the BBC to continue. Jones cowrote all the shows with Palin, but appeared only in the first.

The shows were all very British, rooted in the stiff-upper-lip stories of English pluck, with a fine, ironic edge. Each story is separate, and the hero (played by Palin) escapes from prisoner-of-war camps, leads an expedition over the Andes, and prevents the Germans from starting World War I ahead of schedule.

The scripts for the shows were published in two volumes, the first six as *Ripping Yarns,* and the last three as *More Ripping Yarns.* The pair also collaborated in 1976 on *Dr. Fegg's Nasty Book of Knowledge,* published in the U.K. under the title *Bert Fegg's Nasty Book for Boys and Girls* (revised and reissued in America in 1985 as *Dr. Fegg's Encyclopedia of All World Knowledge*).

The money Jones earned from *Holy Grail* was in part invested in an old restaurant and brewery in the English countryside. Jones is a fierce proponent of CAMRA, the Campaign for Real Ale. He insists that his beer be brewed in line with the most traditional methods.

The *Grail* profits also allowed Jones the time and money to pursue another pet project that had been brewing for years. He wrote a book, *Chaucer's Knight: Portrait of a Medieval Mercenary,* the scholarly study of a few lines of the *Canterbury Tales,* "explaining some 700-year-old jokes" that he felt had been misinterpreted for too long. It was published in 1980, and was followed

Watching videotaped results of some **Erik the Viking** *scenes with costar Mickey Rooney. "Terry is a very wonderful person with a tremendous amount of enthusiasm," says the show business veteran. "He's not intimidating—he's basically an actor himself."* **Photo copyright KHJ**

the next year by something completely different, an original collection of *Fairy Tales,* short stories that he wrote for his daughter Sally. He followed this up in 1983 with *The Saga of Erik the Viking,* written for his son Bill. Yet another children's book, *Nicobobinus,* was issued the following year. Jones wrote screenplays based on the latter two, filming *Erik the Viking* for release in 1989. A book of children's poetry, *The Curse of the Vampire Socks,* was released late in 1988.

Jones's *Fairy Tales* was adapted for television, first as a series of seven shows, with another series to follow; titled *East of the Moon,* they were nominated for an Emmy Award. And 1988 saw the publication of *Attacks of Opinion,* a collection of columns written by Jones for the *Young Guardian* "Input" column earlier in the year.

His interest in the Middle Ages also led him to write a serious screenplay based on the Peasants' Revolt, called *1381.* "It's glossed over in most history books, and it was a most extraordinary, apocalyptic event. These people actually won, and took over London! They revolted not because they lived under such terrible oppression, but because they suddenly realized a much better, more equal life was in their grasp, and they could actually do something about it," Jones says.

Jones's reputation as one of Britain's leading children's authors resulted in his collaboration with Jim Henson on *Labyrinth.* He ended up writing the text for the Brian Froud illustrations done for the film, published as *Goblins of the Labyrinth* in 1986.

His varied interests also found an outlet on TV. He hosted a series of shows called *Paperbacks* in June and July, 1981, and directed a tribute to one of his boyhood favorites on Channel Four's *The Rupert Bear Story,* in December 1982.

Film appearances by Jones have become less frequent recently. One of his few non-Python roles had him fall victim to Gilliam's Jabberwocky in the first few minutes of that film.

Directing has occupied much of Jones's time as of late. Although he took an active interest in the direction and editing of the Python TV shows, he did not actually get involved until he and Terry Gilliam codirected *Holy Grail.* Jones then went on to tackle the same chores by himself on *Life of Brian* and *Meaning of Life.* Although he is chiefly interested in directing his own projects, he did win acclaim for his work at the helm of 1987's *Personal Services,* the story of celebrated madame Cynthia Payne. The followup, *The Saga of Erik the Viking* (released in 1989), is the first non-Python feature both written and directed by the increasingly busy Terry Jones.

☞ RIPPING YARNS

The first major post-Python project for Terry Jones and Michael Palin was the series *Ripping Yarns.* The first of them was "Tomkinson's Schooldays," the story of life at a very strange British public school. Beautifully photographed and with outstanding production values, the half-hour, broadcast early in 1976, impressed the BBC enough to authorize the next five.

Written by Jones and Palin, Jones only appeared on screen in *Tomkinson,* though Palin starred in all the episodes. "They all have a little hero figure, who really isn't a hero," Palin described them at the time. "In one, I play a boy of about eighteen, which is getting increasingly difficult; in another, I play a man of sixty, which is getting increasingly easier . . ."

Directed by Terry Hughes and Jim Franklin, the six satirical stories of British pluck and stiff-upper-lip adventure were popular enough for three more to be written and filmed in the autumn of 1979, directed by Franklin and Alan J.W. Bell. That, however, would be the last of the *Yarns.* As critically acclaimed as the shows were, they proved too expensive to continue. Palin once expressed a wish to see them in a theater rather than on a TV screen.

The pilot was aired in the U.K. on January 7, 1976, and the other five, broadcast from September 27 to October 25, 1977, completed the first series. The second series of three shows appeared October 10–24, 1979.

FIRST SERIES

Show 1: "Tomkinson's Schooldays" A young boy at a very peculiar public school, where students must beat the headmaster and runaways are hunted down by the school leopard, rises through the ranks to become the new school bully.

Show 2: "The Testing of Eric Olthwaite" A young man so boring that his parents run away from home (all he can speak of is rainfall, shovels, and black pudding) is idolized when he becomes the leader of an outlaw gang.

Show 3: "Escape From Stalag Luft 112B" A British P.O.W. who holds the record for escaping from German camps is sent to the most impregnable camp of all, but his plans are thwarted by his fellow Englishmen.

Jones on the set of **The Saga of Erik the Viking,** *looking very relaxed and in charge in the midst of a Viking village on a fiord constructed inside a London soundstage.* **Photo copyright KHJ**

Show 4: "Murder at Moorstones Manor" Trouble breaks out at a country estate when a family beset by murder finds there are more confessions than corpses.

Show 5: "Across the Andes by Frog" Capt. Snetterton leads the first High Altitude Amphibian Expedition across the Andes, but the natives and his crew are more interested in schoolgirls and listening to football.

Show 6: "The Curse of the Claw" An old man recounts the story of his youth, and the mysterious claw given to him by his Uncle Jack (who was totally unconcerned about contagious diseases).

Show 7: "Whinfrey's Last Case" While on holiday, a British hero foils a German plot to begin World War I ahead of schedule.

Show 8: "Golden Gordon" The Barnestoneworth Football team's most fanatical supporter takes action when his team is sold.

Show 9: "Roger of the Raj" A wealthy young soldier-of-fortune stoops to the most despicable act known to the British Army.

Michael Palin

A fervent-looking Michael Palin (here in the title role of The Missionary). Handmade Films/The Missionary

The son of an engineer, Michael Palin was born May 5, 1943, in Sheffield, Yorkshire. He began attending Birkdale Preparatory School in 1948, where he made his first dramatic appearance as Martha Cratchit in *A Christmas Carol,* and fell off the stage. He then attended Shrewsbury School in 1957.

Majoring in history, Palin began studying at Brasenose College, Oxford, in 1962, where he wrote and performed his first comedy material at the Oxford University Psychology Society Christmas Party. He began acting with the Oxford University Dramatic Society and the Experimental Theatre Company, where he first met future writing partner Terry Jones.

The two were featured in one of the Experimental Theatre Company's most notable productions, *Hang Down Your Head and Die,* a musical anthology which carried a strong anti-capital punishment message; the show was specifically designed around the talents of a few ETC members, including Palin and Jones, who both contributed material, as well. It was presented at Oxford during the winter term of 1964, and played forty-four performances at London's Comedy Theatre in March 1964. Later that year, Palin appeared with Jones and others in *The Oxford Revue* at the Edinburgh Festival, and also played Mc-Cann in the ETC production of Pinter's *Birthday Party.*

The following year, after Jones graduated, Palin wrote, directed, and appeared in *The Oxford Line* revue at the Edinburgh Festival in 1965, and received a degree in Modern History. He appeared briefly as the co-compère of *Now,* a TV pop show produced in Bristol for the now-defunct Television West Wales, and simultaneously

***Michael Palin with the un-Gwen Dibley-like Maggie Smith in* The Missionary; *the pair subsequently teamed up again for Alan Bennett's* A Private Function. Handmade Films/The Missionary**

resumed his partnership with Jones, rewriting a Jones script called *The Love Show,* a documentary dealing with sex. In April of 1966, he married Helen Gibbins.

Palin and Jones began contributing to a number of TV shows around this time, including *The Billy Cotton Band Show, The Ken Dodd Show,* and *The Illustrated Weekly Hudd,* as well as writing for *The Two Ronnies* and Marty Feldman. The two of them also wrote and performed in short films for the BBC's *Late Show. The Frost Report* found them working with Cleese, Chapman, and Idle, while the pair of them were script editors on *A Series of Birds* and *Twice a Fortnight.* It was on the latter program, a late-night satirical show in 1967, that Palin and Jones got their first chance to perform. Palin and Jones also wrote pantomimes of *Aladdin* and *Beauty and the Beast* for the Watford Palace Theatre in 1967 and 1968, the latter of which Palin characterized as "fairly dreadful."

It was in 1967 that Palin teamed with Jones and Eric Idle to write and perform the first of two seasons of *Do Not Adjust Your Set,* a forerunner to Monty Python. Between the first and second series, Palin and Jones wrote their own six-part

series, a historical comedy called *The Complete and Utter History of Britain,* for London Weekend Television. Palin also appeared in a TV special written by and starring Cleese and Chapman, called *How to Irritate People.* Cleese and Chapman had written a sketch for the show based on Palin's experiences with a defective car, which was later rewritten and turned into the "Dead Parrot" sketch for Python. Palin and Jones also appeared in *The Late Show,* and did more writing for Frost, the Two Ronnies, and Marty Feldman's series as Python got underway in 1969.

During the Monty Python years, Palin managed to keep busy with other activities outside the group. In 1973, he and Jones cowrote a BBC play, *Secrets,* an hour-long black comedy about a worker in a chocolate factory who falls into a vat; the play was later adapted into the 1988 film *Consuming Passions* starring Vanessa Redgrave. On New Year's Eve, 1975, Palin appeared in a Tom Stoppard adaptation of Jerome K. Jerome's *Three Men in a Boat,* directed by Stephen Frears and costarring Tim Curry.

Palin and Jones also wrote two short "Their Finest Hours" plays for the Crucible Theatre, Shef-

Palin at home in 1978, strangling one of his sons with the Claw used in the Ripping Yarn *"Curse of the Claw."* **Photo copyright KHJ**

field, the following year. *Underhill's Finest Hour* took place in a hospital delivery ward, where a woman giving birth finds that her doctor is more interested in listening to cricket; *Buchanan's Finest Hour* took place entirely inside a large box.

Charles McKeown, who went on to cowrite and appear in *Brazil,* appeared in both of them. Of the latter, he says "It was about an international packaging organization that had been taken for a ride by an even bigger packaging organization, in which there were three of us inside a large crate. We never saw the audience, and the audience never saw us. We sat in this crate.

"There was a conservative M.P. and his agent, and a French escapologist who also turned out to be inside the box with-

in about ten minutes of the start of the play. A little later, his decapitated wife was also found to be inside the box. We thought we had been delivered to a place where we were going to receive tremendous publicity in front of an audience, and it becomes clear to us that something has gone tremendously wrong, and there's nobody there at all. Later we hear a truck, and another box is brought in containing the Pope. He has also been duped by this even larger international marketing company to be part of their publicity campaign."

Contributing to the Python books, Palin and Jones also wrote *Dr. Fegg's Nasty Book of Knowledge* (released in the U.K. as *Bert Fegg's Nasty Book for Boys and Girls,* and subsequently retitled in 1985 as *Dr. Fegg's Encyclopedia of All World Knowledge*) in 1974. Palin has also contributed articles to *Esquire* magazine, *The New York Times, The Sunday Telegraph Magazine,* and *Punch.*

Palin's writing following Python, however, tended to be more concerned with teleplays and screenplays. He and Jones wrote and performed "Tomkinson's Schooldays" for the BBC, a travesty on English schoolboy stories popular in comics and juvenile books in the '20s. The story of a young man who rises to the post of School Bully became the first in a series of six *Ripping Yarns,* which won a Broadcasting Press Guild award for Best Comedy Series of 1977. Three more shows

Here, Palin insisted that the above picture be taken, as proof that the director kept them on the set until 6:45 P.M. Photo copyright KHJ

Called upon to minister to the fallen women of London (which his wife interprets to mean those women who have hurt their knees), Palin takes an active role in his work. **Photo copyright Handmade Films/The Missionary**

were aired late in 1979. Although Jones only appeared in the first show, Palin starred in all nine of the *Yarns*. Two books of scripts were released containing all the scripts from both seasons, *Ripping Yarns* and *More Ripping Yarns*.

Perhaps inspired in part by Jones's success, Palin also tried his hand at writing children's books, beginning in 1982 with *Small Harry and the Toothache Pills*. He also wrote *The Mirrorstone,* a book illustrated with holograms, and penned two Cyril books, including *Cyril in the House of Commons*.

Palin made a number of appearances hosting *Saturday Night Live,* beginning on April 8, 1978, where he showed a brief clip from "Tomkinson's Schooldays." He next appeared in January 1979 (with the Doobie Brothers as musical guests) and again in May (with James Taylor). Palin had a small role in Eric Idle's *The Rutles: All You Need*

Is Cash on NBC in March 1978, in which he is interviewed on Rutle Corps by George Harrison. He also appeared on an NBC effort called *The News is the News* on June 15, 1983.

More serious efforts were made for the BBC. Palin was featured on one episode of *Great Railway Journeys of the World* on November 22, 1982, which traced a journey across Great Britain. And in late 1988, he set out with a BBC crew to trace the around-the-world route taken in *Around the World in 80 Days,* titled, *Around the World in 80 Days?,* airing on the BBC in late 1989, and on America's Arts and Entertainment network in January 1990. Palin has also written a book based on his adventures during the trip.

Beginning with his lead role in Terry Gilliam's *Jabberwocky* in 1977, Palin also launched a successful solo film career following Python. He cowrote and played a dual role in 1981's *Time*

Bandits, also written and directed by Terry Gilliam. The following year, Palin wrote, coproduced, and starred in *The Missionary* for Handmade Films, his first major solo film project. As the title character, returning from Africa, he is called to work among the fallen women of Victorian London. His subdued, low-key humor stood as a marked contrast to his Python work, and the film was generally received well by critics and audiences. In 1984 he was reunited with Maggie Smith, his *Missionary* costar, performing Alan Bennett's screenplay of *A Private Function,* the story of a social-climbing family and their pig in the heavily rationed days of post-World War II Britain. Palin's acting was again well received, and he continued to be the busiest acting Python.

In 1985, Palin returned to yet another Gilliam project. In *Brazil,* he played Jack Lint, the hero's best friend who eventually becomes his torturer. And 1988 saw Palin in a much lighter role in Cleese's *A Fish Called Wanda,* playing the stuttering animal lover Ken, who inadvertently kills three dogs and runs over Kevin Kline with a steamroller.

Palin is also hoping to film *American Friends* from his original script, for release in 1990.

Although Palin loves his acting career, he still looks forward to writing and acting in his own projects. He continues to wrote teleplays for the BBC, including the 1986 *East of Ipswitch,* and is planning collaborations with Terry Jones and Terry Gilliam, and hopes to work on a project with all of Python once again.

THE RECORDS THE BOOKS, AND THE VIDEOS

With the success of the TV series, it wasn't long before record companies and publishing houses took notice of Python. Although the group wasn't wildly enthusiastic about the ideas, they went on to success in both of those fields. The first books utilized some material from the TV shows, but with new twists and insights.

"It was Geoffrey Strachan at Methuen who actually proposed the idea of a book," explains Terry Jones, "and we'd all come to it rather half-heartedly. We always had somebody supervising our different projects, and it was Eric who edited the Python books. We were all quite surprised by how successful the *Big Red Book* was."

Their first album was a BBC recording of the soundtrack of the TV series, but they began incorporating new sketches and experimenting with the possibilities of audio scenes with their first independent record.

"Mike and I supervised the first record album, *Another Monty Python Record,* with the Beethoven sleeve crossed out," says Jones. "We had been approached by a record company—Mike and I handled that first one, and then Mike took over. We had such a horrendous time doing the first record! It got terribly involved, and everything seemed to be crucial, recording and using the stereo effect. . . . We recorded in this studio where the guys were on marijuana most of the time, and it just took forever. They recorded piles and piles of tapes, and they never made any record of what was on what. It was so ridiculous—it took forever to record. I didn't enjoy that at all."

Monty Python: On the Record

There are numerous variations in both the packaging and the contents of Python albums that have surfaced over the years, but the following discography is intended as a representative guide. There are special banded, promotional copies released to radio stations that have been censored, and in fact, the Pythons themselves have had to delete certain material, mostly for legal reasons (such as the "Farewell to John Denver" on the first release of the *Contractual Obligation Album*).

The Pythons always tried to innovate, and their records are no exception. *Matching Tie* was, on its initial release, the first three-sided record album: one side played normally, while the other had two sets of grooves cut into it, each with different material—the sketch that was heard depended on which groove the needle dropped into. The album was also packaged with an inner sleeve decorated with a tie and handkerchief visible through a hole cut out of the outer jacket. Unfortunately, cost-cutting attempts on later pressings resulted in the two double-sets of grooves pressed as only one, and the Gilliam-designed inner sleeve replaced with plain white paper, completely ruining the joke.

Instant Record Collection fell victim to the same cost-cutting measures as well. Its original release in Britain saw it packaged in an elaborate, Gilliam-designed fold-out cover, that could be assembled into a box that looked exactly like a stack of record albums, providing the title. Unfortunately, the record packages reportedly kept breaking open and unfolding in store bins, and all subsequent pressings, including the American versions, were released in a much more ordinary album jacket. Likewise, later pressings of *Another Monty Python Record* are lacking the "Be a Great Actor" inserts, including the instructions, effects sheet, and two plays.

☞ THE ALBUMS

MONTY PYTHON'S FLYING CIRCUS (1970) BBC Records REB 73M
(U.K.)/Pye 12116 (U.S.)
      The contents here are taken from the soundtrack of the TV shows.

SIDE ONE
Flying Sheep
Television Interviews/Arthur
  Frampton
Trade Description Act/
  Whizzo Chocolates
Nudge, Nudge
The Mouse Problem
Buying a Bed
Interesting People
The Barber/Lumberjack
  Song
Interviews/Sir Edward Ross

SIDE TWO
More Television Interviews/Arthur
  "Two Sheds" Jackson
Children's Stories
The Visitors
The Cinema/Albatross
The North Minehead By-Election
Me Doctor
Pet Shop (Dead Parrot)
Self-Defense

ANOTHER MONTY PYTHON RECORD (1971) Charisma 1049
      Packaged as "Beethoven Symphony No. 2 in D Major" and
defaced by the Pythons to serve as their own record jacket. Most of the
material is rerecorded versions of TV sketches, although some have
been altered slightly; there are also a few new sketches and new linking
material.

SIDE ONE
Apologies*
Spanish Inquisition
World Forum
Gumby Theatre, etc.*
The Architect
The Piranha Brothers

SIDE TWO
Death of Mary, Queen of Scots
Penguin on the TV
Comfy Chair/Sound Quiz*
Be a Great Actor*/Theatre Quiz*
Royal Festival Hall Concert*
Spam
The Judges/Stake Your Claim*
Still No Sign of Land/Undertaker

MONTY PYTHON'S PREVIOUS RECORD (1972) Charisma 1063 (U.K.)/
Charisma 0598 (U.S.)
      Contains a mixture of material from the TV shows, largely the
third series, as well as new material. "A Fairy Tale" is a shortened
version of a sketch done by John Cleese and Connie Booth for one of
the German Python shows.

SIDE ONE
Embarrassment/A Bed-Time
  Book*
England 1747—Dennis
  Moore
Money Programme
Dennis Moore Continues
Australian Table Wines*
Argument Clinic
Putting Budgies Down
Eric the Half a Bee*
Travel Agency

SIDE TWO
Radio Quiz Game*
A Massage/City Noises Quiz*
Miss Anne Elk
We Love the Yangtse*
How-to-do-it Lessons
A Minute Passed*
Eclipse of the Sun*/Alistair
  Cooke*
Wonderful World of Sounds*
A Fairy Tale*

*Denotes sketches not in the original TV shows or film sound-
tracks, or at least significantly different from the TV and film
versions.

THE WORST OF MONTY PYTHON (1976) Kama Sutra KSBS2611-2

This is actually a repackaging of *Another Monty Python Record* and *Monty Python's Previous Record,* with a new album jacket. The two records were also packaged as a double-album set with their original covers, and sold as a two-record set.

THE MONTY PYTHON MATCHING TIE AND HANDKERCHIEF (1973) Charisma 1080 (U.K.)/Arista AL 4039 (U.S.)

Released as the world's first three-sided record, one side actually contains a pair of grooves cut into it, each containing different material; the material that played depended on where the needle dropped. Subsequent pressings have not included the double groove.

SIDE TWO
Dead Bishop on the
  Landing/The Church
  Police
Who Cares/The Surgeon
  and the Elephant Mr.
  Humphries*
Thomas Hardy/Novel
  Writing*
Word Association*
Bruces/Philosophers' Song*
Nothing Happened/Eating
  Dog*
Cheese Shop
Thomas Hardy*
Tiger Club*
Great Actors*

SIDE TWO
Infant Minister for Overseas
  Development
Oscar Wilde's Party
Pet Shop Conversions
Phone-in*
SIDE TWO
Background to History*/Medieval
  Open Field Farming Songs*
World War I Soldier/Stuck
  Record*
Boxing Tonight with Kenneth Clark

MONTY PYTHON LIVE AT THE THEATRE ROYAL, DRURY LANE (1974) Charisma Class 4 (U.K. only)

SIDE ONE
Introduction*/Llamas
Gumby Flower Arranging
Secret Service*
Wrestling*
Communist Quiz
Idiot Song (Neil Innes)*
Albatross/The Colonel
Nudge, Nudge/Cocktail Bar*
Travel Agent

SIDE TWO
Spot the Brain Cell
Bruces
Argument
Four Yorkshiremen*
Election Special
Lumberjack Song
Parrot

THE ALBUM OF THE SOUNDTRACK OF THE TRAILER OF THE FILM OF MONTY PYTHON AND THE HOLY GRAIL (1975) Charisma 1103 (U.K.)/Arista AL 4050 (U.S.)

Contains excerpts from the film soundtrack, plus other film-related linking material.

SIDE ONE
Congratulations/Welcome to
  the Cinema*
Opening/Coconuts
Bring Out Your Dead
King Arthur Meets Dennis/
  Class Struggle
Witch Test

Professional Logician*
Camelot/The Quest
The Silbury Hill Car Park*
Frenchmen of the Castle
Bomb Threat*/Executive
  Announcement*

SIDE TWO
Story of the Film So Far*
The Tale of Sir Robin
The Knights of Ni
Interview/Director Carl French*
Swamp Castle/The Guards/Tim
   the Enchanter

Great Performances/Angry
   Crowd*
Holy Hand Grenade
Announcement—Sir Kenneth
   Clark*
French Castle Again
Close*

MONTY PYTHON LIVE AT CITY CENTER (1976) Arista AL 4073
(U.S. only)

SIDE ONE
Introduction*/Llama
Gumby Flower Arranging
Short Blues (Neil Innes)*
Wrestling*
World Forum
Albatross/Colonel Stopping
   It
Nudge, Nudge/Crunchy Frog
Bruces Song*
Travel Agent

SIDE TWO
Camp Judges/Blackmail
Protest Song (Neil Innes)*
Pet Shop
Four Yorkshiremen*
Argument Clinic
Death of Mary, Queen of Scots
Salvation Fuzz/Church Police
Lumberjack Song

THE MONTY PYTHON INSTANT RECORD COLLECTION (1977) Charisma 1134 (U.K.)
   Originally designed by Terry Gilliam and packaged to fold out into a cardboard box resembling a large stack of record albums, and now released in a normal record sleeve because the package kept breaking open in stores, this is essentially a "greatest hits" album, or, as it is billed, "The pick of the best of some recently repeated Python hits again, Vol. II." Most of the material here has been on previous albums.

SIDE ONE
Introductions
Alistair Cooke
Nudge, Nudge
Mrs. Nigger-Baiter
Constitutional Peasants
Fish License
Eric the Half a Bee
Australian Table Wines
Silly Noises
Novel Writing
Elephantoplasty
How to Do It
Gumby Cherry Orchard
Oscar Wilde

SIDE TWO
Introduction
Argument
French Taunter
Summarized Proust Competition
Cheese Emporium
Funerals at Prestatyn
Camelot
Word Association
Bruces
Parrot
Monty Python Theme

MONTY PYTHON'S LIFE OF BRIAN (1979) Warner Bros. K 56751 (U.K.)/
BSK 3396 (U.S.)
Contains excerpts from the film, with brief linking material by Eric
Idle and Graham Chapman.

SIDE ONE
Introduction*
Three Wise Men
Brian Song
Big Nose
The Stoning
Ex-Leper
Bloody Romans
Link*
People's Front of Judea
Short Link*
Latin Lesson
Missing Link*
Revolutionary Meeting
Very Good Link*
Ben
Audience with Pilate
Meanwhile*

SIDE TWO
The Prophets
Haggling
Lobster*
Sermon on the Wall
Lobster Link*
Simon the Holy Man
Sex Link*
The Morning After
Lighter Link*
Pilate and Biggus/Welease Bwian/
   Nisus Wettus
Crucifixion
Always Look on the Bright Side of
   Life
Close*

*THE WARNER BROTHERS MUSIC SHOW: MONTY PYTHON EXAM-
INES "THE LIFE OF BRIAN"* (1979) WBMS 110
A promotional album released to radio stations as part of the
Warners series and never sold. It consists of an hour-long interview with
the Pythons conducted by Dave Herman, along with excerpts from the
soundtrack.

MONTY PYTHON'S CONTRACTUAL OBLIGATION ALBUM (1980) Charisma 1152 (U.K.)/Arista AL 9536 (U.S.)
Exactly what its title claims it is, this record contains all-new
material, except for "String" and "Bookshop," both of which predate
Python. "Farewell to John Denver" was deleted from later pressings for
legal reasons, while "Sit on My Face" reportedly faced legal threats, as
it is sung to the tune of "Sing As We Go," an old Gracie Fields tune. This
is easily the most musical of any Python album, with over half of the
twenty-four tracks consisting of songs.

SIDE ONE
Sit on My Face*
Announcement*
Henry Kissinger*
String*
Never Be Rude to an Arab*
I Like Chinese*
Bishop*
Medical Love Song*
Farewell to John Denver*
Finland*
I'm So Worried*

SIDE TWO
I Bet You They Won't Play This
   Song on the Radio*
Martyrdom of St. Victor*
Here Comes Another One*
Bookshop*
Do What John*
Rock Notes*
Muddy Knees*
Crocodile*
Decomposing Composers*
Bells*
Traffic Lights*
All Things Dull and Ugly*
A Scottish Farewell*

MONTY PYTHON'S THE MEANING OF LIFE (1983) MCA Records MCA 6121

Contains excerpts from the film, with new linking material.

SIDE ONE
Introduction*
Fish Introduction
The Meaning of Life Theme
Birth
Birth Link/Frying Eggs*
Every Sperm is Sacred
Protestant Couple
Adventures of Martin
   Luther*
Sex Education
Trench Warfare
The Great Tea of 1914–18*
Fish Link*

SIDE TWO
Terry Gilliam's Intro*
Accountancy Shanty
Zulu Wars
Link*
The Dungeon Restaurant
Link/Live Organ Transplants
The Galaxy Song
The Not Noel Coward (Penis)
   Song
Mr. Creosote
The Grim Reaper
Christmas in Heaven
Dedication (to Fish)*

MONTY PYTHON'S THE FINAL RIPOFF (1988) Virgin Records Virgin 7 90865-1

Another "greatest hits" compilation, released when Virgin took over the Monty Python catalogue. This represents their first double-record set. All material here has been performed on previous records, except for some brief links by Michael Palin.

SIDE ONE
Introduction
Constitutional Peasants
Fish License
Eric the Half a Bee
Finland Song
Travel Agent
Are You Embarrassed
   Easily?
Australian Table Wines
Argument
Henry Kissinger Song
Parrot (Oh, Not Again!)

SIDE TWO
Sit on My Face
Undertaker
Novel Writing (Live From Wessex)
String
Bells
Traffic Lights
Cocktail Bar
Four Yorkshiremen
Election Special
Lumberjack Song

SIDE THREE
I Like Chinese
Spanish Inquisition Part 1
Cheese Shop
Cherry Orchard
Architects' Sketch
Spanish Inquisition Part 2
Spam
Spanish Inquisition Part 3
Comfy Chair
Famous Person Quiz
You Be the Actor
Nudge, Nudge
Cannibalism
Spanish Inquisition
   Revisited

SIDE FOUR
I Bet You They Won't Play This
   Song on the Radio
Bruces
Bookshop
Do Wot John
Rock Notes
I'm So Worried
Crocodile
French Taunter Part 1
Marilyn Monroe
Swamp Castle
French Taunter Part 2
Last Word

☛ THE SINGLES

THE LUMBERJACK SONG/SPAM SONG Charisma CB 268

ERIC THE HALF A BEE (1972) Charisma CB 200

SPAM SONG/THE CONCERT Charisma CB 192

THE SINGLE (1975) Arista AS 0130 (U.S.)
    This is a promotional single for the *Matching Tie* album, containing shortened versions of: Who Cares/The Elephant Mr. Humphries; Infant Minister for Overseas Development; Pet Shop Conversions

PYTHON ON SONG (1976) Charisma MP 001
    A two-record set released in the U.K.
RECORD 1, Side A: Lumberjack Song (Produced by George Harrison)
Side B: Spam Song
RECORD 2, Side A: Bruces Song (with Neil Innes, from *Drury Lane*)
Side B: Eric the Half a Bee

ALWAYS LOOK ON THE BRIGHT SIDE OF LIFE/BRIAN (1978) Warner Bros. K 56751 (U.K.)

I LIKE CHINESE/FINLAND/I'LL BET YOU THEY WON'T PLAY THIS SONG ON THE RADIO (1980) Charisma CB 374

THE GALAXY SONG/EVERY SPERM IS SACRED (1983) CBS Records WA 3495
    This is an over-sized picture disc released with *Meaning of Life,* shaped like a fishbowl and with a photo of the Python fish from the film.
    Python also released flexi-discs inserted into various British music magazines, some containing new material.

MONTY PYTHON'S TINY BLACK ROUND THING Election '74/Lumberjack Song, taken from *Drury Lane,* with a new introduction by Michael Palin; included with *New Musical Express.*

TEACH YOURSELF HEATH contains original material, with an introduction by Michael Palin, lesson by Eric Idle, and examples by Edward Heath; included in the December 1972 *Zigzag.*

Python is also represented on several compilation/sampler albums:
ONE MORE CHANCE Charisma Class 3 (U.K.) Eric the Half A Bee
SUPERTRACKS Vertigo Sport 1 (U.K.) The Money Song
25 YEARS OF RECORDED COMEDY (1978) Warner Bros. Argument Clinic

RECORDS FEATURING MEMBERS OF PYTHON

SEVEN-A-SIDE (1965) MJB Recording and Transcription Service
Oxford University Experimental Theatre Club and Oxford Theatre Group
Features Michael Palin and Terry Jones
Recorded at Oxford in November 1964, this was apparently a private recording made for cast members, families, and friends, and contains material from the 1964 Oxford cabaret and theater shows *Hang Down Your Head and Die,* the Edinburgh *Oxford Revue,* and *Keep This to Yourself.*
Palin/Jones compositions and performances include:
"Grin" (Palin/Gould), performed by Palin
"Song About a Toad" (Jones/Gould)
"Forgive Me" (Jones/Gould)
"Song of British Nosh" (Palin/Gould), performed by Palin, David Wood, and Bob Scott
"I've Invented a Long-Range Telescope" (Palin/Gould) Palin
"Last One Home's a Custard" (Fisher/Palin/Jones/Gould), performed by Solomon, Sommerville, Sadler, Palin, Wood, Weston, and Scott

CAMBRIDGE CIRCUS (1965) Odeon PCS 3046 Original Broadway Cast
Features John Cleese
The soundtrack album from the show as it ran on Broadway.

THE FROST REPORT ON BRITAIN (1966) Parlophone PMC 7005
Features John Cleese and Jean Hart
Produced by James Gilbert; writing credits: David Frost and John Cleese, with Tim Brooke-Taylor, Graham Chapman, Barry Cryer, Tony Hendra, Terry Jones, Herbert Kretzner, Peter Lewis and Peter Dobereiner, David Nobbs, Bill Oddie, and Ludwig Van Beethoven.

SIDE ONE
Matter of Taste (Cleese)
Schoolmaster (Cleese)
Just Four Just Men (Cleese)
Internal Combustion
Deck of Cards
Top of the Form (Cleese)
Unknown Soldier (Cleese)

SIDE TWO
Scrapbook (Cleese)
Adventure (Cleese)
Numbers
Bulletin
Hilton
Zookeeper (Cleese)

THE FROST REPORT ON EVERYTHING (1967) Janus JLS-3005
Features David Frost, Ronnie Barker, John Cleese, Ronnie Corbett, and Sheila Steafel
Writing credits include Frost, Terry Jones, Michael Palin, Eric Idle, Graham Chapman, and John Cleese (misspelled "Clease")

SIDE ONE
The State of England
Theatre Critic (Cleese)
Frost, What People Really Mean

Three Classes of People (Cleese)
Narcissus Complex (Cleese)

SIDE TWO
Frost on Agriculture, Speech   Selling String
The Secretary (Cleese)   Executive and the Teaman
Frost on Commercials   Three Classes (Cleese)

I'M SORRY, I'LL READ THAT AGAIN (1967) EMI M-11634
    Features John Cleese, Tim Brooke-Taylor, Graeme Garden, David Hatch, Jo Kendall, and Bill Oddie
    Among other roles, Cleese plays the Doctor, Mary's John, Little John, Sir Angus of the Prune, the MC, Baby Rupert, Captain Cleese, and Wong Tu

SIDE ONE
The Auctioneer
The Day After Tomorrow's
  World
The Doctor (written by
  Oddie/Cleese)
Blimpht
John and Marry (Cleese/
  Oddie)
Robin Hood (Garden/Cleese)

SIDE TWO
Identikit Gal
Baby Talk
Family Favorites
The Curse of the Flying Wombat
Closing/Angus Prune Tune

I'M SORRY, I'LL READ THAT AGAIN (1967) BBC Records REH 342

FUNNY GAME, FOOTBALL (1972) EP from "The Group" from *Funny Game, Football* Charisma CB 197 Music by Neil Innes
    Features Michael Palin, Terry Jones, Arthur Mullard, Bryan Pringle, Bill Tidy, Joe Steeples, Michael Wale
    Written by Joe Steeples, Bill Tidy, Michael Wale

SIDE ONE
Piraeus Football Club
Crunch!
Rangers Abroad
An Open Letter to George
  Best
The Missionary
Sir Alf Speaks
World War III
Newsnight with Coleman
Soccer Laureate
Bovver Boys

SIDE TWO
Scilly Season
Government Policies
I Remember It Well
Floor's the Limit*
Director's Song
Blackbury Town
A Joke

* A Python-ish quiz show with Palin as host, and Jones the unfortunate contestant.

THE RUTLAND WEEKEND SONGBOOK (1975) BBC Records REB 233 (U.K.)/(1976) ABC/Passport Records PPSD-98018 (U.S.)
    Features Eric Idle and Neil Innes, containing material from the BBC series

SIDE ONE
L'Amour Perdue
Gibberish
Wash with Mother/Front
  Loader
Say Sorry Again

The Rutles in "Rutles for
  Sale" ("I Must Be in
  Love")
24 Hours in Tunbridge Wells
The Fabulous Bingo
  Brothers

SIDE ONE (cont.)
In Concrete—Concrete
    Jungle Boy
The Children of Rock and
    Roll
Startime—Stoop Solo
Song O' the Insurance Men
Closedown

SIDE TWO
I Give Myself to You
Communist Cooking/Johnny Cash
    Live at Mrs. Fletchers
The Old Gay Whistle Test
Accountancy Shanty
Football/Boring
Good Afternoon/L'Amour Perdue
    Cha Cha Cha
Disco—the Hard to Get
Closedown—the Song O' the
    Continuity Announcers

A POKE IN THE EYE WITH A SHARP STICK (1976) Transatlantic TRA
331 (U.K. only)
    Recording of the 1976 Amnesty International Benefit
    Features John Cleese, Graham Chapman, Terry Gilliam, Terry
Jones, Michael Palin, Carol Cleveland, Neil Innes, Alan Bennett, John
Bird, Eleanor Bron, Tim Brooke-Taylor, Peter Cook, John Fortune, Jonathan Miller, Jonathan Lynn, Graeme Garden, Bill Oddie

SIDE ONE
A Brief Introduction (Cleese)
Asp (Cook, Fortune)
Happy, Darling? (Bron,
    Fortune)
The Last Supper (Cleese,
    Lynn)
Telegram (Bennett)
Funky Gibbon (The
    Goodies—Brooke-Taylor,
    Garden, Oddie)
Appeal (Bron)

SIDE TWO
Courtroom (Chapman, Cleese,
    Cleveland, Gilliam, Jones, Palin,
    with Cook)
Portraits from Memory (Miller)
You Say Potato (Bird, Fortune)
Baby Talk (Bron, Fortune)
So That's The Way You Like It—
    Beyond the Fringe (Miller,
    Bennett, Cook with Jones)
Lumberjack Song (All)

THE MERMAID FROLICS (1977) Polydor Special 2384101
    Recording of the second Amnesty International Benefit, recorded
May 8, 1977
    Features John Cleese, Terry Jones, Connie Booth, Jonathan
Miller, and Peter Ustinov
    The first side is all music; the comedy side contains skits by
Cleese, and Jones performs a song.

THE RUTLES: ALL YOU NEED IS CASH (1978) Warner Bros. HS 3151
(U.S.)Warners K 56459 (U.K.)
    Features Eric Idle
    Soundtrack of the NBC/BBC 2 film with songs by Neil Innes, and
a twenty-page booklet enclosed

SIDE ONE 1962–67
Hold My Hand
Number One
With a Girl Like You
I Must Be in Love
Ouch!
Living in Hope
Love Life
Nevertheless

SIDE TWO 1967–70
Good Times Roll
Doubleback Alley
Cheese and Onions
Another Day
Piggy in the Middle
Let's Be Natural

THE RUTLES (1978) Warner Bros. Pro. E723
A five-song promotional EP, released on yellow vinyl
I Must Be in Love
Doubleback Alley
With A Girl Like You
Another Day
Let's Be Natural

THE SECRET POLICEMAN'S BALL (1979) Island ILPS 9601
A recording of the 1979 Amnesty International Benefit, released on two records in the U.K., one containing the comedy portion of the show, the other with the music, including Pete Townshend
Features John Cleese, Terry Jones, Michael Palin, Rowan Atkinson, and Peter Cook. Python-related tracks include the following:

SIDE ONE
Interesting Facts (Cleese, Cook)
How Do You Do It? (Jones, Palin)
The Names the Game (Cleese, Jones)
Stake Your Claim (Palin, Atkinson)

SIDE TWO
Cheese Shop (Cleese, Palin)
Four Yorkshiremen (Cleese, Jones, Palin, Atkinson)
The End of the World (Cook and cast)

FAWLTY TOWERS (1979) BBC Records REB 377
Features John Cleese and Connie Booth
The soundtrack to the TV shows "The Hotel Inspectors" and "Mrs. Richards"

FAWLTY TOWERS: SECOND SITTING (1981) BBC Records REB 405
Features John Cleese and Connie Booth
The soundtrack to the TV shows "The Builders" and "The Rat"

THE SECRET POLICEMAN'S OTHER BALL (1981) Island HAHA 6003
A recording of the 1981 Amnesty International Benefit, also released as a comedy record, and as a separate music album, which included Eric Clapton and Jeff Beck, Phil Collins, and Sting
Features John Cleese, Graham Chapman, with Rowan Atkinson, Alan Bennett, Billy Connolly, John Fortune, Alexei Sayle, and Pamela Stephenson

FAWLTY TOWERS: AT YOUR SERVICE (1982) BBC Records REB 449
Features John Cleese and Connie Booth
The soundtrack to the TV shows "The Germans" and "Death"

FAIRY TALES (1982) A recording of several stories from Terry Jones's children's book, read by a cast including Bob Hoskins and Helen Mirren

THE MIKADO (1987) MCA Classics MCAD-6215
Highlights from the English National Opera production starring Eric Idle (as Koko), and directed by Jonathan Miller. Additional lyrics to "I've Got a Little List" are apparently by Eric.

THE SCREWTAPE LETTERS (1988) Audio Literature, Inc. ISBN 0-944993-15-X

    Available on tape only, this is a three-hour, two-cassette version of the C. S. Lewis book as read by John Cleese.

THE ADVENTURES OF BARON MUNCHAUSEN (1989) Warner Brothers Records 9 25826-2

    Instrumental soundtrack from the film; most songs are instrumentals except for "What Will Become of the Baron?" and "The Torturer's Apprentice" medley (the latter is cowritten by Eric Idle).

☞ *ADDITIONAL SINGLES*

SUPERSPIKE, PARTS 1 and 2 Bradley 7606

    "The Superspike Squad" with John Cleese and Bill Oddie

    All profits were donated to the International Athlete's Club's fundraising campaign.

I MUST BE IN LOVE/DOUBLEBACK ALLEY Warner Bros. WBS 8560

    The Rutles (the single from the soundtrack album)

    Features Eric Idle and Neil Innes

GING GANG GOOLIE/ MR. SHEENE EMI 2852 (U.K. only)

    Dirk and Stig (Eric Idle and Rikki Fataar) of the Rutles

George Harrisons *33⅓* album includes Eric Idle on "This Song," in which he delivers a few spoken lines during a bridge in a Pepperpot voice.

The Beatle bootleg *Indian Rope Trick* contains "Cheese and Onions," as performed by Neil Innes on *Saturday Night Live,* and credits it as a Beatle song; also on the bootleg is "The Pirate Song," cowritten by Eric Idle and George Harrison, and performed on *Rutland Weekend Television.*

A bootleg anthology album on the Kornyfone label, *T'anks for the Mammaries,* includes "Get Up and Go," featured on *All You Need is Cash,* but not included on the soundtrack album.

Python Press

After the first season of Python proved a success, the group was approached by Methuen Books about doing a tie-in with the television show. Eric Idle, in particular, was quite keen on assembling a book consisting of material from the TV series, but by the time he had finished, it looked much more like an original collection of humor. Most of the material used the Python sketches as a starting point, with Idle and the others extrapolating from them to develop new premises.

Lavishly illustrated with photo stills, original art, and Gilliam animation, *The Big Red Book* (with, naturally, a bright blue cover) was successful enough to warrant a followup. *The Brand New Monty Python Bok* (accompanied later by, of course, *The Brand New Monty Python Papperbok* edition) was even more elaborate, original, and innovative, with cutout pages and inserts to delight fans looking for more than just an ordinary book. Idle again assembled the material for the followup, which actually contained even more new material than the first volume. The hardcover edition included a white dust jacket (with smudged fingerprints on the back) over a cover that announced "Tits and Bums: A Weekly Look at Church Architecture," which the paperback did not have.

The books have always been steady, consistent sellers, but the group didn't decide to do another volume until *Monty Python and the Holy Grail (Book),* as the group itself was moving on from television to film. In addition to the final draft of the screenplay, the edition also includes the first draft, which enables the reader to view the process the story went through (with much of the first draft material ending up in Monty Python Series 4). The book is loaded with photos and sketches, as well as the Cost of Production Statement. Appropriately enough, it was even designed to look like a script, and was edited by Terry Jones, the codirector.

It took another film for another book to result, although in the Python spirit of innovation—or simply trying to stir things up—it was packaged *Monty Python's Life of Brian/Montypythonscrapbook* as two books under one cover. The back cover of one book is actually the front cover of the other when it is flipped over. One is the reproduction of the script, illustrated with stills throughout. It is very nearly the final version, but a few items removed from the film at the last moment, including the scene with Eric Idle as Otto, leader of a suicide squad, remain in the book. The other portion of the book is indeed a scrapbook, with deleted scenes from various stages of the movie, excerpts from diaries, bits of animation, and a variety of other material (including the Bruces' "Philosophers' Song") not necessarily related to the film.

At the moment, the final official Python book is, of course, a tie-in to their final official movie, *The Meaning of Life;* this trade paperback reprints the script with numerous color photos.

Each member of the group has been responsible for original books of a surprising variety, ranging from psychology to autobiography, literature, fiction, and children's books, in addition to all their movie tie-ins, and there is the bright prospect of many more to come.

👉 The BOOKS

MONTY PYTHON'S BIG RED BOOK   Methuen, 1971 (U.K.)/Warner Books, 1975 (U.S.) ISBN 0-446-87077-3
Letter of Endorsement from Television Newscasters
"Juliette," featuring Ken Shabby and Rosemary
Why Accountancy is Not Boring, by A. Putey
Campaign Literature for the Silly Party
Batley Ladies' Townswomen's Guild
Sports Page, with Jimmy Buzzard and Ken Clean-Air System
The Importance of Being Earnest—a new version by Billy Bremner
Sir Kenneth Clarke—Are You Civilized?
The Greatest Upper-Class (Twit) Race in the World
Goat's Page
Johnson's Novelties ("Guaranteed to break the ice at parties")
Letter Retracting the Endorsement of the Book
Lumberjack Song
Whizzo Chocolate Assortment
How to Walk Silly
Poems of Ewan McTeagle
Piranha Brothers

THE BRAND NEW MONTY PYTHON BOK (hardcover)   Methuen, 1973 (U.K.)/Henry Regnery, 1976 (U.S.) ISBN 0-8092-8046-9
Contents are identical to the paperback, except for the "Tits and Bums" cover under the dust jacket of this edition.

THE BRAND NEW MONTY PYTHON PAPPERBOK   Methuen, 1974 (U.K.)/Warner Books, 1976 (U.S.) ISBN 0-446-87-078-1
Biggles is Extremely Silly (1938)
Notice of the Availability of Film Rights to Page Six
The Bigot (a newsletter)
The London Casebook of Detective René Descartes
The Adventures of Walter Wallabee (comic strip)
Film Review with Phillip Jenkinson
Rat Recipes and Chez Rat (menu)
The British Apathy League
Let's Talk About Bottoms
Page 71
Ferndean School Report for God
Cheeseshop (The Word Game)
The Official Medallic Commemoration of the History of Mankind
The Anagrams Gape (4) and the Anagram-Haters Page
Teach Yourself Surgery

THE COMPLETE WORKS OF SHAKESPEARE AND MONTY PYTHON: VOLUME ONE—MONTY PYTHON   Methuen, 1981, ISBN 0-413-49450-0
     A British compilation of Big Red Book and Brand New Monty Python Bok.

THE MONTY PYTHON GIFT BOKS Methuen, 1988, ISBN 0-413-14520-4

    A repackaging of the first two books, with an additional poster.

MONTY PYTHON AND THE HOLY GRAIL (BOOK) Methuen, 1977, ISBN 0-458-92970-0

    Contains the first draft, final draft, production notes, sketches, and both production and candid photos, and is packaged to look like an actual script.

MONTY PYTHON'S THE LIFE OF BRIAN/MONTYPYTHONSCRAP-BOOK Methuen, 1979 (U.K.)/Fred Jordan Books/Grosset & Dunlap, 1979 (U.S.) ISBN 0-448-16568-6 (oversized trade paperback)

    One half of the book contains the final script of the film, profusely illustrated with photos from the movie; while the other half contains the following assortment:

How It All Began: a comic strip featuring three shepherds
Diaries of Terry Jones and Michael Palin
What to Take on Filming
Python Cinema Quiz
Brian Feeds the Multitude
"Sharing" Magazine with "Sharing a Caravan with John Cleese"
The Gilliam Collection of Famous Film Titles
Cleese vs. The Evening Standard
Doc. Chapman's Medical Page

MONTY PYTHON'S LIFE OF BRIAN Ace Books, 1979, ISBN 0-441-48240-6

    The small paperback version of the script originally printed in the oversized Grosset & Dunlap edition, including all the photos, but without any *Montypythonscrapbook* material

MONTY PYTHON'S THE MEANING OF LIFE Methuen (U.K.)/Grove Press (U.S.) 1983, ISBN 0-394-62474-2

    This trade paperback reproduces, in full color, the entire script; a great number of stills accompany it.

MONTY PYTHON: JUST THE WORDS Methuen (U.K.)/Pantheon (U.S.) (1989)

    A 20th anniversary collection of Python TV show scripts.

☞ BOOKS ABOUT MONTY PYTHON

THE LAUGHTERMAKERS, by David Nathan, Peter Owen Ltd., 1971

    Published in the U.K., Chapter 10 is devoted to "Monty Python's Flying Breakthrough."

FROM FRINGE TO FLYING CIRCUS, by Roger Wilmut, Eyre Methuen, 1980, ISBN 0-413-46950-6

    Another U.K. book, a significant portion of it is devoted to Python and its place in modern British humor.

MONTY PYTHON'S COMPLETE AND UTTER THEORY OF THE GRO-TESQUE, edited by John O. Thompson, British Film Institute, ISBN 0-85170-119-1

A series of forty-eight essays on various facets of Python, with an index.

MONTY PYTHON: THE CASE AGAINST, by Robert Hewison, Eyre Methuen, 1981, ISBN 0-413-48660-5 (published in hardback and paper-back)

A thorough study of the Pythons' battles against censorship, from the TV shows to the ABC lawsuit to the *Life of Brian* controversy, including script excerpts from the material in question.

LIFE OF PYTHON, by George Perry, Pavilion Books, 1983, ISBN 1-85145-057-2

A biography of the group, with individual chapters devoted to each of the six members, with an index.

☞ OTHER PYTHON-RELATED BOOKS

FUN AND GAMES, by Harvey Kurtzman, assisted by Terry Gilliam, 1965, Gold Medal Books

A book of brain-teasers assembled from Kurtzman's *Help!* maga-zine, assisted by Terry Gilliam.

BERT FEGG'S NASTY BOOK FOR BOYS AND GIRLS, by Terry Jones and Michael Palin, Methuen, 1974; retitled *Dr. Fegg's Nasty Book of Knowledge* for its American release in 1976, and republished as *Dr. Fegg's Encyclopedia of All World Knowledge* in 1985; ISBN 0-87226-005-4
Natural History—Across the Andes by Frog
Fashion—Items from the House of Fegg
Sports—Soccer My Way, by the Supremes
Magic—Conjuring by Feggo!
Sex—All You Need to Know About Sex Education (with a revised version by a proper doctor)
Theatre—Aladdin and his Terrible Problem: a new pantomime
Religion—I Fought the Mighty Anaconda and Lived

HELLO, SAILOR, by Eric Idle, Futura Publications, 1975 (paperback), ISBN 0-8600-7235-5 (U.K. only)

The only novel-length fiction by a Python, Idle's novel features the Prime Minister's secret, the seduction of the daughters of every Minister in the Cabinet, astronaut Sickert's "space first," and much, much more.

THE RUTLAND DIRTY WEEKEND BOOK, by Eric Idle, Methuen/Two Continents, 1976, ISBN 0-846-70185-5

      Contains material inspired by *Rutland Weekend Television,* with Neil Innes, and a guest page by Michael Palin.

The Vatican Sex Manual

A History of *Rutland Weekend Television* from 1300

The Rutland TV Times

Saturday RWT World of Sport Listings

Sunday Listings—Misprint Theatre presents The Wife of Christ

Rutland Stone

The Wonderful World of Sex

New Publications from Rutland University Press

THE STRANGE CASE OF THE END OF CIVILISATION AS WE KNOW IT, by John Cleese, Jack Hobbs, and Joe McGrath, Star Book, 1977 (U.K.), ISBN 0-351-30109-0

      Contains the script and stills of the London Weekend Television film. Two editions of the paperback were published: a TV tie-in with a photo cover, and a "humour" edition with a painted cover; contents of both are the same.

FAWLTY TOWERS, by John Cleese and Connie Booth, Futura/Contact Publications, 1977, ISBN 0-8600-7598-2 (paperback) (U.K.)

      Reprints the scripts of "The Builders," "The Hotel Inspectors," and "Gourmet Night" from the first series; illustrated with a generous portion of photos.

JABBERWOCKY, by Ralph Hoover, Pan Books, 1977 (U.K. only), ISBN 0-330-25012-4

      Paperback adaptation of the script by Charles Alverson and Terry Gilliam.

ANIMATIONS OF MORTALITY, by Terry Gilliam, with Lucinda Cowell, Methuen, 1978, ISBN 0-458-93810-6 (published as a hardcover and trade paperback in Britain, and as a trade paperback in the U.S.)

      A delightful collection of Gilliam artwork loosely disguised as a guide to animation; includes pre- and post-Python works, as well as material from the TV shows, and Brian the Badger guides the reader through The Wonderful World of Animation.

Lesson 1   Creating Something Out of Nothing

Lesson 2   How to Ruin the Pleasure of a Painting Forever

Lesson 3   Discovering the Secret of Cut-Out Animation

Lesson 4   Where Ideas Come From

Lesson 5   Looking the Part

Lesson 6   Meaningless Political Statements

THE ODD JOB, by Bernard McKenna and Colin Bostock-Smith, Arrow Books, 1978, ISBN 0-09-918950-X (British paperback)

      The novelization of the Graham Chapman film.

RIPPING YARNS, by Terry Jones and Michael Palin, Methuen, 1978 (U.K.)/Pantheon Books, 1979 (U.S.) ISBN 0-394-73678-8 (published as a hardcover and trade paperback in the U.K., and as a trade paperback in the U.S.)

Contains the scripts and photos from the six shows of the first series:
Tomkinson's Schooldays
Across the Andes by Frog
Murder at Moorstones Manor
The Testing of Eric Olthwaite
Escape from Stalag Luft 112B
The Curse of the Claw

FAWLTY TOWERS TWO, by John Cleese and Connie Booth, Weidenfeld and Nicolson, 1979, ISBN 0-7088-1547-2 (paperback)

Contains these scripts, illustrated with photos throughout:
The Wedding
A Touch of Class
The Germans

MORE RIPPING YARNS, by Terry Jones and Michael Palin, Pantheon Books, 1980, ISBN 0-394-74810-7 (paperback)

Contains the scripts and stills from the three shows of the second series:
Whinfrey's Last Case
Golden Gordon
Roger of the Raj

CHAUCER'S KNIGHT: PORTRAIT OF A MEDIEVAL MERCENARY, by Terry Jones, Weidenfeld and Nicolson (U.K.)/University of Louisiana Press (U.S.) 1980, ISBN 0-8071-0691-7

Long a pet project of Terry Jones, this scholarly volume illuminates a short section of *The Canterbury Tales,* which he feels has been misinterpreted throughout the years. Or, as Jones puts it, he's just "explaining a lot of 600-year-old jokes."

A LIAR'S AUTOBIOGRAPHY, by Graham Chapman, Methuen, 1980 (published in hardcover and paperback in the U.K., and in hardcover in the U.S.) ISBN 0-413-47570-0

The first Python autobiography, Chapman begins with lengthier fantasy passages, and eases into his own real-life story. He frankly discusses his battle with alcohol, his homosexuality, his medical studies, and of course, his involvement with Python.

FAIRY TALES, by Terry Jones, Pavilion Books, 1981 (hardcover) ISBN 0-907516-03-3/Penguin (paperback) (U.K.) ISBN 0-14-032262-0

An acclaimed collection of children's short stories, originally written for his daughter Sally and read to her each night at bedtime; a record album, radio, and TV adaptations have resulted.

TIME BANDITS, by Michael Palin and Terry Gilliam, Hutchinson (U.K.)/Doubleday (U.S.) 1981, ISBN 0-385-17732-1 (paperback)

Contains the illustrated script of the film.

TIME BANDITS, by Charles Alverson, Arrow Books, 1981 (U.K. only) (paperback) ISBN 0-09-926020-4
> Contains the novelization of the film.

TIME BANDITS, Marvel Comics, February 1982
> A one-shot comic book adaptation of the film.

THE SECRET POLICEMAN'S OTHER BALL, Methuen, 1981 (U.K. only) (paperback) ISBN 0-413-50080-2
> Proceeds donated to Amnesty International
> This book of the Amnesty Stage show contains scripts and photos, with program notes throughout by Terry Jones and Michael Palin. The book includes "Introduction," by John Cleese and the cast; "Beekeeping," an interview sketch with Cleese and Rowan Atkinson; "Top of the Form," with Cleese, Graham Chapman, and others; and "Clothes Off," with Cleese, Chapman, and Pamela Stephenson; several backstage photos are included, as well.

NO MORE CURRIED EGGS FOR ME, edited by Roger Wilmut, Methuen, 1982 (U.K. only) ISBN 0-413-53680-7
> A collection of scripts from comedy sketches and scenes going back to the Marx Brothers; Python-related material includes "Bookshop" (from . . . *the 1948 Show*), an excerpt from *Fawlty Towers* and "The Germans," and of course, the "Parrot."

THE MISSIONARY, by Michael Palin, Methuen, 1982 (paperback) ISBN 0-413-53680-7, (hardback) 1983 ISBN 0-413-51010-7 (U.K.)
> Contains the script and photos of the film.

PASS THE BUTLER, by Eric Idle, Methuen, 1982, ISBN 0-413-49990-1
> The script of Idle's play, which ran in London's West End.

SMALL HARRY AND THE TOOTHACHE PILLS, by Michael Palin, Methuen/Magnet Books, 1982, ISBN 0-416-27160-5
> The first of Palin's children's books.

FAMILIES AND HOW TO SURVIVE THEM, by John Cleese and Robin Skynner, Methuen, 1983 (hardcover) ISBN 0-413-52640-2 (paperback) ISBN 0-413-56520-3
> A series of dialogues between Cleese and his former therapist, dealing with the variety of human relationships, from love and marriage to children.

GREAT RAILWAY JOURNEYS OF THE WORLD, with one chapter written by Michael Palin; "Confessions of a Train-Spotter" is based on this journey, which involved his rail trip across Britain in 1983. A long-time train afficionado, Palin had an opportunity to travel across Britain for this BBC 2 series, which included railway routes all over the world. The text of his program is printed here, along with photos.

THE SAGA OF ERIK THE VIKING, by Terry Jones, Pavilion Books, 1983, ISBN 0-14-03.1713-9, (paperback) (U.K.) Penguin ISBN 0-14-032261-2

This followup to *Fairy Tales* is a book of stories Jones wrote for his young son, Bill; actually one long story broken up into shorter episodes, it served as the rough outline for the 1989 film.

A PRIVATE FUNCTION, by Alan Bennett, Faber and Faber, 1984, ISBN 0-571-13571-4

The novelization of the film starring Michael Palin.

THE COURAGE TO CHANGE, by Dennis Wholey, Houghton Mifflin, 1984, ISBN 0-395-35977-5

A collection of interviews with well-known alcoholics and their families, in which they discuss their battles with alcohol; included is a chapter on Graham Chapman.

THE LIMERICK BOOK, by Michael Palin, Hutchinson Publishing, 1985

A children's book of original limericks.

NICOBOBINUS, by Terry Jones, Pavilion Books (U.K.); paperback ISBN 0-14-032091-1 (U.K.)/Peter Bedrick Books (U.S.) 1985, ISBN 0-87226-065-8

Jones's third children's book is the story of the title character, who sets off to discover the Land of Dragons (Jones has also written a screenplay based on this story).

THE GOBLINS OF LABYRINTH, by Brian Froud and Terry Jones, Pavilion, 1986 (hardcover) ISBN 0-85145-058-0

After writing the script of the film for Jim Henson (although his version was changed significantly), Jones also wrote the text for this tie-in, based on Froud's drawings.

CYRIL AND THE HOUSE OF COMMONS, by Michael Palin, Pavilion, 1986 (U.K. only) ISBN 0-85145-078-5

A Palin children's book.

CYRIL AND THE DINNER PARTY, by Michael Palin, Pavilion, 1986 (U.K. only) ISBN 1-85145-069-6

Anohter Palin children's book.

THE MIRRORSTONE, by Michael Palin, Alan Lee, and Richard Seymour, Jonathan Cape, 1986 (hardback) ISBN 0-224-02408-6

This children's book is thoroughly illustrated and contains several holograms as part of the story.

THE UTTERLY, UTTERLY MERRY COMIC RELIEF CHRISTMAS BOOK, Fontana Trade Paperback, ISBN 0-00-637-128-0; proceeds donated to charity

Contains "Biggles and the Groupies," by Michael Palin (with an introduction by George Harrison), "A Christmas Fairly Story," by Terry Jones and Douglas Adams, and "The Private Life of Genghis Kahn," from a sketch by Graham Chapman and Douglas Adams.

THE GOLDEN SKITS OF WING COMMANDER MURIEL VOLESTRAN-GLER FRHS & BAR, by Muriel Volestrangler, Methuen, ISBN 0-413-415-60-0 (paperback)

    A collection of sketches written and cowritten by John Cleese ranging back to Cambridge.

Architect Skit*
Shirt Shop Skit
Goat Skit
Sheep Skit*
Top of the Form
Word Association Football**
Bookshop Skit
Arthur "Two Sheds"
   Jackson*
The Last Supper Skit
Merchant Banker Skit*
Cricket Commentators Skit
Fairly Silly Court Skit*
Crunchy Frog Skit*
Regella Skit
Hearing Aid Skit
Argument Skit*
The Good Old Days Skit
Lucky Gypsy Skit
Mrs. Beulah Premise & Mrs.
  Wanda Conclusion Visit
  Mr. & Mrs. J. P. Sartre*

Undertaker Skit*
Railway Carriage Skit
Cheese Shop Skit*
String Skit
Chapel Skit***
"Ones" Skit
Army Protection Racket Skit*
Slightly Less Silly Than the Other
   Court Skit Court Skit
Courier Skit
Ethel the Frog Skit*
Dead Parrot*

* Performed in the Python TV show
** From the *Matching Tie and Handkerchief* album
*** From *The Meaning of Life*

THE SECRET POLICEMAN'S THIRD BALL, Sidgwick and Jackson, 1987 (paperback) ISBN 0-283-99530-0

    Contains the script of the Amnesty International show, as well as portraits of the cast; includes a brief appearance by John Cleese accepting an award.

THE BATTLE OF BRAZIL, by Jack Mathews, Crown Books, 1987 (hardback) ISBN 0-517-56538-2

    The chronicle of Terry Gilliam's battle with Universal to release his own *Brazil,* rather than the less-disturbing version; ultimately, it comes across as the David vs. Goliath story of the maverick director fighting against the giant studio for the integrity of his work.

THE COMPLETE (U.K.) FAWLTY TOWERS, by John Cleese and Connie Booth, Methuen, 1988 (hardback) ISBN 0-413-18390-4; Pantheon Books, 1989 (U.S.) (paperback) ISBN 0-679-72127-4

    The scripts from all twelve shows, with a brief photo section.

A FISH CALLED WANDA, by John Cleese, Methuen (U.K.)/Applause Theatre Book Publishers (U.S.) 1988 (paperback) ISBN 0-413-19550-3

    Contains the final script of the film, and is illustrated with stills of the cast.

CURSE OF THE VAMPIRE SOCKS, by Terry Jones, Pavilion Books, 1988 (hardback) (U.K.) ISBN 1-85145-233-8

    An original collection of children's poetry.

ATTACKS OF OPINION, by Terry Jones, Penguin Books (U.K.), 1988 (paperback) ISBN 0-14-032895-5

A collection of columns for the *Young Guardian* "Input" column, with Jones giving his opinion on a variety of timely, controversial subjects.

THE ADVENTURES OF BARON MUNCHAUSEN, by Terry Gilliam and Charles McKeown, Methuen (U.K.)/Applause Theatre Book Publishers (U.S.) 1989 (trade paperback) ISBN 1-55783-039-8

The novelization of the Gilliam film by its cowriters, with line drawings.

THE ADVENTURES OF BARON MUNCHAUSEN, by Terry Gilliam and Charles McKeown, Methuen (U.K.)/Applause Theatre Book Publishers (U.S.) 1989 (paperback) ISBN 1-557-83-041-X

The script of the film, complete with photos, all of the credits, plus twenty-five additional pages of material deleted from the final cut of the movie.

AROUND THE WORLD IN 80 DAYS?, by Michael Palin, BBC Books, 1989

Contains Palin's account of his trip re-creating the Jules Verne story.

LIFE AND HOW TO SURVIVE IT, by Robin Skynner and John Cleese, Methuen, 1989

The followup to their book on families, this investigates psychology in the business world.

Monty Python's Flying Circus: The Videos

The original TV shows are in the process of being released on videocassette. Paramount Home Video is releasing the shows, two per tape, in no particular order. Contents are as follows.

Vol. 1 THE FIRST MONTY PYTHON'S FLYING CIRCUS VIDEOCASSETTE (PAR 12543) Contains "Dinsdale" and "The Buzz Aldrin Show"

Vol. 2 THE SECOND (IN SEQUENCE, NOT QUALITY) MONTY PYTHON'S FLYING CIRCUS VIDEOCASSETTE (PAR 12544) Contains "The Spanish Inquisition" and "The Monty Programme"

Vol. 3   THE THIRD (BUT STILL DRASTICALLY IMPORTANT ABSOLUTE-LY NECESSARY TO HAVE) MONTY PYTHON'S FLYING CIRCUS VIDEO-CASSETTE (PAR 12545) Contains "The Attila the Hun Show" and "The All-England Summarize Proust Competition"

Vol. 4   THE FOURTH (EAGERLY AWAITED, IMPATIENTLY ANTICIPAT-ED, ARDENTLY SOUGHT AFTER, RARING-TO-GO AND REAL GOOD) MONTY PYTHON'S FLYING CIRCUS VIDEOTAPE (PAR 12560) Contains "How to Recognise Different Parts of the Body" and "Mr. and Mrs. Brian Norris' Ford Popular"

Vol. 5   MONTH PYTHON'S FIFTH VIDEOCASSETTE (PAR 12561) Con-tains "Spam" and "The War Against Pornography"

Vol. 6   VOLUME SIX AND VIOLENCE (PAR 12582) Contains "How Not to Be Seen" and "Salad Days"

Vol. 7   PIPE DREAMS (PAR 12583) Contains "Live From the Grillomat" and "The Nude Man"

Vol. 8   BEHIND THE EIGHT BALL (PAR 12600) Contains "Royal Episode 13" and "E. Henry Thripshaw's Disease"

Vol. 9   SILLY PARTY AND OTHER FAVORS (PAR 12601) Contains "School Prizes" and "Njorl's Saga"

Vol. 10   BLOOD, DEVASTATION, DEATH, WAR, HORROR, AND OTHER HUMOROUS EVENTS (PAR 12652) Contains "Show 5" and "Blood, Devastation, Death, War, and Horror"

Vol. 11   DIRTY VICARS, POOFY JUDGES, AND OSCAR WILDE, TOO! (PAR 12653) Contains "Archeology Today" and "The British Royal Awards Programme"

Vol. 12   KAMIKAZE HIGHLANDERS (PAR 12654) Contains "Dennis Moore" and "A Book at Bedtime"

Vol. 13   "I'M A LUMBERJACK" (PAR 12736) Contains "Whither Cana-da?" and "The Ant—an Introduction"

Vol. 14   CHOCOLATE FROGS, BAFFLED CATS, AND OTHER TASTY TREATS (PAR 12737) Contains "Man's Crisis of Identity in the Latter Half of the Twentieth Century" and "The BBC Entry for the Zinc Stoat of Budapest"

Vol. 15   "DEAD PARROTS DON'T TALK" AND OTHER FOWL PLAYS (PAR 12738) Contains "Oh, You're No Fun Anymore" and "Full Frontal Nudity"

Vol. 16   A MAN WITH THREE CHEEKS, OR BUTT NAUGHT FOR ME
(PAR 12739) Contains "Sex and Violence" and "Untitled"

Vol. 17   THE UPPER-CLASS TWIT COMPETITION (PAR 12740) Contains "The Naked Ant" and "Intermission"